N7L

6

D0025219

WITHDRAWN

THE LAW OF TREASON
IN THE UNITED STATES

Contributions in American History

Series Editor: Stanley I. Kutler

THE LAW
OF TREASON
IN THE UNITED STATES
Collected Essays

James Willard Hurst

Contributions in American History
Number 12

Greenwood Publishing Corporation
Westport, Connecticut

Contents

Preface

IN 1943 FOR THE first time the United States Supreme Court undertook to review a conviction for treason. The Court granted a writ of certiorari in *Cramer* v. *United States,* 320 U. S. 730 (1943). After a first argument at the October Term, 1943, the Court, on May 2, 1944, returned the case to its docket and invited reargument in an order which said that "Further briefs and argument are desired as to the questions raised under the treason clause of the Constitution, particu larly as to the meaning of 'treason' and of 'overt act' and as to the requirement that such overt acts be proved by testimony of two witnesses; also as to whether each overt act submitted to the jury complied with constitutional requirements." (88 L. Ed. 1598, 64 Sup. Ct. 1149 [1944]) At the request of the Department of Justice, the Navy Department assigned me to work for some months for the Solicitor General to prepare an historical appendix for the government's brief on reargument to deal with the English and American background of the treason offense. Solicitor General Charles Fahy put no restrictions on the materials or findings which I prepared for

vii

this appendix to the government's brief. The Court's opinion in *Cramer* v. *United States,* 325 U. S. 1, 8, note 9 (1945) took note of the relation between the work of several scholars in addition to that of counsel:

> Counsel for petitioner [Mr. Harold R. Medina], although assigned by the trial court, has responded with extended researches. The Solicitor General engaged scholars not otherwise involved in conduct of the case [including Dr. Elio Gianturco, Research Assistant to the Foreign Law Section of the Law Library of Congress, Dr. V. Gsovski, Chief of the Foreign Law Section of that Law Library, and Dr. Stephan G. Kuttner, Professor of the History of Canon Law, The Catholic University of America] to collect and impartially to summarize statutes, decisions and texts from Roman, Continental, and Canon Law as well as from English, Colonial, and American law sources. . . . Counsel have lightened our burden of examination of the considerable accumulation of historical materials.

These essays owe much to the invaluable assistance given in their preparation by Professor Eldon James, then Law Librarian of Congress, and members of his staff. For the opportunity to prepare material on developments in the law since the *Cramer* decision, I am indebted to the Trustees of the William F. Vilas Trust Estate, under whose auspices I hold a chair as Vilas Professor of Law in the University of Wisconsin. The opinions stated in the original essays and in the updated material are mine, and do not purport to reflect the official position either of the Department of Justice or of the United States Navy, or any position of the Vilas trustees or of the University of Wisconsin.

A student of the subject may wish to take note in particular of several other sources of materials and comment published since the *Cramer* case. Most general is a legal survey by Arthur M. Stillman and Frederick R. Arner, of the American Law

Division of the Library of Congress, *Federal Case Law Concerning the Security of the United States* (83d Congress, 2d Session. Printed for the use of the Senate Committee on Foreign Relations. Government Printing Office. Washington. 1954).

Simon, "The Evolution of Treason," 35 *Tulane Law Review* 667 (1961), and Hill, "The Two-Witness Rule in English Treason Trials," 12 *American Journal of Legal History* 95 (1968), provide more material on the political and older legal context of English origins than the essay in this collection, which focuses on the analysis of the crime in the standard treatises. Especially useful in adding a different dimension of source materials to the doctrinal aspects of treason on which these essays center is the monograph by Bradley Chapin, *The American Law of Treason: Revolutionary and Early National Origins* (University of Washington Press. Seattle. 1964). After sketching colonial developments, this book gives the bulk of its text to the American Revolution and the remainder to the years from 1789 through the trial of Burr. The study is especially useful for its attention to executive, administrative, and trial court documents, and for its focus on action taken under the law in the Revolution. What it principally shows of this period is a readiness to confiscate property, but a marked lack of enthusiasm for mass jailings or executions under charges of treason—a pattern which fits with the generally restrictive attitude taken in legal doctrine on the offense. I would raise one substantial caveat as to the Chapin monograph: I doubt its claim that there is continuing life in the idea of treason by constructive levying of war, in forcible resistance to enforcement of particular laws. I find more persuasive the material presented in these essays, indicating that this branch of the crime has become obsolete by nonuse and by critical reaction against it at the bar and in the courts.

The development of treason doctrine was not just the product of courts. As in other fields of law, doctrinal movement was also affected by the strategy and tactics of contending counsel. A reader interested in the legal process aspects of the matter should take note of the work and comments of a distinguished Washington lawyer, Mr. Frederick Bernays Wiener, on the relation between the history of treason law and the argument and decision of particular treason cases. Mr. Wiener criticizes the manner in which legal history materials were used in presenting *Cramer* to the Supreme Court, in his paper, "Uses and Abuses of Legal History (A Lecture to the Selden Society)," 59 *The Law Society's Gazette* 311 (1962). The government was ably represented in *Cramer*. But skilled lawyers inevitably differ in the approaches they take in presenting issues to a court. The observer should find instruction in comparing the government's briefs in *Cramer,* and especially its brief on reargument, with the brief for the United States before the Supreme Court in *Haupt* (1947), in which Mr. Wiener had a shaping hand as special assistant to the Attorney General. These documents will be found in any of the major law libraries in this country which keep records and briefs of cases in the United States Supreme Court. Mr. Wiener, it should be noted, also led for the government in the argument which lies back of the leading decision of the First Circuit Court of Appeals in *Chandler* v. *United States* (1948).

Acknowledgments

GRATEFUL acknowledgment is made to the editors of the journals listed in which these pages first appeared for their kind permission to reprint them.

Chapter 1 was originally entitled "The Historic Background of the Treason Clause of the United States Constitution" and appeared in 6 *The Federal Bar Journal* 305–313 (1945). Chapter 2, originally entitled "English Sources of the American Law of Treason," first appeared in 1945 *Wisconsin Law Review* 315–356. Chapters 3, 4, and 5 were originally published as a three-part essay, "Treason in the United States," in 58 *Harvard Law Review* 226–272, 395–444, 806–857 (1944–1945). The notes in chapters 3–5 have been renumbered, beginning with "1" in each chapter.

THE LAW OF TREASON
IN THE UNITED STATES

1

The Historic Background
of the Treason Clause
in the Constitution

IN ITS MOST original aspects, as in the commerce clause, the Constitution of the United States expresses policies the strength of which lies in their capacity to embrace and take new vigor from changed circumstances since 1787. But there are other aspects in which the strength of constitutional policy lies in the definiteness and the distillation of experience given by the invoking of historic concepts. This has been most marked, perhaps, in regard to institutions recognized by the Constitution, or some of the procedural decencies guaranteed to the individual facing the power of the state.

Article III, Section 3, bears the mark of a provision the primary reference of which is to history:

> Treason against the United States, shall consist only in levying War against them, or in adhering to their Enemies, giving them Aid and Comfort. No person shall be convicted of Treason unless on the Testimony of two Witnesses to the same overt Act, or on Confession in open Court. . . .

The Congress shall have Power to declare the Punishment of Treason, but no Attainder of Treason shall work Corruption of Blood, or Forfeiture except during the Life of the Person attainted. [1]

The framers did not choose to contrive their own definition of the crime of attempting the subversion of the government. "Treason" is itself a term which—to speak only of the Anglo-American background—was familiar to the common law before it was used in the Statute of 25 Edward III, from which the Constitution derives its language concerning the levying of war, and adhering to enemies, giving them aid and comfort. [1] The record makes it clear that terms thus weighted with historic significance were deliberately chosen, in order better to deal with a problem the practical dangers of which history was believed to teach. [2]

The appeal of *Cramer* v. *United States,* recently heard on reargument in the Supreme Court of the United States, illustrates both the need to resort to history and the limitations of the assistance which history can give, in applying the policy of the treason clause. [3] As has been noted, the propriety or wisdom of resort to history is implicit in the framers' deliberate use of a tradition-weighted concept of the crime of subversion of the state. This of course does not mean that constitutional policy is to be straitjacketed or to be easily evaded by skirting the edges of the peculiar situations which make up the history of the policy involved. The American decisions are uniform to the effect that the restrictive policy of the treason clause is to be understood in the light of history, but, likewise, that it is to be vigorously and sympathetically enforced out of respect to the lessons of that history. [4] Thus, there is of course no difficulty in ruling that, within the terms borrowed from a fourteenth century statute, aid may be rendered an enemy by means familiar to the commercial world of the twentieth century. [5]

Granted that the treason clause calls for careful examination of the history evoked by its terms, how far may that inquiry be pressed? It would beg the question offhandedly to borrow English experience, for in large part the balance between acceptance and rejection of the English inheritance is that which gives its peculiarly American flavor to our law. Some dicta have gone so far as to intimate the necessity of a wholesale repudiation of the English background of the law of treason.[6] This seems illogical: if one accepts the relevance of history, it is the logic of history and not of some juristic theory which must decide what evidence is proper and pertinent. The clear weight of American authority accordingly takes the common-sense approach, that English materials may properly be used to help explore the policy behind the concepts borrowed from the Statute of Edward III.[7] But American judges also have recognized that the very inclusion of a restrictive definition of "treason" in the Constitution plainly evidences a repudiation of some part of the English experience. In one respect, the comparison between what the framers took from English history, and what they pointedly omitted, is most striking. The treason clause contains no provision analogous to that by which the Statute of Edward III penalized the compassing of the king's death. In the light of the record, it is too shallow an explanation to hold that this omission occurs simply because that provision had no analogue in a republic.[8] Charges of compassing the king's death had been the principal instrument by which "treason" had been employed in England for the most drastic, "lawful" suppression of political opposition or the expression of ideas or beliefs distasteful to those in power.[9] At the time of the adoption of the Constitution, the treason clause was most praised for the reason that it prevented the use of treason trials as an instrument of political faction; and the link here to the omission of any provision similar to the charge of compassing seems clear.[10] Judges have accordingly denied the general relevance of English precedents peculiarly derived from the charge of compassing the king's death and have agreed that the mere expression of beliefs cannot be deemed "treason" within the constitutional definition.[11]

In a respect less clearcut, but as important, the lesson of history has called for careful distinction between aspects of English history which help explain the policy of the treason clause and others which run counter to it. An elementary caution which must be observed in the use of legal history is to avoid equating it with judge-made law alone. Indeed, the greatest usefulness of an historical approach to the determination of policy should be the recognition of the interaction of legal and non-legal institutions and pressures in the shaping of law. No better illustration could be wished than the story of the desuetude of the crime of "constructive" levying of war. According to the decisions of the English courts, in 1787, the levying of war upon the king could consist in any effort by violence to fix or enforce public policy; and this was taken to include forcible resistance to the general execution of a law, or the attempt by force to deprive any class of the people of their rights under law, or to influence the king's choice of counsellors. This amounted to saying that the line between treason and riot was unpredictable and would shift towards the more serious crime largely according to the ruthlessness or strong-mindedness of the administration. This, however, was doctrine better suited to an age of royal rather than of parliamentary power, and by the end of the eighteenth century English juries had reflected this basic shift in constitutional politics by acquitting of "treason" several notable defendants who, like Horne Tooke or Lord George Gordon, had been at most guilty of inciting to riot.[12] In the first years under the Constitution, Federalist judges applied the broad scope of English legal doctrine in cases arising out of the Whiskey Rebellion and the disturbances against the House Tax of 1799, which were at least on the borderline between subversion and riot. Since the Constitution had deliberately chosen to define "treason" in terms broadly interpreted by English judges in the interest of the state, and at the same time had clearly indicated a policy favoring restriction of the scope of the crime, there was room for doubt, if a narrow reading of history were applied to the treason clause. But President John Adams pardoned the rioters in 1799, because he believed that their convictions imported into the law concepts inconsistent with contemporary policy.[13] And subsequently, Justices Livingston and Grier, on circuit, insisted that not the formal doctrine of the English reports but the living practice of the English constitution was the proper background to understand the restrictive policy which Article III, Section 3, expresses.[14] As long since in England, so in the United States since the Civil War, with one abortive exception, no effort seems to have been made to charge the crime of treason by levying war simply on the basis of a breach of the peace without a showing of a specific intent to overthrow the government.[15]

The relevance of English history to the constitutional definition of treason introduces also the more specific question of determining the sources of that history. There is historic logic in beginning with the English materials in a subject like "treason," because American policy was derived from American ideas concerning the meaning of English experience as well as American professional familiarity with English statutes and treatises. This means giving attention to those aspects of English materials which the evidence indicates were most significant to Americans, or which best illuminate the development of the branches of treason which concerned American law, rather than trying to trace all the ramifications of the English law as such. Thus, in the analysis of "treason," it proves sound to place first the analysis of the accounts of the crime given in the great English law treatises prior to the adoption of the United States Constitution,

because only in them do we find any careful attempt to
analyze the policy behind and elements of the offense and
because the Americans obtained their knowledge of the
English law and experience primarily from the treatises.
Americans likewise had access to English statutory materials,
which are thus relevant to our inquiry. The English State
Trials seem, however, to deserve only third rank in value for
exploring the historic background of the treason clause. True,
this is partly because of inherent limitations; the impressive
volumes of the State Trials contain a maximum of pleadings,
tedious testimony, and records of executions and a minimum
of helpful analysis. Moreover, one famous trial after another
proves on careful examination to be so interwoven with the
peculiar politico-religious motives and pressures of its time as
to be of little value beyond furnishing cumulative evidence
that careful and realistic definition of the offense is necessary
if "treason" is not to be readily abused as an instrument of
faction. But, the ultimate reason which must make the State
Trials a dubious source for understanding the constitutional
provision is that there is little satisfactory evidence that
Americans had access to or extensive knowledge of the
records of English trials, as distinguished from their familiarity with the basic English statutes and treatises.[16]

When one turns to the American sources of the period
prior to the framing of the Constitution, the most obvious
feature is the overwhelming predominance of materials of a
legislative nature. This of course presents merely an example
of a familiar problem of the assessment of historical sources:
since history is necessarily based on records, one must ask
whether the matter which chanced to be recorded and
preserved can be taken as typical of the general run of what
men were doing and thinking. Records of executive and
judicial action in the earlier periods are less voluminous than
the statute books. But this does not necessarily mean that
there was no significant activity in the executive or judicial

fields. Thus there is a handful of "treason" trials recorded for
the period of the Revolution. The reason for the paucity of
civil trials, on further examination, proves to be the widespread resort to summary administrative or court martial
handling of cases. Again, the evidence of the statute books
would suggest that "treason" was handled with great severity.
But such evidence as is available of the judicial and executive
practice suggests that in the whole picture severity was felt in
the drastic confiscation of property rather than in the imposi-
tion of capital punishment.[17] There is, however, no evidence
to suggest that the legislative materials do not fairly reflect the
prevailing notions of the desirable scope of "treason" and the
elements of the crime. The statute books thus in this, as in so
many instances, furnish an important and too often ignored
type of evidence of the evolution of policy.

A search for the legislative type of source material leads to
various avenues. There are, for example, colonial charters,
proprietary grants, and colonial and state "Fundamental
Articles" and constitutions for each of the original thirteen
states. Moreover, this type of material suggests an important
link to the English sources. Instructions to royal governors
must be checked. There was, likewise, royal surveillance of
the action of colonial legislatures and executive and judicial
agencies under these fundamental colonial documents, and
this control may be observed through the records of the
Board of Trade and the Privy Council.[18] An adequate picture
of American policy as reflected in legislation before the
Constitution requires search of the statute books of the
thirteen original states through 1790, and of Vermont from
its separation from New York in 1776 through 1790. Similarly, the Declaration of Independence, the Articles of Confederation and the "Ordinance of 1787 for the government
of the territory of the United States northwest of the river
Ohio" (as well as the legislation of the Northwest Territory), together with the Journals of the Continental Congress consti-

tute basic sources for the study of policy evolving before 1787. Especially in the case of the colonial and state statute books, the inadequacy or absence of indexing will frequently require a check item by item or even by paging of volumes. [19]

The familiar law reports contain no decisions in treason cases prior to 1790, except for a handful of Pennsylvania cases in the volumes of Dallas, reflecting a burst of prosecuting zeal following the recovery of Philadelphia from the British. After the adoption of the Constitution, the reports contain between thirty-five and forty instances of treason prosecutions carried to the point of judicial decision. Though not up to the standard of inclusiveness set by Howell's English State Trials, Wharton's *State Trials of the United States* (Philadelphia, 1849), and Lawson's *American State Trials* (17 volumes, St. Louis, 1914–1926) contain also a number of important cases not elsewhere easily accessible, notably the trials of Thomas Wilson Dorr (1844) and of John Brown (1859) on charges of treason by levying war against the States of Rhode Island and Virginia, respectively. Local histories contain references to other abortive efforts to employ treason indictments against individuals who and groups which had incurred the wrath of more powerful elements in the community. The troubled history of the Mormons provides outstanding examples in indictments brought against Mormon leaders in Missouri in 1838 and in Illinois in 1844. [20] The incomplete as well as the finished stories of history may cast helpful light on the growth and meaning of public policy; and the inconclusive result of such charges as those in the Mormon cases contribute to the phenomenon already noted, of the practical abandonment of any broad resort to the crime of levying of war.

For the Philadelphia Convention and its sequel, the basic sources are, of course, Farrand's *Records of the Federal Convention of 1787, The Federalist,* and Elliott's *Debates in the Several State Conventions on the Adoption of the Federal Constitution.* The history of the treason clause presents an especially clear example of the illumination to be had from Elliott's collection of the debates in the state ratifying conventions, for it is there that the proud citation of the treason clause by the Constitution's proponents makes most clear the intent that its restrictive definition safeguards normal political processes against repressive prosecutions. Our constitutional tradition is not expressed only in the formal records, however. The private papers, speeches and draftsmanship of American statesmen are contributing factors. Thus further light on the restrictive policy expressed in Article III, Section 3, may be had from such diverse sources as Thomas Jefferson's letter of November 1, 1778, to Chancellor Wythe concerning the former's proposed Virginia "bill for proportioning Crimes and Punishments in cases heretofore Capital," and James Wilson's Lectures on Law, delivered in the College of Philadelphia in 1790 and 1791.[21]

Thus, even a brief canvass of the variety of historical sources of potential help in explaining the policy background of the Constitution's treason clause suggests the complex wealth of material which such an approach may add to the case-trained lawyer's familiar tools of decision and opinion. But, likewise, it suggests that since the historical approach seeks nothing less than to comprehend the whole pattern of causes which shape a given policy, it requires of the advocate an imaginative readiness to forego the abstract logic of doctrine for the living logic of events.

NOTES

1. See Glanvill, De Legibus et Consuetudinibus Regni Angliae (Woodbine, ed. New Haven, 1932) Lib. 1, cap. 2, Lib. 14, cap. 1; Bracton, De Legibus et Consuetudinibus Angliae (Woodbine, ed. New Haven, 1932) f.

118b; Coke, Institutes of the Laws of England, Third Part (5th ed. London, 1671) 2–3.

2. See 2 Farrand, ed., Records of the Federal Convention of 1787 (New Haven, 1937) 345–350; Wilson, Lectures on Law, delivered in the College of Philadelphia, 1790 and 1791, in 3 Works of Hon. James Wilson (Bird Wilson, ed., Philadelphia, 1804) 99–100.

3. See *United States* v. *Cramer*, 137 F. (2d) 888 (C.C.A. 2d. 1943), reversed, 325 U.S. 1 (1945). The case in essence posed the problem of the relation between the "intent" and the "act" elements in the crime. On two separate occasions, the defendant, a naturalized American citizen, was observed by two F.B.I. agents to meet over a meal with an enemy agent. The two witnesses could testify only to the fact of the meeting; the defendant's admissions on the witness stand furnished the only evidence from which it could be argued that he knew that he was dealing with the enemy and that in fact he gave aid to the enemy by holding funds for the latter's convenience and by putting him in contact with a likely friend. The defense contended that if the constitutional requirement of two witnesses to the same overt act were to give substantial protection to innocent persons, only an act would suffice which "manifested" the treason, and that an act innocent on its face was not enough. The Government replied that this analysis seemed to mean that the act must be in itself at least some evidence of the treasonable intent, that such a construction deprived the intent element of the offense of its separate significance and so narrowed the practical scope of the crime as unreasonably to imperil the community. This is a much simplified statement of the case presented, but will suffice, since it is not the purpose of this discussion to explore the merits of the issue, but rather the use of historical materials in its solution.

4. *E.g.,* Iredell, Circ. J., in Case of Fries, Fed. Cas. No. 5126, 9 Fed. Cas. 826, 912 (Circ. Ct., D. Pa., 1799); Marshall, Circ. J., in *United States* v. *Burr,* Fed. Cas. No. 14,693, 25 Fed. Cas. 55, 159–160 (Circ. Ct., D. Va., 1807); Field, Circ., J., in *United States* v. *Greathouse,* Fed Cas. No. 15,254, 26 Fed. Cas. 18, 21 (Circ. Ct., N.D. Cal., 1863).

5. *Cf. United States* v. *Fricke,* 259 Fed. 673 (S.D.N.Y., 1919).

6. See Charge to Grand Jury, by Nelson, Circ., J., Fed. Cas. No. 18,271, 30 Fed. Cas. 1034, 1035 (Circ. Ct., S.D.N.Y., 1861).

7. See note 4, *supra.*

8. See 2 Swift, A System of the Laws of the State of Connecticut (Windham, 1796) 297; Rawle, A View of the Constitution of the United States (2d ed. Philadelphia, 1829) 141.

9. 8 Holdsworth, History of English Law (2d ed. 12 vol. London, 1937) 309, 311.

10. See Madison, in The Federalist (Lodge, ed. N. Y., 1908) No. XLIII, pp. 269, 463; James Wilson, in the Pennsylvania Convention, 2 Elliott, Debates in the Several State Conventions on the Adoption of the Federal Constitution (2d ed. Washington, 1854) 469, 487.

11. See Peters, J., in Case of Fries, Fed. Cas. No. 5126, 9 Fed. Cas. 826, 909 (Circ. Ct., D. Pa., 1799) (first trial), and Chase, Circ. J., in same case, Fed. Cas. No. 5127, 9 Fed. Cas. 924, 927 (Circ. Ct., D. Pa., 1800) (second trial); *Wimmer v. United States*, 264 Fed. 11, 13 (C.C.A. 6th, 1920), cert. den. 253 U. S. 494.

12. 8 Holdsworth, *op. cit. supra*, note 9, p. 335 ff.

13. See *United States* v. *Vigol*, Fed. Cas. No. 16,621, 28 Fed. Cas. 376 and *United States* v. *Mitchell*, Fed. Cas. No. 15,788, 26 Fed. Cas. 1277 (Circ. Ct., D. Pa., 1795); Case of Fries, note 11, *supra;* 9 Works of John Adams (Boston, 1856) 58, 10 *id.* 153, 154.

14. Livingston, Circ. J., in *United States* v. *Hoxie*, Fed. Cas. No. 15,407, 26 Fed. Cas. 397, 400, 402 (Circ. Ct., D. Vt., 1808); Grier, Circ. J., in *United States* v. *Hanway*, Fed. Cas. No. 15299, 26 Fed. Cas. 105, 127 (Circ. Ct., E.D. Pa., 1851).

15. The exception was the short-lived attempt to charge the leaders of the Homestead strike with treason. See Paxson, C. J., in *Commonwealth* v. *O'Donnell*, 12 Pa. Co. 97, 104–105 (O. & T. Allegheny Cty. 1892); Burgoyne, Homestead (Pittsburgh, 1893) 294.

16. Coke, Hale, Hawkins, and Foster are the English treatises of which Americans had the greatest familiarity. As to American access to English legal sources in general, see Aumann, The Changing American Legal System (Columbus, 1940); Goebel and Naughton, Law Enforcement in Colonial New York (N. Y. 1944) xxiii, xxv; Morris, Studies in the History of American Law (N. Y. 1930) 44 ff., 67; Warren, A History of the American Bar (Boston, 1911) Ch. VIII.

17. Palsitts, Minutes of the Commissioners for detecting and defeating Conspiracies in the State of New York, 1778–1781 (3 vol. Albany, 1909); Van Tyne, The Loyalists in the American Revolution (N. Y. 1929) 271, 272.

18. See Labaree, Royal Instructions to British Colonial Governors, 1670–1776 (2 vol. N. Y. 1935); Thorpe, The Federal and State Constitutions, Colonial Charters, and Other Organic Laws (7 vol. Washington, 1909).

19. See Babbitt, Hand-List of Legislative Sessions and Session Laws, Statutory Revisions, Compilations, Codes, etc., and Constitutional Conventions of the United States and Its Possessions and of the Several States, to May, 1912 (State Library of Massachusetts. Boston, 1912).

20. See Culmer, New History of Missouri (Mexico, Mo., 1938) 212; 1 Roberts, Comprehensive History of the Church of Jesus Christ of Latter-Day Saints (Salt Lake City, 1930) 499, 500, 529, 530; 2 *id.* 254; Ford, History of Illinois (Chicago, 1854) 337.

21. See 1 Writings of Thomas Jefferson (Library ed. Washington, 1903) 216, 218, 220–221; Wilson, Lectures on Law, *op. cit. supra,* note 2 Ch. V.

2

English Sources of the Law of Treason

ARTICLE III, Section 3 of the United States Constitution provides:

> Treason against the United States, shall consist only in levying War against them, or in adhering to their Enemies, giving them Aid and Comfort. No Person shall be convicted of Treason unless on the Testimony of two Witnesses to the same overt Act, or on Confession in open Court.
>
> The Congress shall have power to declare the Punishment of Treason, but no Attainder of Treason shall work Corruption of Blood, or Forfeiture except during the Life of the Person attainted.

Accurate definition of the intent and act elements and the policies underlying their definition provides the central and most difficult problems in the law of treason. Treason is the betrayal of allegiance owed a political sovereign either because of citizenship or because of acceptance of the protection

14

of laws. Obviously the intention is at the heart of such a crime. Is an act a distinct element of the offense, in addition to the showing of the intent to betray? Must the act be of some peculiar character, or must it be such as to furnish some evidence, or evidence beyond a reasonable doubt, of the existence of the treasonable intention? The crime is the most serious against the safety of the state; but, by the same token, the stigma it carries, and the vagueness of its reach have made it a notorious instrument of arbitrary power and political faction. This contrast poses the further question, whether in a doubtful case policy calls upon the court to extend the scope of the offense for the protection of the state, or to restrict it for the protection of the individual.

The treason clause of the United States Constitution was written, debated, and adopted by men whose ideas regarding the policy and historical implications of the law of treason were derived from English law. The very terms of Article III, Section 3 are in large part derived from the statute of 25 Edward III (1350), among whose seven categories of high treason the most important were to "compass or imagine the death of our lord the King," to "levy war against our lord the King in his realm," or to adhere to his enemies, giving them aid and comfort. The omission of any provision analogous to that against compassing the king's death, and the constitutional limitation of "treason" to the other two of the three principal branches of the Statute of Edward III, form the heart of the restrictive policy evidenced in the definition in Section 3 of Article III. Clearly, it is relevant to an understanding of the terms of that section to examine the English doctrine with which the Americans of 1787 were familiar. First importance in this undertaking should be given to the analysis of the accounts of "treason" in the great English law treatises prior to the adoption of the United States Constitution. This is both because only in the treatises do we find any careful effort to analyze the policy and the elements of the crime, and because the Americans obtained their knowledge of the English law and experience primarily from the treatises. Granting always the fundamental importance of the Statute of Edward III, other English legislative materials contribute little to explicit analysis of the crime. The case materials deserve only third rank in value; the impressive volumes of the State Trials contain a maximum of pleadings, tedious testimony and records of executions, and a minimum of helpful examination of the policy and elements of the offense. Moreover, one famous case after another proves, on close inspection, to be so interwoven with the peculiar political and religious motives and pressures of its time as to be of little value beyond furnishing cumulative evidence of the readiness with which the crime has been abused as an instrument of faction. Finally, there is little satisfactory evidence that Americans had access to, or extensive knowledge of the records of the English trials, as distinguished from their familiarity with the basic statute and the treatises.

This study, therefore, examines the accounts given in the basic English treatises of the elements of the crime of treason, and the policy which should guide application of the law in doubtful cases. The discussion is supplemented by brief consideration of 19th and 20th century texts.

(a) Early English Treatises[1]

Significantly, there is no word of any policy restrictive of the scope of "treason" in the brief definitions and discussions of the early books (Glanvill, Bracton, Britton, Staundford). The crime is simply set forth in positive terms, looking to the interest in the security of the king and his authority. Staundford notes that the Statute of Edward III asserted the need for resolving the uncertainties of the common law regarding the extent of the offense, but he does not feel impelled to add any special words of praise for the endeavor.[2] Appropriately, the new emphasis on safeguarding the liberty of the subject first appears in Coke. His discussion is not wholly consistent in this respect,[3] and in one instance especially, he avows a principle of liberal construction in favor of the king:

> This compassing, intent, or imagination, though secret, is to be tryed by the peers, and to be discovered by circumstances precedent, concomitant, and subsequent, with all endeavour evermore for the safety of the King.[4]

This is said, however, with reference to the most vague and precautionary head of the Statute, which is pointedly omitted in the restrictive terms of the Constitution of the United States. Apart from this, the general terms of Coke's analysis are all such as to stress that the distinguishing mark of the Statute of Edward III is its limitation of the scope of the crime.

> And albeit nothing can concern the King, his crown and dignity, more then *Crimen laesae Majestatis,* High Treason: Yet at the request of his Lords and Commons, the blessed King by authority of Parliament made the Declaration, as is above-said; and therefore, and for other excellent laws made at this Parliament, this was called *Benedictum Parliamentum,* as it well deserved. For except it be *Magna Charta,* no other Act of Parliament hath had more honour given unto it by the King, Lords spirituall and temporall and the Commons of the Realm for the time being in full Parliament, then this Act concerning Treason hath had, For by the Statute of *1 H. 4 cap. 10.* reciting that where at a Parliament holden *21 R. 2* divers pains of treason were ordained by Statute, in as much as there was no man did know how to behave himself to doe, speak, or say, for doubt of such pains: It is enacted by the King, the Lords and Commons, that in no time to come any

treason be judged otherwise, then it was ordained by this Statute of *25 E. 3.* . . . [After reciting other acts to the same effect:] And all this was done in severall ages, that the faire Lillies and Roses of the Crown might flourish, and not be stained by severe and sanguinary Statutes. . . . [5]

At the outset of his discussion, he emphasizes the importance of the clause referring the declaration of new treasons to Parliament, and subsequently he points out that this means, broadly, that the judges "shall not judge à simili, or by equity, argument, or inference of any treason," and that the statutory injunction that nothing be taken to be treason thereunder which is not "specifically" so declared, is

A happy sanctuary or place of refuge for Judges to flye unto, that no mans blood and ruine of his family do lie upon their consciences against law. And if that the construction by arguments *à simili or à minori ad majus* had been left to Judges, the mischiefe before this statute would have remained, *viz.* diversity of opinions, what ought to be adjudged treason, which this statute hath taken away by expresse words.[6]

He cautions, though, that "the clause . . . of restraint of like cases, *&c.* extends onely to offences, and not to tryals, judgements, or executions"[7] But this seems to refer to matters of procedure and sentence, and, in view of the general emphasis of the treatise, does not mean that the scope of the offense might in effect be extended by new definitions of the evidence which would suffice to make out a charge under one of the classic headings.[8] Coke applies the doctrine of strict construction to limit the offense of adherence to enemies:

A. is out of the Realm at the time of a Rebellion within England, and one of the Rebels flie out of the Realm, whom A. knowing his treason doth aide or succour, this is no treason in A. by this branch of 25 E. 3. because the traytor is no enemy, as hereafter shall be said; and this statute is taken strictly.[9]

Again, since the words of the statute punished him who should bring counterfeit money "en cest roialme," it was not an offense within this clause if the counterfeit was brought from Ireland, which for some purposes is a part of the realm — ". . . so wary are Judges to expound this statute concerning Treason, and that in most benigne sense."[10]

There is nothing in Coke's discussion more explicit than the passages quoted above, to indicate that his praise of the restrictive policy evidenced by the Statute of Edward III was given with particular thought to prevention of oppressive resort to "treason" prosecutions in domestic political controversy, as distinguished from charges of dealing with external enemies. But, it will be noted that his reference to strict construction in the case of the crime of adhering to enemies points towards keeping that clause of the Act out of the sphere of home politics. And the fact is, that the "divers pains of treason . . . ordained by Statute," which are cited as oppressive and threatening in their vague scope, all focussed on the struggle for power immediately between essentially English factions. This seems true even of legislation directed against the assertion of papal power. This matter is more explicitly treated in Hale, and will be noted further at that point.

The earliest books are thoroughly ambiguous as to the kind of overt act, if any, required to make out a case under the various headings of "treason." Glanvill recognizes the existence of the "crimen quod in legibus dicitur crimen laesae maiestatis, ut de nece vel seditione personae domini regis vel regni vel exercitus," and this he later described as existing "cum quis itaque de morte regis vel de seditione regni vel exercitus infamatur"[11] but these definitions—though inter-

esting for the hint of Roman influence ("laesae maiestatis")—
shed no light on the types of conduct which would fit these
general descriptions. At only one point, in describing the
steps in procedure, does he approach specifications:

> Ad ultimum autem accusatore proponente se vidisse vel alio modo
> in curia probato certissime se scivisse, ipsum accusatum machina-
> tum fuisse vel aliquid fecisse in mortem regis vel seditionem regni
> vel exercitus, vel consensisse vel consilium dedisse vel auctoritatem
> praestitisse. . . .
>
> At length, however, when the accusor has charged that he saw,
> or that, by another way proved in court, he knew for a certainty
> that the accused had plotted or had done something toward the
> death of the king [against the life of the king] or insurrection in
> the kingdom or in the army or had consented or given counsel or
> conferred authority therefor. . . . [12]

This seems to put simple conspiracy or plotting of the named
ends on a par with their execution, so far as the offense goes.
If conspiracy is put aside, however, Glanvill seems to refer to
overt acts ("vel aliquid fecisse") not as inherently reflecting
evil intent, but simply as an independent element of the
crime; and this seems reinforced by the fact that, as he puts it,
the relevance of the "something" which was done was that it
put a train of events in motion, looking toward one of the
specified purposes or results ("in mortem regis vel seditionem
regni vel exercitus": the use of the accusative with "in"). Thus
when action is referred to as an element in the completed
offense—whatever the significance of the act in a charge of
conspiracy to commit the offense—Glanvill does not indicate
that the action is significant as evidence of intent but as
evidence of the fact of beginning execution of the intent. It is
also interesting to note that at this early reference, there is the
idea that contact or conference with dangerous persons
presents *per se* a social danger.

These implications—including the suggestion of Roman ideas of the basic policy of protecting the head of the state—are reinforced in the terse definition of Bracton:

> Habet enim crimen laesae maiestatis sub se multas species, quarum una est ut si quis ausu temerario machinatus sit in mortem regis, vel aliquid egerit vel agi procuraverit ad seditionem domini regis vel exercitus sui, vel procurantibus auxilium et consilium praebuerit vel consensum, licet id quod in voluntate habuerit non perduxerit ad effectum.

> For the crime of lèse majesté includes many types, one of which is, if anyone out of rash daring [by a deed of rash daring?] should plot the death of the king, or do something or cause something to be done towards the betrayal of our lord the king or his army or gives aid and counsel to those procuring these things, or gives consent thereto, though he does not carry through to accomplishment what he had in intention.[13]

Whether or not "ausu temerario" means that an overt act was necessary in Bracton's view for the offense of compassing the king's death—Coke thought not[14]—Bracton seems clearly to require overt acts for the offense denominated "seditionem domini regis vel exercitus sui," and the something which must be shown to have been done ("aliquid egerit vel agi procuraverit") is treated as important not as evidence of intent, but because it puts in train a course of action leading to the forbidden result (the use of "ago" with "ad" seems significant, i.e.). The importance of the fact of action taken towards the prohibited purpose seems implied in the contrast of "machinatus sit in mortem regis" and "aliquid egerit . . . ad seditionem . . . , " and by the final contrast of the intention and the incomplete course of action.

Britton and Fleta are of no assistance in defining the scope of the offense, though the former's definition is interesting for the sweeping principle of punishing "betrayal" which he announces and for his concentration on plotting the king's death.[15] Staundford notes that at common law "cestuy qui succorda as enemyes le roy" was guilty of treason; this is probably the offense of adherence ("succurro"?) and implies an overt act as an independent element of the crime.[16] His most interesting discussion concerns the offense of compassing the king's death, as set out in the Statute of Edward III, of which he comments,

> Cest compassement, ou imagination, sauns reducer ceo al effect, est grand treason, come apiert. M. 19. H. 6. f. 47. & P. 13 H. 8. fo. 13. Mes intant que compassement & imagination sont secrete, & ne poient etre conus sinon per un overt fait, est requisit daver ascun chose fait, a signifier le dit compassement ou imagination. Per que ie query, si le dit compassement ou imagination uttere per parolx soit sufficient signification de ceo ou nemye . . . Bracton. Semble que cy . . . Britton in semblable manner. . . . [17]

He notes that the Statute of Edward III adopts the same terms used by the early treatises regarding the offense of compassing the king's death, and so indicates his belief that the statute is to be interpreted according to the scope of the previous authorities. Coke disagreed, emphasizing the overall and explicit requirement of an overt act under that statute, though he felt that a writing might be an overt act.[18] Staundford does not mention the overt act requirement of the Statute of Edward III, and in view of his broad language it is questionable whether he did not overlook it in connection with his analysis of the offense of compassing the king's death. In any event, he introduces us to an ambiguous terminology which bedevils discussion henceforth. When he says that an "overt fait" is necessary, because compassing is secret and cannot be known without such, he seems to regard the act as relevant simply as evidence of the treasonable intent; but he sums up by saying that "ascun chose fait" is necessary "a signifier" ("declare" or "show") the compassing. The overt act might "declare" the compassing, however, either in the sense of evidencing a treasonable intent, or of translating the intent into the world of action by some thing done towards its execution. There seems to be no further help in Staundford to resolve this difficulty, and his discussion is of limited usefulness in any case, because it deals only with the crime of imagining the death of the king.

Coke uses this ambiguous wording, in repeated statements that the offenses of compassing the king's death and adhering to his enemies include the element of "declaring the same by some overt deed."[19] There are important passages in which he seems to regard the overt act as relevant, because and insofar as it helps prove treasonable intent. Thus, speaking of the Statute of Edward III, he states,

> The composition and connexion of the words are to be observed, *viz.* [thereof be attainted by overt deed]. This relateth to the severall and distinct treasons before expressed, (and specially to the compassing and imagination of the death of the King, &c. for that it is secret in the heart) and therefore one of them cannot be an overt act for another. As for example: a conspiracy is had to levie warre, this (as hath been said, and so resolved) is not treason by this Act untill it be levied, therefore it is no overt act or manifest proofe of the compassing of the death of the King within this Act; for the words be *(de ceo &c.)* that is, of the compassing of the death. For this were to confound the severall Clauses. . . . [20]

Thus he puts special emphasis on the overt act requirement as applied to that one of the offenses embraced by the statute the gist of which most clearly is the intent. Previously, in constructing an analytical table of the crimes defined by the act, he included in the offenses of compassing the king's death and adhering to his enemies the element of "declaring the same by some overt deed," as has been noted; but he omits this reference regarding the levying of war.[21] Clearly he views an overt act as an element of the last named crime, but it would seem that he felt that the conduct which would amount to levying war so plainly, of its intrinsic character, "declared" the treasonable intent, that no special emphasis was called for in his analysis. Note also, in the passage quoted above, that if a conspiracy to levy war were treated as a sufficient overt act to establish the offense of compassing the king's death, in Coke's view its relevance would be as an "overt act or manifest proofe of the compassing."

Further, he explains his view that words will not generally make an overt act, in terms which might seem to indicate that the relevance of the overt act is to prove clearly the existence of treasonable intent:

> . . . the wisdome of the makers of this law would not make words only to be Treason, seeing such variety amongst the witnesses are about the same, as few of them agree together. But if the same be set downe in writing by the Delinquent himselfe, this is a sufficient overt act within this statute. . . .
>
> In the Preamble of the statute of *1. Mar.* concerning the repeale of certaine Treasons, &c. It is agreed by the whole Parliament, that lawes justly made for the preservation of the Common-wealth without extreame punishment, are more often obeyed and kept, then lawes and statutes made with great and extreame punishments; and in speciall, such lawes and statutes so made: whereby not only the ignorant and rude unlearned people, but also learned and expert people minding honesty, are oftentimes trapped and snared, yea, many times for words only, without other fact or deed done or perpetrated: therefore this Act of *25 E. 3.* doth provide, that there must be an overt deed. But words without an overt deed are to be punished in another degree, as an high misprision.[22]

However, a close examination of these famous passages suggests that, in the first, Coke is merely saying that—

regardless whether offered to prove intent or overt act—mere spoken words are inherently too unreliable in witnesses' memories to be a just basis for establishing so high a crime. And in the approving recital of the Statute of 1 Mary, it is important to note that the objection is particularly to a case where the spoken words are the *sole* evidence, to prove all elements of the crime. Rather than reading this to mean that the overt act must always be such as itself evidences treasonable intent, it would seem more natural to construe the criticism as being simply that in many cases the spoken words, being offered as sole proof of the intent, were not adequate for that purpose, quite apart from their adequacy as an overt act. If spoken words are not generally a sufficient overt act, it will then be, as Coke later suggests was the general common law doctrine, simply because they generally do not represent a sufficient advance beyond the stage of thought into that of execution.[23] Though the interpretation of Coke's words here set out seems a reasonable one, his marginal note to the quotation from the preamble of the Statute of 1 Mary throws the matter back into doubt, for there he warns, "*Nota,* this Act of 25 E. 3 saith, *per overt fait, per apertum factum,* and not *per apertum dictum,* by word or confession." Coke here created an ambiguity which continues to fog analyses of the law of treason, as may be seen, for example, in Hale.

Throughout his discussion, Coke gives examples of overt acts which, without exception, seem acts which themselves are some evidence of treasonable intent. It is not clear whether he would hold that a meeting of conspirators to plot the king's death was a sufficient overt act for that broadest of offenses.[24]

On the other hand, there is evidence that Coke thought of the overt act as a separate element of the offense, whose function was not to furnish more objective evidence of the treasonable intent, but to establish that the business had moved from the realm of thought into the realm of action. He does not clearly link this with a general policy of the criminal law, that men are not prosecuted for wicked thoughts alone; but the belief that, after the Statute of Edward III at least, treason was in this respect no different from other crimes seems implicit in his treatment. Thus he begins by contrasting the common law crime of compassing the king's death with the general common law offense of compassing the death of an ordinary subject. He cites the maxim "Voluntas reputabatur pro facto," endorsed by Bracton, but points out that even under this principle, to be guilty, the defendant "must declare the same [i.e., his "voluntas"] by some open deed tending to the execution of his intent, or which might be cause of death" and that the crime was made out,

> So as it was not a bare compassing or plotting of the death of a man, either by word, or writing, but such an overt deed as is aforesaid, to manifest the same. So as if a man had compassed the death of another, and had uttered the same by words or writing, yet he should not have died for it, for there wanted an overt deed tending to the execution of his compassing.[25]

The examples he gives are of aggravated attempts falling short of success, but his emphasis is not that the deeds evidence the intent, but—a more objective stress—that they "tend to the execution of his intent." He then points out that the requirement of an overt act, under the Statute of Edward III, applies to all of the offenses defined therein, including compassing the king's death; and, as he has asserted that the Statute "is for the most part Declaratory of the ancient Law," it is a fair inference that he would interpret the overt act requirement now inserted in the offense of compassing the king's death in the same manner which he had interpreted that element in the general common law offense of plotting the death of a subject. The objective tendency of the act to forward a course of conduct seems the aspect which is stressed when he explains that the words "Per overt fait" doth also strengthen the former exposition of the word [provable-ment] that it must be probably, by an open act, which must be manifestly proved. As if divers do conspire the death of the King, and the manner how, and thereupon provide weapons, powder, poison, assay harnesse, send letters, &c. or the like, for execution of the conspiracy. Also preparation by some overt act, to depose the King, or take the King by force, and strong hand, and to imprison him, until he hath yeelded to certain demands, this is a sufficient overt act to prove the compassing, and imagination of the death of the King: for this upon the matter is to make the King a subject, and to dispoyl him of his kingly office of royall government.[26]

This seems also true of the statement that

if a subject conspire with a foraine Prince beyond the seas to invade the Realme by open hostility, and prepare for the same by some overt act, this is a sufficient overt act for the death of the King, for by this Act of Parliament in that Case there must be an overt act.[27]

And the emphasis upon the objective tendency of the act to further a plan of conduct appears in his explanation of the significance of the statute of 3 Henry VII, which made it a felony to plot the king's death:

By this Act it expressly appeareth by the judgement of the whole Parliament, that besides the confederacy, compassing, conspiracy, or imagination, there must be some other overt act or deed tending thereunto, to make it treason within the statute of *25 E. 3*. And therefore the bare confederacy, compassing, conspiracy, or imaginations by words only, is made felony by this Act. But if the Conspirators do provide any weapon, or other thing, to accom-plish their devilish intent, this and the like is an overt act to make it treason.[28]

So also when Coke pronounces that "a compassing or conspiracy to levy war is no Treason, for there must be a levying
of war *in facto,*"[29] he seems sharply to distinguish the overt act
from the showing of intent, since his statement clearly as-
sumes that a treasonable intent appears, and yet the offense
of levying war is not made out, for lack of the overt act. And
he points up the sharp distinction between intent and act as
separate elements of the crime, by citing the words of a
proper indictment:

> For first it is alledged according to this act, *Quod proditoriè
> compassavit, & imaginatus jult mortem & destructionem dñi regis, &
> ipsum dom. regem interficere, & c.* In the second part of the
> indictment is alledged the overt act, *& ad illam nephandam, &
> proditoriam compassationem, imaginationem, & propositum suum
> perficiend & perimplend,* and then certainly to set down the overt
> fact for preparation to take, and imprison the King, or any other
> sufficient overt act, which of necessity must be set down in the
> Indictment.[30]

Thus Lord Coke may be cited, with some conviction, to
both purposes: that the significance of the overt act is that it
confirms the evidence of evil intent, or that it is relevant
wholly apart from evidence of intent, in order to show that
the defendant's guilt had moved from the realm of thought
alone into that of action. Coke's attention was apparently not
directed to the problem of defining the precise function of
the overt act element, and hence his words must be taken in
either case with caution. However, on the whole, in view of his
over-riding emphasis on the distinct quality of the overt act
element under the Statute of Edward III, it seems that he
does not mean to insist that it be an act which in itself is
evidence of the treasonable intent.

(b) Treatises Published in the 18th Century

Hale comments frequently on the uncertain scope of "treason" at common law and during certain periods of legislative activity, notably under Richard II, and on the resultant uncertainty and insecurity of the individual. Thus, after stating the statute of 1 Henry IV, which restored the terms of the Statute of Edward III as the guide in defining the offense, he warns,

> Now altho the crime of high treason is the greatest crime against faith, duty, and human society, and brings with it the greatest and most fatal dangers to the government, peace, and happiness of a kingdom, or state, and therefore is deservedly branded with the highest ignominy, and subjected to the greatest penalties, that the law can inflict; yet by these instances, and more of this kind, that might be given, it appears, 1. How necessary it was, that there should be some fixed and settled boundary for this great crime of treason, and of what great importance the statute of *25 E. 3* was, in order to that end. 2. How dangerous it is to depart from the letter of that statute, and to multiply and inhanse crimes into treason by ambiguous and general words, as *accroaching of royal power, subverting of fundamental laws,* and the like; and 3. How dangerous it is by construction and analogy to make treasons, where the letter of the law has not done it: for such a method admits of no limits or bounds, but runs as far as the wit and invention of accusers, and the odiousness and detestation of persons accused will carry men.[31]

He is clearcut, in pointing out that the policy and the terms of the Statute of Edward III limit the power of judges, praising

> The great wisdom and care of the parliament to keep judges within the bounds and express limits of this act, and not to suffer

them to run out upon their own opinions into constructive treasons, tho in cases, that seem to have a parity of reason (*like cases of treason*) but reserves them to the decision of parliament: this is a great security, as well as direction, to judges, and a great safeguard even to this sacred act itself.[32]

Despite these general assertions of the strength of the restrictive policy embodied in the basic Statute, Hale has little to say in specific explanation of the historic bases of that policy. His only detailed comment, however, seems to rest the policy on the abuse of "treason" in domestic factionalism:

And we need no greater instance of this multiplication of constructive treasons, than the troublesome reign of king *Richard* II. which, tho it were after the limitation of treasons by the statute of *25 E. 3.* yet things were so carried by factions and parties in this king's reign, that this statute was little observed; but as this, or the other party prevailed, so the crimes of high treason were in a manner arbitrarily imposed and adjudged to the disadvantage of that party, that was intended to be suppressed; so that *de facto* that king's reign gives us as various instances of these arbitrary determinations of treasons, and the great inconveniences that arose thereby, as if indeed the statute of *25 E. 3.* had not been made or in force. And tho most of those judgments and declarations were made in parliament; sometimes by the king, lords, and commons; sometimes by the lords, and afterwards affirmed and enacted, as laws; sometimes by a plenipotentiary power committed by acts of parliament to particular lords and others, yet the inconvenience, that grew thereby, and the great uncertainty that happened from the same, was exceedingly pernicious to the king and his kingdom.[33]

In expounding the meaning of the overt act element in the crime,[34] Hale frequently uses the sort of ambiguous terminology which we have seen take its start in Staundford and Coke. Thus when he says that the overt act is necessary to "prove," or "manifest," or "declare" the compassing of the king's death or the adhering to his enemies, this might imply that the act is relevant because it helps prove the intent, and that therefore only such an act as is some evidence of the intent will satisfy this requirement of the offense.[35] Like Coke, he does not, however, use even these doubtful terms regarding the levying of war.

Explaining the scope of the offense of compassing the king's death, he further notes:

> Tho the conspiracy be not immediately and directly and expressly the death of the king, but the conspiracy is of something that in all probability must induce it, and the overt-act is of such a thing as must induce it; this is an overt-act to prove the compassing of the king's death. . . .

But this states what kind of an overt act will surely satisfy the requirements of proof, and does not necessarily exclude acts less forthright than those which "must induce" the king's death.

We have seen that Coke rejected spoken words as an overt act of treason in terms which might seem to imply that this was because they were inherently insufficient evidence of the treasonable intent, thereby mingling the two basic elements of the crime. Hale, more plainly restating Coke, objects to the use of spoken words for their intrinsic unreliability as proof of any element of such offense:

> Regularly words, unless they were committed to writing, are not an overt-act within this statute. *Co. P. C. p. 14;* and the reason given is, because they are easily subject to be mistaken, or misapplied, or misrepeated, or misunderstood by the hearers.[37]

But, he likewise, is not clearcut in his analysis, since for the further support of his position, he cites *Pyne's Case,* which both on its facts and opinion seems to turn on the finding that the spoken words, offered as the sole evidence in the case, were insufficient to make out the intent, without a ruling on their sufficiency as an overt act.[38]

In two respects, however, Hale's analysis of the offense of compassing the king's death seems to make clear that the overt act need not be such as is evidence of a treasonable intent, and that it may even be "indifferent" in character. Thus, after developing the thesis that spoken words are not alone enough to make out an overt act of treason, he lays down these qualifications:

(1.) That words may expound an overt-act to make good an indictment of⋅ treason of compassing the king's death, which overt-act possibly of itself may be indifferent and unapplicable to such an intent; and therefore in the indictment of treason may be joined with such an overt-act, to make the same applicable and expositive of such a compassing, as may plainly appear by many of the precedents there cited [in *Pyne's case,* Cro. Car. 125, q. v.].

(2.) That some words, that are expressly menacing the death or destruction of the king, are a sufficient overt-act to prove that compassing of his death, *M. 9 Car. B. R. Crohagan's* case in *Croke* [Cro. Car. 332], who being an *Irish* priest, *7 Car. 1* at *Lisbon* in *Portugal* used these words, *"I will kill the king* (innuendo dominum *Carolum* regem *Angliae*) *if I may come unto him,"* and in *Aug. 9 Caroli* he came into *England* for the same purpose. This was proved upon his trial by two witnesses, and for that his traitorous intent and the imagination of his heart was declared by these words, it was held high treason by the course of the common law, and within the express words of the statute of *25 E. 3.* and accordingly he was convicted, and had judgment of high treason; yet it is observable, that there was somewhat of an overt-act joined with it, namely, his coming into *England,* whereby it seems to be within the former consideration, namely, tho the coming into *England* was an act indifferent in itself, as to the point of treason; yet it being laid in the indictment, that he came to that purpose, and that in a great measure expounded to be so by his minatory words, the words coupled with the act of coming over make his coming over to be probably for that purpose, and accordingly applicable to that end.[39]

This passage might be interpreted to mean that the "indifferent" overt acts would not suffice, standing alone, without being coupled with obviously harmful words, here also regarded as in the nature of overt acts. But it seems a fairer reading, that the words are not treated as an essential part of the overt act in these cases, but only as evidence linking the overt act to the intention. Further, it is a fair inference from the foregoing quotation, and especially from the first explanation offered of *Crohagan's Case,* that what was really in Hale's mind in his general assertion of the insufficiency of spoken words as an overt act was a judgment that in many cases where the words were the only evidence in the case, they were insufficient *qua* evidence of intent, rather than *qua* evidence of overt act.

Secondly, Hale declares that the mere meeting of persons, with the intent of plotting the king's death, is a sufficient overt act to make out the crime of compassing that end:

If there be an assembling together to consider how they may kill the king, this assembling is an overt-act to make good an indictment of compassing the king's death. This was *Arden's* case [1 Anderson 104], 26 *Eliz.* and accordingly it was ruled *Decem. 14 Caroli* at *Newgate* in the case of *Tonge* and other confederates [Kelyng, 17]. . . .

Vide Anderson's Reports Placito 154, which was the case of *Arden* and *Somerville* and others, who conspired the death of queen

Elizabeth, resolved by all the justices, that a meeting together of these accomplices to consult touching the manner of effecting it was an overt-act to prove it, as well as *Somerville's* buying of a dagger actually to have executed it.[40]

The fact that both of the foregoing propositions are laid down with reference to the overt act in compassing the king's death naturally raises the question whether they are peculiar to that branch of the Statute of Edward III. The second ruling, that a mere meeting with intent to plan the effectuation of a treasonable intent is a sufficient overt act, is, at any rate according to Hale, inapplicable to the crime of levying war against the king, for—agreeing with Coke—he declares that "a bare conspiracy of consultations of persons to levy a war, and to provide weapons for that purpose; this, tho it may in some cases amount to an overt-act of compassing the king's death, yet it is not a levying of war within this clause of this statute."[41] Hale gives no more explanation of this than does Coke, and seems to rest the dogma simply on the statutory terms themselves: "the act saith *levy guerre.*"[42] The crime of "adhering to the king's enemies . . . giving them aid or comfort" seems stated no less bluntly; but neither Coke nor Hale raises the question whether a meeting of conspirators to plan such giving of aid or comfort would be an overt act of adherence.[43] One might argue that the first offense (compassing the king's death) is defined in a term referring to thought, and the other two in terms referring to action, and that this indicates that the danger involved in the first was regarded as greater, or the offense more heinous, so that the overt act requirement is properly satisfied, in the case of the first offense, by conduct less close to accomplishment of the treasonable intention than in the cases of the other two branches of the crime. At least as applied to modern conditions, however, this seems to place too much weight on the words alone, and the proposition that the offenses of levying war and adhering to enemies present less serious perils to the security of the community than that of compassing the king's death is dubious enough in the circumstances of the present-day state to cast the burden of proof on him who urges it. The Statute of Edward III has always been treated, as it was treated in the adoption of its words in American law, as declaring broad policy for an indefinite future, and one should, therefore, be slow to narrow it to the peculiar political circumstances of medieval or Renaissance England. Moreover, so far as the logical pertinence of Hale's analysis is concerned, a proper understanding of the significance of the overt act in any of the branches of treason makes his argument applicable to all. It is fallacious to hold that any act has a character in and of itself. What it means depends on many other facts, of memory, present perception, and logical prediction, in the mind of the observer. There is, therefore, no reason to believe that in the case of levying war or adhering to enemies, a person might not be proved to have committed acts highly dangerous to the security of the community, but which, in the absence of extrinsic evidence linking them to the actor's general purpose, would seem "innocent on their face." There is, in other words, nothing peculiar to the offense of compassing the king's death which would bring it about that only there might one be presented with acts "indifferent" except when appraised in the light of accompanying words or other evidence of intent. Whether Lord Chief Justice Hale would agree to this analysis must be admitted to be conjectural, for he does not spell out his thought more directly than is indicated in the passages quoted. However, in discussing the action taken in *Rot. Parl. 21 R. 2 n. 18,* Hale seems to indicate quite clearly that he did not believe that there was any fundamental difference in the significance of the overt act element in the offenses of compassing the king's death and levying war against him. The Parliament had there declared:

Chescun qe compasse, et purpose la mort le roy, ou de lui deposer, ou de susrendre son homage liege, ou celuy, qe levy le people, et chivache encountre le roy a faire guerre deins son realme, et de ceo soit dument attaint, et adjugge en parlement, soit adjuggez come traytor de haut treason encountre la corone.

Hale declares of this act that

> these four points of treason seem to be included within the statute of *25 E. 3* as to the matter of them . . . ; but with these differences, *viz* . . . 3. But that, wherein the principal inconvenience of this act lay, was this, that whereas the statute of *25 E. 3.* required an overt-act to be laid in the indictment, and proved in evidence, this act hath no such provision, which left a great latitude, and uncertainty in point of treason, and without any open evidence, that could fall under human cognizance, subjected men to the great punishment of treason for their very thoughts, which without an overt-act to manifest them are not triable but by God alone.[44]

Kelyng and Hawkins give little which further illuminates the definition of the offense.[45] Kelyng does add great emphasis to the doctrine that a meeting of conspirators is a sufficient overt act in compassing the king's death, by the resolutions of the judges which he reports concerning knowing attendance upon a meeting of conspirators. Thus in the consideration of the case of Tong and others, he notes:

> It was resolved by all the Judges, that the meeting together of Persons, and consulting to destroy the King, was of itself an Overt Act to prove the compassing the King's Death.
> It was resolved that where a Person knowing the Design does meet with them, and hear them discourse of their traiterous Designs, and say or act nothing; This is High-Treason in that Party, for it is more than a bare Concealment, which is *Misprision,*

because it sheweth his liking, and approving of their Design; but if a Person not knowing of their Design before, come into their Company, and hear their Discourses, and say nothing, and never meet with them again at their Consultations, that Concealment is only Misprision of High-Treason. But if he after meet with them again, and hear their Consultations and then conceal it, this is High-Treason. For it sheweth a liking, and an approving of their Design [citing Sir Everard Digby's Case, 1 St. Tr. 234].[46]

So, also, he reports that in considering the case of the conspiracy to levy war in the North Riding of Yorkshire,

It was agreed that the bare knowledge of Treason, and the concealment of it was not High-Treason, but Misprision of Treason. But in Case any thing be proved upon Evidence, that the Party liked or approved of it, then it is High Treason; or if the Party knew of the Design, and after such Knowledge, met with the Conspirators at their Consultation; or if he went knowingly to their Consultations several Times, this is Evidence of his Approbation of the Design, and is High Treason.[47]

These passages are not without ambiguity, as to whether the emphasis is on the evidence as evidence of intent, or as adequate evidence, also, of an overt act; but since Kelyng notes the general, basic ruling, that a conspiratorial meeting is a sufficient overt act, it seems that the intent is to find the more borderline case to involve a sufficient overt act as well. Though the broad doctrine reported by Kelyng might be thought of dubious authority, since it originates in the period of reprisals following the Restoration, it has been accepted without such criticism by modern English authority.[48]

Foster gives us the most illuminating discussion of the 18th century writers on the nature of the overt act element in treason. His analysis rests on the familiar declaration that wise policy calls for careful definition of the scope of the offense,

in the interest of individual security.[49] Thus he makes it clear
that an overt act is an essential element of the crime under
each branch of the Statute of Edward III.[50] But, despite his
fundamentally cautious approach to the definition of the
offense, he does not permit it to be wrongly narrowed by a
muzzy analysis of the relation of its elements to each other.
He insists that the overt act is required, not merely as
cumulative evidence of the intent, but for the distinct purpose
of demonstrating that the defendant had moved from the
realm of thought into that of execution.

> The words of the statute descriptive of the offence must be strictly
> pursued in every indictment for this species of treason. It must
> charge, that the defendant did traitorously *compass and imagine
> &c,* and then go on and charge the several overt acts as the means
> employed by the defendant for executing his traitorous purposes.
> For the compassing is considered as the treason, the overt acts as
> the means made use of to effectuate the intentions and imagina-
> tions of the heart: and therefore in the case of the regicides the
> indictment charged, that they did traitorously compass and imag-
> ine the death of the King; and the taking of his head was laid,
> among others, as an overt act of compassing; and the person who
> was supposed to have given the stroke was convicted on the same
> indictment.
>   From what hath been said it followeth, that in every indictment
> for this species of treason, and indeed for levying war, or adhering
> to the King's enemies, an overt act must be alleged and proved.
> For the overt act is the charge, to which the prisoner must apply
> his defense.[51]

Foster particularly deserves our gratitude for introducing the
first clarity into the discussion of words and writings as overt
acts. He points out that, considered as evidence of intent,
mere spoken words are generally unreliable evidence, because of the likelihood that they "are often the effect of mere

heat of blood"; and that, considered as evidence of anything, they are unreliable because they "are always liable to great misconstruction from the ignorance or inattention of the hearers, and too often from a motive truly criminal."[52] So much is familiar. Foster pushes beyond prior analyses when he clearly points out that the objection to basing treason on unpublished writings (*Peacham's* and *Sidney's* cases), is that there the written words are being made to do double duty as evidence both of intent and overt act, and that they will generally not, of themselves, bear such weight. But, if other satisfactory evidence of intent is present, the writing, though "unpublished," suffices as an overt act:

> In Mr. *Sidney's* case it was said, *Scribere est agere.* This is undoubted-ly true under proper limitations, but it was not applicable to his case. Writing being a deliberate act and capable of satisfactory proof certainly may, under some circumstances *with publication,* be an overt act of treason: and I freely admit, that had the papers found in Mr. *Sidney's* closet been plainly relative to the other treasonable practices charged *in the indictment,* they might have been read in evidence against him, though not published.
>
> The papers found in Lord *Preston's* custody, those found where Mr. *Layer* had lodged them, the intercepted letters of Doctor *Hensey,* were all read in evidence as overt acts of the treason re-spectively charged on them; and *William Gregg's* intercepted let-ter might, in like manner, have been read in evidence, if he had put himself upon his trial. For those papers and letters were writ-ten in prosecution of certain determinate purposes, which were all treasonable and then in contemplation of the offenders, and were plainly connected with them. But papers not capable of such connection, while they remain in the hands of the author unpub-lished, as Mr. *Sidney's* did, will not make a man a traitor. Lord *Hale* . . . mentioneth two circumstances as concurring to make words reduced into writing overt acts of compassing the King's death, *that they be published, and that they import such compassing.*

True it is, that in *Peacham's* case a Ms. sermon, in which were some treasonable passages, found in his study, never, for aught appearing, preached or published or intended to be so, was thought to bring him within this branch of the statute; and accordingly he was found guilty, *but not executed.* For whatever rule the court of King's Bench, where he was tried, might lay down, "many of the judges, saith *Croke,* were of opinion, that it was not treason." This case therefore weigheth very little; and no great regard hath been paid to it ever since.[53]

The reference in the second paragraph of this quotation, to Hale, introduces the familiar confusion, as to whether the overt act must evidence the intent; but in the context of Foster's analysis, it seems a fair inference that he here uses Hale's words—whether rightly or wrongly—to mean that the overt act must be adequately related, by evidence, to the evidence of the plan or design into which the act fits. This same lingering confusion in terminology appears when Foster, referring now to mere spoken words, says, after detailing the reasons already noted as to their general unreliability as evidence,

And therefore I choose to adhere to the rule which hath been laid down on more occasions than one since the revolution, that loose words, *not relative to any act or design,* are not overt acts of treason. But words of advice or persuasion, and all consultations for the traiterous purposes treated of in this chapter are certainly so. They are uttered in contemplation of some traiterous purpose actually on foot or intended, and *in prosecution* of it.[54]

If the thesis here advanced as to Foster's basic line of analysis is correct, he should more properly say that in the case put, the "loose words" are not adequate evidence of intention, rather than that they are not sufficient overt acts; for in the same passage, it will be seen that he reiterates that mere spoken words are a sufficient overt act when linked to other satisfactory evidence of a treasonable design into whose execution they fit. That this is a reasonable interpretation of Foster is supported by his comments on *Crohagan's Case,* in which he plainly insists that one must not confuse the appraisal of the adequacy of words as evidence of intent with their sufficiency as an overt act:

> . . . words connected with facts, or expressive of the intention of the speaker, may, under some circumstances, bring him within the statute of treasons. *Crohagan* being beyond sea said, "I will kill the King of *England,* if I can come at him," and the indictment, after setting forth the words, charged, that *he came into* England *for that purpose.*
>
> In this case the words, though laid in the indictment as one of the overt acts, could not be so properly deemed an overt act of treason, as an evidence against the man out of his own mouth, QUO ANIMO *he came into* England. The traiterous intention, proved by his words, converted an action, innocent in itself, into an overt act of treason.

Foster criticizes Kelyng for stating this case as involving words alone as an overt act: "It is true, the words were laid as an overt act, but they were not the *only* overt act laid; for the indictment farther charged, that the man came into *England for the purpose of killing the King."* And he continues his criticism of Kelyng in terms which clearly establish his distinction between the evidence of intent and of an overt act:

> The author in the same page endeavoureth to put writings and words upon one and the same foot; "Words, saith he, set down in writing are an overt act to prove the compassing the King's death, and words *spoken* are the same thing, *if they be proved;* and words are the natural way for a man whereby to express the imagination of the heart."

His Lordship reasoneth in this passage as if he considered the overt acts, required by the statute, merely as *matters of evidence,* tending to discover the imaginations of the heart. Overt acts undoubtedly do discover the man's intentions; but, I conceive, they are not to be considered merely as evidence, but as *the means made use of to effectuate the purposes of the heart.* With regard to homicide, while the rule *voluntas pro facto* prevailed, the overt acts of compassing were so considered. In the cases cited by *Coke* there were plain flagitious attempts upon the lives of the parties marked out for destruction: and though in the case of the King overt acts of less malignity, and having a more remote tendency to his destruction, are with great propriety, deemed treasonable; yet still they are considered as *means to effectuate,* not barely *as evidence* of the treasonable purpose. Upon this principle words of advice or encouragement, and, above all, consultations for destroying the King, very properly come under the notion of *means made use of* for that purpose. But loose words not relative to facts are, at the worst, no more than bare indications of the malignity of the heart.[55]

It follows that Foster has no difficulty in contemplating that actions harmless on their face may yet be sufficient overt acts to make out the offense, when linked to adequate evidence of the treasonable design into which they fit. This appears from his reference in the quotation above to Crohagan's coming into England as "an action, innocent in itself," but converted into treason by the evidence of intention. It appears also in his repeated statement that the mere fact of a meeting of several persons, when coupled with evidence that their intention in meeting was to plan the king's death, is a sufficient overt act; and in his approval of the doctrine that attendance at a meeting with knowledge of its treasonable purpose, or return to a meeting after knowledge is gained of its treasonable purpose, is treason and not merely misprision of treason.[56]

Foster's discussion raises the same question noted in connection with Hale, whether, since his analysis refers almost entirely to problems under that branch of the Statute of Edward III dealing with compassing the king's death, it extends as well to the crimes of levying war or adhering to enemies. There is material in Foster's discussion of the first offense which may reasonably be construed to mean that he viewed it as of specially broad scope, perhaps validating as overt acts conduct more remote from the intended object than in the other crimes:

The antient writers, in treating of felonious homicide, considered the felonious intention manifested *by plain facts,* not by bare words of any kind, in the same light in point of guilt, as homicide itself. The rule was *voluntas reputatur pro facto*: and while this rule prevailed, the nature of the offence was expressed by the term *compassing* the death.

This rule hath been long laid aside as too rigorous in the case of common persons. But in the case of the King, Queen, and Prince, the statute of treasons hath, with great propriety, retained it in its full extent and rigour: and in describing the offence hath likewise retained the antient mode of expression. . . .

The principle upon which this is founded is too obvious to need much enlargement. The King is considered as the head of the body-politick, and the members of that body are considered as united and kept together by a political union with him and with each other. His life cannot, in the ordinary course of things, be taken away by treasonable practices without involving a whole nation in blood and confusion; consequently every stroke levelled at his person is, in the ordinary course of things, levelled at the publick tranquility. The law therefore tendereth the safety of the King with an anxious concern, and, if I may use the expression, with a concern bordering *upon jealousy.* It considereth the wicked imaginations of the heart in the same degree of guilt as if carried into actual execution, from the moment *measures appear to have been taken to render them effectual*: and therefore, if conspirators meet and consult how to kill the King, though they do not fall upon any scheme for that purpose, this is an overt act of compassing his death; and so are all means made use of, be it advice, persuasion or command, to incite or incourage others to commit the fact, or to join in the attempt; and every person who but assenteth to any overtures for that purpose will be involved in the same guilt.[57]

It is in this connection that he first mentions *Lord Preston's Case*:

Offences which are not so personal, as those already mentioned, have been with great propriety brought within the same rule; as having a tendency, though not so immediate, to the same fatal end; and therefore the entering into measures in concert with foreigners and others in order to an invasion of the kingdom, or going into a foreign country, or even purposing to go thither to that end *and taking any steps in order thereto,*—these offences are overt acts of compassing the King's death.[58]

However, his approval of the scope of the ruling there is given in terms of implying that he is fully ready to see the same liberality applied to traffic with an external enemy, whenever it can be brought under another branch of the statute:

The offence of inciting foreigners to invade the kingdom is a treason of signal enormity. In.the lowest estimation of things and in all possible events, it is an attempt, on the part of the offender, to render his country the seat of blood and desolation; and yet, unless the powers so incited happen to be actually at war with us at the time of such incitement, the offence will not fall within any branch of the statute of treasons, except that of compassing the King's death: and therefore, since it hath a manifest tendency to endanger the person of the King, it hath, in strict conformity to the statute, and to every principle of substantial political justice, been brought within that species of treason of compassing the King's death; *ne quid detrimenti respublica capiat.*[59]

In the light of this comment, it is impossible to think that Foster would hold that the same action held a sufficient overt act of compassing the king's death, in *Lord Preston's Case,* was not equally good to make out the offense of adherence to the king's enemies, given the other requisite circumstances. This is made clear by his adducing the indictment in that case, with approval, as an example of the fact that, contrary to Coke's mechanical logic, an offense falling under one branch of the statute may be deemed an overt act of a different type of treason:

> . . . in *Lord Preston's case,* before cited, he and the other gentlemen were indicted upon both branches of the statute, *compassing the death, and adhering*; and the composing, procuring, and secreting the treasonable papers, their taking boat to go on board the smack, and carrying the papers with them in order to be made use of in *France* for the treasonable purposes charged in the indictment,— these facts were all laid as overt acts of *both* species of treason.[60]

That Foster would not require a stricter showing of an overt act in the crimes of levying war or adherence to enemies than in that of compassing the king's death, is further indicated by his strong approval of the doctrine that the former offenses, as much as the last, are made out, where it is attempted to send supplies or information to rebels or enemies,

> though the money or intelligence should happen to be intercepted: for the party in sending did all he could; the treason was complete *on his part, though it had not the effect he intended.* [citing cases]
>
> The cases cited . . . did not in truth turn singly upon rule here laid down, though I think the rule may very well be supported.

For *Gregg* was indicted for *compassing the death* of the Queen, and also for *adhering to her* enemies; and *Hensey's* indictment was in the same form, and so was Lord *Preston's* . . . ; and the writing and sending the letters of intelligence, which, in the cases of *Gregg* and *Hensey, were stopped at the post-office,* was laid as an overt act of both the species of treason: so that admitting for argument's sake, which is by no means admitted, that it was not an overt act of *adhering,* since the letters never came to the enemy's hands and consequently no *aid or comfort* was actually given, yet the bare writing and sending them to the post-office, in order to be delivered to the enemy, was undoubtedly an overt act of the other species of treason. In *Gregg's* case the judges did resolve, that it was an overt act of both the species of treason charged on him; and in *Hensey's* the court adopted that opinion cited it with approbation. [61]

As was suggested in the discussion of the same point in Hale, it would seem a difficult argument to maintain, that, at least in the case of trafficking with enemies in time of war, the safety of the state demanded less broad definition of the overt act in the case of adherence to enemies than in that of compassing the king's death. There is nothing in Foster's chapter on levying war or adhering to enemies which suggests a policy of more closely limiting the scope of those offenses, except for his evident caution regarding the broad extension of the concept of constructive levying of war as a means to proceed against purely domestic disturbances.

However, the specific issue, whether a meeting with intention to plan treason, is a sufficient overt act of levying war or adhering to enemies, is not clearly resolved in Foster. He does not discuss the doctrine of previous writers, that a conspiracy to levy war is not a sufficient overt act to establish that particular offense, though he does declare it to be a sufficient overt act in compassing the king's death. However, developing a brief reference in Hale, Foster states a rule regarding the trial of accessories in treason which may imply that a meeting is not an adequate overt act to establish the crimes of levying war or adhering to enemies. Though in treason all are principals, as concerns the degree of guilt and of punishment, he argues that, except where the charge is compassing the king's death, one accused of advising or encouraging the commission of another of the treasons should be tried only after the principal actor:

> For instance, *A.* adviseth *B.* to counterfeit the King's coin or seals, or indeed to commit any of the offences declared treason by the 25 *Edw.* III, and furnisheth him with means for that purpose: (that species of treason which in judgement of law falleth within the clause of compassing the death of the King, Queen, or Prince always excepted:) if *B.,* in consequence of this advice and encouragement, doth the fact, *A.* is a principal in the treason; for such advice and assistance in the case of felony would have made him an accessary before the fact; and in high treason there are no accessaries, all are principals. But if *B.* forbeareth to commit the fact, to which he is incited, *A.* cannot be a traitor merely on account of this advice and encouragement, though his behavior hath been highly criminal; for bare advice or incitement, how wicked soever, unless in the cases already excepted, will not bring a man within the statute, where no treason hath been commited in consequence of it. . . .
>
> . . . with regard to every instance of incitement, approbation, or previous abetment in that species of treason which falleth under the branch of the statute touching the compassing of the death of the King, Queen, or Prince, every such treason is in it's own nature, independently of all other circumstances or events, a complete overt-act of compassing; though the fact, originally in the contemplation of the parties, should never be affected, nor so much as attempted. . . .

Blackstone is disappointing in his analysis of the nature of the overt act in treason, and gives us nothing but summary restatements of the authorities which we have already examined. In view of the influence of his work in America, however, it is worth while to notice the points which he particularly makes. The desirability of a policy restrictive of the scope of the offense is briefly stated in familiar terms, with the addition of a quotation from Montesquieu, which subsequently also turns up in James Wilson's law lectures in Philadelphia in 1790.[63] An overt act must be shown under each branch of the Statute of Edward III.[64] There is no satisfactory analysis of the distinction between the evidence of intent and that of the overt act, the statement of the problem being put with an ambiguity which we have seen begin with Staundford:

> But, as this compassing or imagination is an act of the mind, it cannot possibly fall under any judicial cognizance, unless it be demonstrated by some open, or *overt,* act. And yet the tyrant Dionysius is recorded to have executed a subject, barely for dreaming that he had killed him; which was held for a sufficient proof, that he had thought thereof in his waking hours. But such is not the temper of the English law; and therefore in this, and the three next species of treason, it is necessary that there appear an open or *overt* act of a more full and explicit nature, to convict the traitor upon. . . .[65]

Likewise ambiguous is his explanation that "words spoken amount only to a high misdemeanor, and no treason," in which he mingles criticism of their unreliability as evidence in general, and as evidence of intent in particular, with the usual distinction that "scribere est agere."[66] There is, at any rate, nothing in Blackstone clear enough to cast material doubt on the analysis which we have seen in Foster. And Blackstone goes so far toward recognizing the distinction between the overt act and the evidence of intent, as to approve the rulings that a mere meeting is a sufficient overt act, where there is evidence of the intent therein to plot the king's death; and that the mere fact of attendance at a meeting known to be treasonable, or the fact of return to a meeting once such knowledge has been gained, make out treason.[67]

(c) Treatises Published in the 19th and 20th Centuries[68]

For all practical purposes, detailed analytical treatment of the law of treason has not interested writers of standard texts since the 18th century; and we have only meager evaluations of the issues of policy involved even from the historians. This is a natural reflection of a period of great political stability, and the Victorian confidence in an ordered world, in which civilization was identified with western Parliamentary government, speaks with naive assurance in Sir James Fitzjames Stephen's apology for the extremes of 16th and 17th century "treasons":

> All these acts were either temporary, or have in one way or another long since expired, and they exercised little or no permanent influence on our law. I have referred to them so fully partly on account of their historical interest, partly because they illustrate in a striking manner the nature of one class of political offences. Convulsions and revolutions have occurred in the history of every nation. Each party in turn, and in particular every successful party, is from the nature of the case obliged to treat the prosecution by their antagonists of the political views and objects which they have at heart, and even in some cases the open avowal of those views, as crimes of the highest nature. It seems to me that such legislation can be fairly criticized only by considering two things, namely, first, the substantial merits of the quarrel, and secondly, the efficiency and approach to necessity of the means

employed for the attainment of the end proposed. The Reformation and the great political revolutions which have followed it were the stormy periods in human history, and the legislation by which different parties have done their best to maintain their respective views in their own dominions, are like orders given by a military commander in time of war. To criticise them upon the false supposition that they were intended to last for an indefinite time, and to apply to the normal state of society, is to misunderstand them pedantically. [69]

The 19th century historians introduce a desirable realism into the discussion of the policy bases of the Statute of Edward III, when they point out that the Parliament's wish to limit the definition of "treason" seems to have stemmed rather from the urge to limit the occasions on which land would forfeit directly and finally to the King, than from any notion of preserving political liberties. [70] But, while noting the politically liberal tradition which became attached to the Statute of Edward III, the typical 19th century discussion does not find it necessary to spend upon this theme the eloquence of great conviction. The alert vigilance of the Philadelphia convention of 1787 seems to have little counterpart in this succeeding period. The historians do, however, focus on the field of domestic politics as the area in which the restrictive policy of the Statute of Edward III has its modern importance. [71] But they place equal stress on the importance of protecting the existence of the state, and in this view find the terms of the Statute of Edward III to be "worded too narrowly, if it is to be construed literally." [72]

The post-18th century writers add nothing to clarify the analysis of the overt act element of the crime. There is recognition that the overt act is a separate element in the offense; indeed, this is so plainly established, in net, by the earlier treatises that it could scarcely be subjected to open question at this date. [73] But the familiar ambiguous language, describing the function of the overt act as being to "prove," "manifest," "declare" the treason, is scattered through all of these works; and some of them contain references which would suggest that, at least in borderline cases, the overt act must be some evidence of treasonable intent.[74] It is also, however, a fair summary of the evidence to say that this latter theory never emerges beyond the stage of innuendo or implication, in the post-18th century writings. And there is recognition that, at least under the charge of compassing the king's death, conduct indifferent on its face, notably mere meetings, may be a sufficient overt act, when linked to proper evidence of treasonable intent. The only references to ambiguous or indifferent conduct as overt acts come under this head of compassing the king's death, and though the writers do not attempt to spin any very explicit theory of the special breadth of this charge, it is quite clear that they all regard it as the broadest category of treason. Holdsworth comes closest to open disapproval, on policy grounds, of the idea that "harmless" conduct may suffice for the overt act element, and he implies emphasis on the fact that the broadest cases have been under the charge of compassing the king's death. This seems the undertone of his comments on *Crohagan's Case*:

> . . . the court seems to have laid some stress upon the facts that the words were accompanied by the overt act of coming to England, and that he had used scornful words when arrested; and this is the manner in which the case was explained and justified by later lawyers. It followed that words could give a treasonable colour to an otherwise innocent overt act. It is, therefore, not suprising that, in 1660, the judges showed a tendency to minimize the importance of the difference between written and spoken words. . . . [75]

This underlying unfriendly note appears also in his comments on *Lord Preston's Case*:

But, except in these two cases [spoken or unpublished written words not linked to a treasonable design], the seventeenth-century decisions, extending the constructive interpretation of this clause, were adopted, and even carried further, after the Revolution. And, here again, the extension was probably inevitable. If a conspiracy to levy war, and the publication of a writing advocating the deposition of the king, or merely arguing that it is lawful to depose him, are overt acts which can be given in evidence to prove the compassing of his death, it will be difficult to draw the line at these acts. It will be difficult to rule out any acts done in preparation for any other act, which, if accomplished, will be an overt act. That no attempt was made to draw the line is clear from the case of Lord Preston.

Quoting Foster's summary, that "Every step taken for those purposes was an overt act," he further comments:

The last sentence contains the gist of the matter. It comes to this—every act, however remotely connected with an overt act of compassing the king's death, is itself an overt act. As the future Lord Eldon contended, when, as attorney-general, he was prosecuting Hardy in 1794, any act which showed that the person doing it intended "to put the king in circumstances in which, according to the ordinary experience of mankind, his life would be in danger," might be given in evidence as an overt act of compassing his death. It followed that this clause of the statute could be made to cover the ground covered both by the clause against levying war against the king, and by the clause against adhering to his enemies.[76]

These remarks should be compared with the same author's emphasis on the basically broader character of the statutory terms regarding the offense of compassing the king's death:

Even in the mediaeval period, the judges had seen that the fact that the gist of the offence was an intention to kill the king, could be used to extend its scope; for they had held that the mere speaking of words might be an overt act which evidenced such an intention. They had seen as clearly as their successors that such an intention can be proved only by overt acts, "for the thought of man is not triable"; and that the statute could be extended by inferring an intention to kill from overt acts which were only remotely connected, if they were connected at all, with a formed intention to kill the king. . . .

. . . the fact that it was the intention to kill the king, and not his murder, which was made treason, was the main reason why this clause could be so extensively construed. . . .[77]

To fill out the picture, it may be worth noting that, referring to the crime of adherence to the king's enemies, Holdsworth points out that this clause "has not been extended by construction in the same way as the first two clauses."[78] He makes no argument, however, to show that there are policy considerations supporting this divergence in the history of the various branches of the Statute of Edward III. Archbold does indicate a difference in scope between the crime of adherence to enemies and that of compassing the king's death, when he asserts that a conspiracy to adhere is not treason under that branch of the statute any more than is a conspiracy to levy war under the levying provision. But he cites no direct authority for his assertion.[79] The specially broad scope of the crime of compassing is stressed to some extent in East's development of Foster's argument that under that heading it is not necessary to postpone the trial of an aider and abetter until the conviction of the principal actors, since advising the king's death is itself the main offense.[80] It is only from such unsatisfactory scraps that one can weave any theory of these writers on the nature of the overt act element, however.

(d) Writers on the Constitution[81]

It is probably significant of a felt connection with fundamental policies in the conduct of politics that most of the
post-18th century writers on the English constitution bring
the law of treason into their discussions. The majority of
these commentators are laymen, and in all of these works the
treatment of the elements of the crime merely derives from
authorities already examined, and casts little additional light
thereon. But, it is worth noting, as evidence of a prevailing
climate of opinion, that these books firmly entrench the
notion of the Statute of Edward III as a desirable delimitation
of a dangerously vague field,[82] and that with striking uni-
formity they emphasize the danger of abuse of broad categories of "treason" in the arena of domestic politics.[83] As a
concrete expression of this general attitude, there appears a
general, if ill-defined, condemnation of "constructive" treasons; and it is especially interesting to see that *Lord Preston's
Case,* in its rulings on the sufficiency of the overt acts, is cited
as the extreme point of extension of construction—
representing "the fictitious interpretation of the crime of
compassing."[84] Hallam alone, however, expressly insists on
linking the overt act to the showing of intent.[85]

Although the texts are by no means wholly consistent, some
reasonably definite conclusions appear from this survey.
Beginning with Coke—in the days of the mounting clash of
Crown and Parliament—the English jurists stress the wisdom
of restricting the scope of "treason" in doubtful cases. This
policy perhaps seems to require less emphatic assertion from
writers living in the confidently stable period at the close of
the 19th and the opening of the 20th centuries; but it is,
nevertheless, an impressive element of continuity in the
general treatment of the subject up to the present time.
Intent and act are, on the whole, seen as distinct elements of

the crime. Frequent ambiguous references imply that the act must, however, be of such a character as to "manifest" the treason: how often this is meant to require that the act be some evidence, or complete evidence, of the treasonable intent, is not clear. The most satisfactorily explicit analyses regard the act element as fulfilling the same function in this as in other crimes: to set ultimate boundaries to the abuse of criminal prosecutions, by insuring that men be not charged or convicted for their thoughts alone, but only on the basis of an evil intent which by some act has been translated into the world of deeds.

At the current Term, in *Cramer v. United States,* the Supreme Court of the United States for the first time reviewed a conviction of treason.[86] In a lengthy survey of the historic roots of the treason clause of the Constitution, the Court follows the current of prior authority in finding basic relevance in the English authority stemming from the Statute of Edward III.[87] The *Cramer* opinion disclaims ability to make "an independent judgment as to the inward meaning of terms used in a six-century-old-statute, written in a form of Norman French that had become obsolete long before our Revolution," and finds the practical meaning of English doctrine in the decisions and in the commentators.[88] Dismissing the few English cases on adherence to the enemy as too entangled with accusations of compassing the king's death to be of certain relevance to American policy, the majority opinion in effect treats the commentaries as the principal source of the law's rationale.[89] From these sources it recognizes the deep historic roots of the general policy restrictive of the scope of the crime. Nevertheless, it concludes that because English law has retained that branch of the offense punishing the compassing the death of the king, even post-17th century English doctrine must be deemed not sufficiently limited to be regarded as similar to the law of the United States Constitution.[90] But, as was seen especially in Foster's acute analysis, the English authorities have apparently felt that the policy underlying the crime of adherence to the enemy in some respects calls for as broad an interpretation of the intent and act elements of "treason" as that taken under the head of compassing.[91] Thus, if the majority means to hold, as apparently it does, that a completed benefit must be shown to have been conferred on the enemy, it does so only by failing to come to grips with the policy indicated by the historic material. Likewise, by ruling that the testimony of two witnesses to a "commonplace" overt act is insufficient, the majority, though disclaiming to do so, seems in practice to insist that the overt act be such as evidences treasonable intent. The opinion rightly does not seek to support such a result by any analogy from English doctrine, and notes the ambiguity inherent in statements that the act must "manifest" the treason. But it does not seem to give fair weight to the persuasive effect of the English material in pointing to the contrary result, that the act need be only such as clearly shows a translation of thought into action. The dissenting Justices found this analogous material convincing.[92]

The English commentaries undertake to implement the general restrictive policy adopted toward the crime of treason particularly by trying to set defined limits to the scope of treasonable intent, and by insisting on the showing of an overt act as a protection against persecution for thought or belief, or peaceful political activity. But after due attention is given to this dominant current of the English treatises, it must be recognized that they still treat the crime as an important weapon for defense of the security of the state. Respect for the wisdom which they distilled from periods of great tension in England might well recommend caution in going beyond historic evidence to extend the traditional policy restrictive of the scope of the offense.

NOTES

1. The following are the treatises referred to in sections (a) and (b), (in chronological order):

Glanvill, De Legibus et Consuetudinibus Regni Angliae (c. 1187–1189) (1) edited by George E. Woodbine (New Haven, 1932); (2) translation by John Beames (Washington, 1900).

Bracton, De Legibus et Consuetudinibus Angliae (c. 1250–1258): (1) edited by George E. Woodbine (4 vol. New Haven, 1932 ff.); (2) translation by Sir Travers Twiss (6 vol. London, 1879).

Fleta (c. 1290) (London, 1647).

Britton (c. 1290), (Nichols, ed. 2 vol. Oxford, 1865).

Fortescue, De Laudibus Legum Angliae (c. 1470) (Chrimes, ed. Cambridge 1942).

Staundford, Les Plees del Corone (1560) (London, 1607).

Coke, Institutes of the Laws of England, Third Part (5th ed. London, 1671).

Hale, History of the Pleas of the Crown (2 vol. Emlyn, ed. London, 1736–1739). (All citations herein are to vol. 1.)

Kelyng: A Report of Divers Cases in Pleas of the Crown, Adjudged and Determined in the Reign of the late King Charles II, etc. Collected by Sir John Kelyng, K^{nt}. (London, 1708) (3d ed., London, 1873).

Hawkins, A Treatise of the Pleas of the Crown or A System of the Principal Matters relating to that subject, digested under proper heads (1716) (7th ed. 4 vol. London, 1795).

Foster, A Report of Some Proceedings on the Commission for the Trial of the Rebels in the Year 1746 in the County of Surry; and of other Crown Cases (1762) (3d ed. London, 1792).

Blackstone, Commentaries on the Laws of England (4 vol. Oxford, 1769) (All citations herein are to volume 4).

2. Staundford, Lib. 1, Cap. 2, 1–0.

3. Note his emphasis on the declaratory aspect of the Statute, and his unquestioning acceptance of the doctrine that in treason all are principals. Coke, 1 (n), 9, 16, 138.

4. *Id.*, 6. This comment is the more striking, because it is made after Coke had emphasized the provision retaining in Parliament the authority to declare new treasons.

5. *Id.*, 2–3. Note that James Wilson, as defense counsel in the Pennsylvania treason trials of 1778, referred to this designation of the "benedictum Parliamentum." 7 Pennsylvania Archives (Hazard, ed. Philadelphia, 1853) 51. Compare Coke's praise and emphasis on the restrictive character of the Statute of 1 Mar., *id.*, 23.

6. *Id.*, 21, 22.

7. *Id.,* 15. Compare 21: "And note this branch extendeth (as hath been said) to the Offence, viz. treason, and not to tryall, judgement, or execution."

8. Thus the remark quoted in the text is made in connection with his pointing out that standing mute or giving a confession may yet be a basis for conviction under the Statute. And compare his emphasis that conviction must be "upon direct and manifest proof, not upon conjecturall presumptions, or inferences, or straines of wit" in view of the Statute's requirement that defendant be "provablement" attained. *Id.* 12, 21.

9. *Id.,* 11.

10. *Id.,* 18; *cf.* 4.

11. Lib. 1, cap. 2 (Woodbine, 42; Beames, 2); Lib. 14, cap. 1 (Woodbine, 174; Beames, 278).

12. *Ibid.* (Woodbine, 174–175; Beames, 281.) (Present author's translation.)

13. F. 118b (2 Woodbine 334; 2 Twiss 259). "Seditio" is often used in this period interchangeably with "seductio." Though, in its context, the word may be more ambiguous in Glanvill, in Bracton it seems a fair inference that it does not mean "sedition" in the phrase "seditionem domini regis," and that hence it does not mean this regarding the army. Compare 2 Pollock and Maitland, History of English Law (2d ed. Cambridge, 1923) 503, n. 2: "We believe that in these passages [Glanvill and Bracton] the best rendering for *seditio* is, not *sedition,* but *betrayal."* Translation in text is by the present author.

Professor George E. Woodbine has given his opinion regarding Bracton's use of "consilium" in this passage in a letter of August 20, 1944, as follows: "In the passage from Bracton (f. 118b) . . . , I would not regard 'comfort' an adequate translation of *consilium.* 'Counsel,' in its usual sense, is apparently what Bracton had in mind. To Bracton *auxilium et consilium* would be a matter of fact and (unlike our technical 'aid and comfort') nontechnical expression. He clearly had in mind the case of the man who stays in the background and gives advice to the one actively engaged in the plotting. I take it that the giving of this advice is with obvious treacherous intent. If the plotter to whom the advice is given is regarded as the 'enemy,' *consilium* should certainly be construed to cover the fact of contact with the enemy."

14. Coke, 6. Foster, 205, would take it not adverbially, regarding the quality of the intent, but as referring to an overt act.

15. See Britton, Liv. 1, Chapitre IX (1 Nichols, 40): "Tresun est en chescun damage qe hom fet a escient ou procure de fere a cely a qi hom se fet ami. . . . Graunt tresoun est a compasser nostre mort, ou de nous desheriter de noster reaume, ou de fauser noster seal, ou de countrefere nostre monee ou de retoundre. . . . " *Cf. id.,* Liv. 1, Chapitre XXIII (1 Nichols, 99): "Et cum il vendrunt en jugement, si face le encusour soen apel pur nous en ceste forme par acun serjaunt. Johan, qi ci est, apele Peres, qi iloeqes est, de ceo qe, com il fu en certeyn leu a tel certeyn jour a tel an, la oy mesmes cestui John purparler tele mort, ou tiel treysoun par entre cestui Peres et un autre, tel par noun, et par tieles alliaunces. . . . " Nichols translates this as, "And when they

appear for trial, let the accuser make his appeal for us by some serjeant in this manner. 'John who is here appeals Peter who is there of this, that being in such a place on such a day and year, the same John there heard such a death or such a treason contrived between the same Peter and another, such an one by name, and by such confederacies," and that John is now ready to prove by his body in any manner the Court shall award that this is the truth. See Fleta, Lib. 1, Cap 21. Cf. The Mirrour of Justices (Robinson, ed. Washington, 1903) 39, 91; see 2 Pollock and Maitland, *op. cit. supra,* note 13, p. 478, n. 1.

16. Staundford, Lib. 1, Cap. 2, 1–S.

17. *Id.,* 2–H. Fortescue has no discussion of the definition of the crime.

18. Coke, 14.

19. *Id.,* 3, 4, 6, 8.

20. *Id.,* 14.

21. *Id.,* 3.

22. *Id.,* 14.

23. Coke, 5. The marginal note on the same page comments, "Sed haec voluntas non intellecta fuit de voluntate nudis verbis, aut scriptis propalata, sed mundo manifestata fuit per apertum factum, Id est, cum quis dederat operam, quantum in ipso fuit, ad occidenda, & sic de similibus." This seems to involve the ambiguity already noted in the use of the word "declare."

24. Coke does not indicate that of his own knowledge he knew of Arden's case (1583–4), referred to by Hale (vol. 1, p. 119); the case was apparently first reported after his death, in 1 Anderson 104 (1664). See note 39, *infra.* In the passages cited in notes 25, 26 and 27, *infra,* it will be noted that his references to persons "conspiring" all include mention of some further overt act. But his assertion that a conspiracy to levy war could not be an overt act of compassing the king's death (note 20, *supra*) seems to rest on a mechanical view of the separateness of the statutory definitions, and not on the view that the "conspiring" was not otherwise a sufficient overt act. Quaere, whether the sending of letters (referred to in the passage quoted at note 25, *infra*), might not involve ambiguous conduct.

25. Coke, 5.

26. *Id.,* 12. Note, however, the ambiguous use of the word "prove," in the last sentence of the quotation.

27. *Id.,* 14.

28. *Id.,* 38.

29. *Id.,* 9.

30. *Id.,* 12.

31. 1 Hale 86. Note that Hale's language is such that it might be interpreted to caution merely against expanding the scope of treason by adding new substantive definitions, and not to embrace the same result when reached by more "liberal" construction of the familiar definitions or of the evidence requisite to satisfy them. But this interpretation seems too narrow, especially in view of the last sentence of the quotation. See also, *id:,* 82, 132, 151, 157, 293.

32. *Id.,* 259.

33. *Id.,* 83. Compare his strong criticism of the ruling of the judges, *Rot. Parl. 11 R. 2.,* that the king could be said to be treasonably "compelled" when pressure was put on him only by the familiar political means of withholding supplies, or by persuasion or strong petition. *Id.,* 109–110; *cf.* 267.

34. See *id.,* 121: "the overt-act is an essential part of the indictment."

35. See *e.g.,* passage quoted at note 43, *infra;* also, 91, 92, 107, 108, 110, 149, 151, 167.

36. *Id.,* 109.

37. *Id.,* 111–112. The notes added by Hale's first editor, Emlyn, are much more clear on this point, and interesting as reflecting an early 18th century understanding of the nature of the requisite overt act. In note (k), p. 111, thus, Emlyn comments that even if certain passages cited by Staundford from Bracton and Britton could be deemed to declare spoken words sufficient overt acts at common law, "yet it does not follow, that they would be so by the statute of *25 E. 3.* which expressly requires the proof of an overt-act, and consequently disallows the evidence of bare words, for *words* and *acts* are contra-distinguished from each other. See *Co. P. C. 14 in margine.* The preamble of *1 Mariae, cap. 1, sess. 1* makes it matter of complaint, *that many had for words only suffered shameful death."* And in note (1), p. 112, Emlyn adds to Hale's explanation of the unreliable quality of testimony regarding spoken words, the comment: "This is one but not the only reason, for another reason was, because men in a passion or heat might say many things, which they never designed to do; the law therefore required, that in a case of so nice a nature, where the very intention was so highly penal, the reality of that intention should be made evident by the doing some act in prosecution thereof." This comment finds evidence of spoken words alone to be insufficient for either of the two purposes the evidence is made to bear: there is deemed insufficient evidence of intent, but also there is not thought to be a sufficient step in execution. *Cf.*note (y), p. 116; note (b), p. 117.

38. Cro. Car. 125. The sole evidence in this case was the speaking of words reflecting upon the ductability and intelligence of the king. The report states: "Upon consideration of the precedents of the statutes of treason it was resolved by the seven judges there named, and so certified to his majesty, that the speaking of the words there mentioned, tho they were as wicked as might be, were not treason; for they resolved that, unless it were by some particular statute, no words will be treason; for there is no treason at this day but by the statute of 25 E. 3. for imagining the death of the king, &c. and the indictment must be framed upon one of the points in that statute; and the words spoken there can be but evidence to discover the corrupt heart of him that spake them; but of themselves they are not treason, neither can any indictment be framed upon them."

39. *Id.,* 115–116.

40. *Id.,* 119, 122.

41. *Id.,* 131; *cf.* 135, 144, 148.

42. *Id.,* 130. Compare Coke, 10, where he explains that though *13 Eliz. cap. 1* declared a conspiracy to levy war to be treason: "It was resolved by all

the Justices, that it was no treason within the statute of 25 E. 3. as hath been said. The words in this law are [levie guerre:] An actuall Rebellion or Insurrection is a levying of war within this Act, and by the name of levying war is to be expressed in the indictment." So also, regarding adherence, Coke merely says that "this is here explained, viz. in giving aid and comfort to the Kings enemies within the Realme or without." *Ibid.* The same reliance on the statutory terms as self-evident in scope appears in his terse declaration that under the words "si home counterface le grand Seale": "A Compassing, intent, or going about to counterfeit the great seale is no treason, but there must be an actuall counterfeiting." *Id.*, 15. *Cf.* Hale, 181.

43. Both seem to think the statutory terms concerning adherence to be so plain as to call for little discussion, and their analyses furnish little help in this connection. It has been noted that in his analytical table of the elements of the different branches of treason under Statute Edward III, Coke stated that both the crimes of compassing the king's death and adhering to his enemies involved the element of "declaring the same by some overt act"; but that he defined the other major offense simply as "Levying war against the King". Coke 3–4. Hale adopts this analysis at one point. (p. 91). But *cf. id.* 149–150. This verbal distinction is obviously a very slender support for arguing that a basic difference was intended in the elements of these offenses, however. But, Coke, 14, states that "If a subject conspire with a foraine Prince beyond the seas to invade the Realme by open hostility, and prepare for the same by some overt act, this is a sufficient overt act for the death of the King, for by this Act of Parliament in that Case there must be an overt act." This may imply that conspiracy to adhere to enemies is not per se a sufficient overt act for that charge, or even for a charge of compassing. As regards adherence, however, it is not clear whether Coke is referring to a foreign prince then at peace with England, in which case, of course, there would as yet be no "enemy" to whom to adhere.

44. Hale, 85; *cf.* 111. This act and its repeal by Hen. IV, ch. 10, are relied on by Judge Hand in U. S. v. Robinson, 259 Fed. 685, 689 (S. D. N. Y. 1919), for his argument that the overt act must evidence intent.

45. Kelyng is a narrative of several treason cases under Charles II. Hawkins foregoes discussion of the political policies involved in the issue of strict or liberal construction of the crime, limiting himself largely to digest-style paragraphs on the statutes and decisions. The overt act is a distinct element under each branch of "treason." 1 Hawkins 92. Words may serve to explain an act in itself indifferent, *id.*, 94; and the meeting of conspirators is a sufficient overt act to make out a compassing the king's death, *id.* 92; Kelyng, *15, 17, 20. Both are as ambiguous as previous writers on the question of whether words are not generally a sufficient overt act. See Hawkins, 93, 94, 96; *cf.* Kelyng, *13. But Hawkins' comment on Peacham's Case, where a writing was the sole evidence, seems to point out that such evidence must be viewed, respectively, in its function of showing intent, and of establishing an overt act, for he finds the evidence in that case inadequate on these distinct grounds: "it has been holden, that written words in a sermon or other writing

may amount to overt acts of compassing the king's death, though the same neither actually were, nor ever were intended to be, preached or published. But this opinion seems to be over-severe; for though it be true that *scribere est agere,* yet surely it cannot with any propriety be said, that to write in such a private manner *est apertè agere,* and it seems rigorous to make that amount to a malicious design against the king, which perhaps was only done by way of amusement or diversion." Hawkins, 93.

46. Kelyng, *17.

47. *Id.,* *21.

48. See 4 Stephen's Commentaries on the Laws of England (18th ed. London, 1925) 157; 8 Holdsworth, History of English Law (2d ed. London, 1937) 323.

49. Foster, 207, 237. There is an intimation that he views the restrictive policy as based on the desire to limit abuse of "treason" in purely domestic factionalism, in his comment that the statute of 1 Ph. & M., in "reducing all treasons to the standard of the *25 E. III,"* brought it about that thereby "the subject was secured in his journey through life against the numerous precipices which the heat and distemper of former times had opened in his way." *Id.,* 237. Compare the breadth which he was eager to give offenses of trafficking with an external enemy, notes 58 and 60, *infra.*

50. *Id.,* 220.

51. *Id.,* 194; compare the third paragraph quoted at note 57.

52. *Id.,* 200.

53. *Id.,* 198–199.

54. *Id.,* 200.

55. *Id.,* 202, 203.

56. *Id.,* 195, 206; see also matter quoted at note 51, *supra,* and note 57, *infra.*

57. *Id.,* 193, 194–195.

58. *Id.,* 196.

59. *Id.,* 196–197.

60. *Id.,* 197–198.

61. *Id.,* 217–218.

62. *Id.,* 210, 342, 346. Coke does not discuss this question. 1 Hale 613, may imply this point, though Emlyn's pointed reference to the ruling in Somerville's case, 1 Anderson 109, on the distinction regarding a charge of compassing the king's death, indicates that Hale's editor believed that the learned author had overlooked the matter. 4 Blackstone 35–36 makes the point that the aider in compassing the king's death has *ipso facto* committed the principal crime. Concerning Foster's underlying caution regarding the scope of constructive levying of war, see Foster, 210.

63. Blackstone, 75, 83, 85, 86. At p. 86 is the reference to "newfangled" treasons, which seems probably behind Madison's similar reference in *The Federalist.*

64. *Id.,* 79.

65. *Ibid.*

66. *Id.,* 79, 80.

67. *Id.,* 79, 120.

68. This section is based on the works hereafter listed. Only those books examined which contained some significant reference to the subject are noted.

Archbold's Pleading, Evidence & Practice in Criminal Cases (31st. ed. Butler and Garsia, editors. London, 1943).

Crabb, History of English Law (1st Am. Ed. Burlington, 1831).

Chitty, Practical Treatise on the Criminal Law (3 vol. 2d ed. London, 1826) (4th Am. ed. Springfield, 1841).

East, Treatise of the Pleas of the Crown (2 vol. London, 1803) (Philadelphia, 1806).

Holdsworth, History of English Law (2d ed. 12 vol. London, 1937).

Jenks, Short History of English Law (5th ed. London, 1938).

Luders, Considerations on the Law of High Treason in the Article of Levying War (Bath, 1808).

Plucknett, Concise History of the Common Law (3d ed. London, 1940).

Pollock and Maitland, History of English Law (2 vol. Cambridge, 1895).

Reeves, History of the English Law from the Time of the Saxons to the End of the Reign of Philip and Mary (4 vol. London, 1814–1829).

Stephen, History of the Criminal Law of England (3 vol. London, 1883).

Stephen's Commentaries on the Laws of England (4 vol. 18th ed. London, 1925).

69. 2 Stephen 262–263; *cf. id.* 251. It may be significant that Stephen begins his discussion with a strong assertion of the importance of defending the basic organization of the community. *Id.,* 241–242; *cf.* 4 Holdsworth 493.

70. Luders, 10: 2 Stephen 247; 2 Pollock and Maitland 508; 2 Holdsworth 449.

71. 3 Reeves, 207, 208, 217, 234–235; 4 *id.* 273, 281, 197; 2 Stephen 247 ("Probably the great importance of the Act of Edward as a protection to what we should now call political agitation and discussion, was hardly recognized till a much later time."); 2 Pollock and Maitland 508; 3 Holdsworth 287, 290, 291; 8 *id.* 309; but *cf. id.* 310.

72. 2 Stephen 263; 4 Holdsworth 496, 498; 8 *id.* 310.

73. 3 Reeves 408; 5 *id.* 104; 1 East 58; 4 Stephen's Commentaries 150; Archbold 1067, 1073, 1077.

74. See 1 East 69, 119; 4 Stephen's Commentaries 150; 8 Holdsworth 309, 311, 315; *cf. id.* 317. From the fact that this ambiguous terminology is almost invariably used in analysis of the offense of compassing the king's death, one might infer that the writers regard the overt acts involved in the other branches of treason to be so clearly evidence of treasonable intent as not to require such comment. But *cf.* A Treatise upon the Law and Proceedings in Cases of High Treason, &c., By a Barrister at Law (London, 1793: printed as an appendix to Kelyng's Crown Cases—reprint, Lond. (1873) 106: "If the treason consists not in the intention, but in the act, as levying war, then it must be laid to have been done traiterously," citing *Cranburn's Case,* 2 Salk. 633.

75. 8 Holdsworth 316.

76. *Id.* 317–318. Compare 2 Stephen 267, which mentions Lord Preston's Case with the comment that "After the Revolution of 1688 the fictitious interpretation of the offence of compassing the king's death was carried much further than it had been under the Stuarts." He states that in the passage from Foster, quoted at note 57, *supra,* that author "proceeds to carry the law laid down in [Lord Preston's Case] . . . a step further," underlining the last clause of Foster's paragraph, and continues, "Foster follows Coke and Hale in holding that "levying war" is an overt act of compassing, and that conspiring to levy war in one sense of the expression is so too. Indeed, he goes so far as to say that "a treasonable correspondence with the enemy" is an act of compassing the king's death, and he refers in support of this to Lord Preston's case, and also to the case of one Harding, in which it was held on a special verdict that enlisting men in England and sending them abroad to join the French forces in an attempt to dethrone King William III was an imagining of his death." Neither Stephen nor Holdsworth takes note of the fact that the overt acts laid in Lord Preston's case were under a charge of adhering to the King's enemies as well as of compasssing his death. See notes 58 and 59, *supra.*

77. 8 Holdsworth 309, 311.

78. *Id.,* 307. Compare 2 Stephen 282: "Instances of this offence have been very rare in our history. England, owing to its insular position, has not for centuries been the scene of war carried on with a foreign enemy. . . . Hence the offence of 'adhering to the king's enemies'—an exceedingly vague expression—has been committed only by a few spies who have in the time of war been detected in giving information to foreign enemies. . . . No questions of legal or constitutional interest have arisen on this branch of the act of Edward III to my knowledge."

79. Archbold 1076. His further comments suggest that he draws this conclusion from rulings on the effect of a conspiracy to levy war, for he declares that a conspiracy to adhere to enemies may probably be laid as an overt act of compassing the king's death, and that "if the prosecution can prove such a conspiracy [to adhere], and connect the prisoner with it by evidence, and can prove an act done by any one of the conspirators in furtherance of the common design, it may be given in evidence against the prisoner, if it tends to prove any of the overt acts laid in the indictment; for the act of one, in such a case, is the act of all: *R. v. Stone,* 25 St. Tr. 1115; 6 T. R. 527."

"A conspiracy to aid or comfort the king's enemies is not within the act," according to A Treatise upon the Law and Proceedings in Cases of High Treason, *op. cit. supra,* note 74, p. *41. This work cites 3 Inst. 9, and 6 Ba. Abr. 5th ed. 516, the latter in turn relying on Coke, Hale, Pleas of the Crown 13, 14 (the one volume work preceding the History), and 1 Hawkins P. C. c. 17, sec. 27 for the same proposition. Coke, Hale, and Hawkins, however, discuss only conspiracy to levy war, in the passages relied on; and in no others do they appear to support the doctrine for which they are here cited.

3 Holdsworth 288 points out a probable historical explanation for the omission of conspiracy to levy war as a branch of treason under the Statute of

Edward III: "As is well known, there is no mention in the statute of a conspiracy to levy war; and, as Maitland points out, [2 Pollock and Maitland 503, 504; but this reference actually discusses only the reason for the late recognition of the crime of levying war against the king], this is probably due to the fact that such a conspiracy was hardly regarded as an offence if the war was properly declared." That is, the feudal bond was in law a reciprocal one, of rights and duties, so that the vassal had a right in some cases to war upon a lord who had broken the bond. Thus, the omission of conspiracy in the statutory definition would not in its origin reflect any policy relevant to present use of the Statute. *Cf.* 2 Hallam, Constitutional History of England (London, 1827) 501.

2 Chitty 69, 73 gives as a sufficient count for adhering to enemies the following allegations, which might be deemed broad enough to include a meeting with an enemy agent as a sufficient overt act of adherence:

And further, &c. . . . He the said William Stone, as such false traitor as aforesaid, during the said war, to wit, on, &c. and on divers other days as well before as after that day, at, &c aforesaid, well knowing the said William Jackson traitorously to have come to and landed in this kingdom, for the traitorous purpose of procuring and obtaining intelligence and information whether the subjects of our said lord the king were or were not well affected to our said lord the king and his government, and were or were not likely to join with and assist the forces of the said persons exercising the powers of government in France, and being enemies of our said lord the king as aforesaid, in case an hostile invasion of this kingdom should be made by them for the prosecution to be sent such intelligence and information to the said persons exercising the powers of government in France, and being enemies of our said lord the king, as aforesaid, for the aid, assistance, direction, and instruction of the said enemies of our said lord the king, in their conduct and prosecution of the said war against our said lord the king, did, with force and arms, maliciously and traitorously receive and treat with the said William Jackson, in the prosecution, performance, and execution of his traitorous purpose aforesaid, and did then and there maliciously and traitorously aid, comfort, abet, and assist the said William Jackson in, about, and concerning the prosecution, performance and execution of his the said William Jackson's traitorous purpose aforesaid.

80. East 100; *cf. id.,* 58. However, the argument that compassing was always a peculiarly broad offense due to ideas no longer prevailing, regarding the special protection of the King's person, is somewhat rebutted by the emphasis which is put on concern for the King, not as a person, but as a symbol of the ordered community. See Foster, note 57, *supra.* This also appears in the distinction taken by Hale and East between the scope of the crime as applied to the king and to his queen or heir apparent. 1 East 65 thus says, of the crime of compassing the death of the queen or of the eldest son and heir: "As to what shall be said to be an overt act of compassing their

death; it must be such as shews an unlawful intent against their *persons,* and not merely against their *state and dignity.* Therefore much of what has been already said concerning overt acts of compassing the death of the king, which are specifically appropriate to him and his sovereign power and royal dignity, does not apply to the queen or prince. Thus a compassing to imprison or otherwise punish them by due course of law is not within the statute; but a compassing to wound them is." See 1 Hale 127–128.

81. This paragraph is based on examination of the following works, among others. Only those containing some substantial discussion of the subject are noted.

Anson, The Law and Custom of the Constitution (3d ed. 3 vol. Oxford, 1907).

Chalmers and Asquith, Outlines of Constitutional Law (5th ed. London, 1936).

Hallam, The Constitutional History of England (2 vol. London, 1827).

Joliffe, Constitutional History of Medieval England from the English Settlement to 1485 (London, 1937).

Keir, Constitutional History of Modern Britain 1485–1937 (2d ed. London, 1943).

May, Constitutional History of England (3 vol. London, 1912).

Morris, Constitutional History of England to 1216 (N. Y., 1930).

Smith, History of the English Parliament (2 vol. London, 1892).

Stubbs, Constitutional History of England (3 vol. 6th ed. Oxford, 1897).

Tanner, Tudor Constitutional Documents A. D. 1485–1603 (Cambridge, 1930).

Taswell-Langmead, English Constitutional History (9th ed. London, 1929).

Thomson, A Constitutional History of England (4 vol. London, 1938).

82. 2 Anson 243; 2 Hallam 499; Jolliffe, 446–447; 1 Smith 211; Taswell-Langmead, 242, n.

83. Joliffe, 446; Keir, 107, 213; 2 May 45, 55, 72 (though *cf. id.,* 43); 2 Smith 340; 3 Stubbs 290, 537; Tanner, 379; Taswell-Langmead, 348.

84. Tanner, 377, note 2; *cf.* 4 Thomson 284.

85. See 2 Hallam 516:

In the vast mass of circumstantial testimony which our modern trials for high treason display, it is sometimes difficult to discern, whether this great principle of our law, requiring two witness to overt acts, has been adhered to; for certainly it is not adhered to, unless such witnesses depose to acts of the prisoner, from which an inference of his guilt is immediately deducible.

Cf. 1 *id.* 177, n. In the light of the quoted comment, and as evidence of the inherent ambiguity of those statements which assert that the act must "manifest" treason, it is interesting to note that elsewhere Hallam says: "The crime of compassing and imagining the king's death must be manifested by some overt act; that is, there must be something done in execution of a traitorous purpose." 2 *id.* 505. In this latter statement, clearly the meaning is that the act must "manifest" the intent in the sense of translating thought into deed.

86. 325 U.S. 1 (1945). On two occasions, the defendant, a naturalized American citizen, was observed by two FBI agents to meet in a public restaurant and engage in long and earnest conversation with an enemy agent. The two witnesses could testify only to the fact of the meeting; the defendant's admissions to a third party, to the FBI agents after his arrest, and while on the witness stand furnished the only evidence that he knew he was dealing with an enemy agent, and that he intended to aid the latter by taking the latter's funds into safekeeping to be held for his convenience. The Court, in a 5–4 decision, apparently ruled that aid must be shown to have been "actually" given the enemy, and that insofar as any conduct of defendant was relied on to show that the overt act was an act giving aid, this must be shown by two witnesses.

87. *Id.,* 16–18.

88. *Id.,* 18.

89. The dissenting opinion also gives first place to the analysis of the treatises. *Id.,* 68-72.

90. *Id.,* 18, 19, and note 25; *cf.* 21.

91. The dissent emphasizes Foster's interpretation. *Id.,* 71. The majority (*Id.,* 18, note 25) refers to Coke and Blackstone as "chief" among the commentators. If this is meant as an evaluation of their analyses of the offense, it seems unduly favorable. Coke's account of the crime is often ambiguous and is quite disorganized in presentation. Blackstone's treatment is relatively short, and contributes nothing new in thought and little in penetration. Hale and Foster seem to deserve by far the highest praise for depth and clarity of analysis. If the *Cramer* opinion means that Coke and Blackstone were the "chief" commentators in the eyes of American lawyers and draftsmen of the 18th century, this is more difficult to weigh. There is no doubt of their great influence, though the *Cramer* opinion cites no evidence that they dominated American analysis of the crime. However, evidence is not lacking that other commentators were also well known to learned Americans. In his notes to Chancellor Wythe, November 1, 1778, regarding his proposed "bill for proportioning Crimes and Punishments, in cases heretofore Capital," Thomas Jefferson cites Hale and Foster, as well as Coke in his discussion of treason. 1 Writings of Thomas Jefferson (Library ed. Washington, 1903) 216, 218, 220–221. And in his argument as defense counsel in the Pennsylvania treason trials of 1778, James Wilson bases his brief on Hale and Hawkins, as well as on Blackstone. See "Notes of C. J. McKean in case of Ab'm Carlisle, 1778," 7 Pennsylvania Archives (Hazard ed. Philadelphia, 1853) 44–52; *cf;* Republica v. Carlisle, 1 Dallas 34, 36 (Pa. Oyer and Terminer, 1778).

92. *Id.,* 18, note 25 (majority opinion); 73, 74 (dissent).

3

Treason Down
to the Constitution

(a) Prior to the Revolution

IN MOST OF the colonies there was at some stage some
legislative definition or at least recognition of the existence of
an offense of treason. Charters and proprietary grants and
the royal instructions to colonial governors sometimes conferred authority to exercise martial law for the suppression of
what might amount to treason. There were scattered prosecutions for treason in the colonies, but we have few reports of
these and no evidence to suggest that there developed a
common law of treason or any substantial gloss upon the
legislative provisions. The statutory offense, however, was
generally outlined or recognized in sufficiently general terms
to give room for a creative role of the executive in deciding
what to prosecute and of the judges in interpreting the scope
of the crime.

Taking the colonial period as a whole, in most of the
colonies the definition of the offense was clearly thought of in
terms of the English legislation stemming from the Statute of

25 Edward III.[1] This is not true, however, of the earliest references to the crime, mainly in the northern colonies. The authority given in charters and grants and in instructions to royal governors was not put in familiar words of art, but merely approved resort to martial law for the suppression of "rebellion," "sedition," or perhaps "mutinies." The North Carolina Charter of 1665 was unusually explicit; but it, like the others, does not use traditional language when it confers power

> to exercise martial law against any mutinous and seditious persons of these parts; such as shall refuse to submit themselves to their government, or shall refuse to serve in the war, or shall fly to the enemy, or forsake their colours or ensigns, or be loiterers, or stragglers, or otherwise offending against law, custom, or military discipline.[2]

The *Laws of New Haven Colony* contained this provision, which has no resemblance to any familiar English model:

> If any person shall conspire, and attempt any invasion, insurrection, or publick Rebellion against this Jurisdiction, or shall endeavour to surprize, or seize any Plantation, or Town, any Fortification, Platform, or any great Guns, provided for the defence of the Jurisdiction, or any Plantation therein; or shall treacherously and perfidiously attempt the alteration and subversion of the frame of policy, or fundamentall Government laid, and setled for this Jurisdiction, he or they shall be put to death. *Num.* 16. *2 Sam.* 18. *2 Sam.* 20. Or if any person shall consent unto any such mischievous practice, or by the space of foure and twenty houres conceale it, not giving notice thereof to some Magistrate, if there be any Magistrate in the Plantation, or place where he liveth, or if none, to some Deputy for the Jurisdiction, or to the Constable of the place, that the publick safety may be seasonably provided

for, he shall be put to death, or severely punished, as the Court of Magistrates weighing all circumstances shall determine.[3]

The biblical citations suggest that this provision was not drawn with any primary attention to English materials. A very similar provision was contained in the *General Laws* of Connecticut (1673), which under the heading "Capital Laws" declared:

> 12. If any person shall conspire or attempt any Invasion, Insurrection or publick Rebellion against this Colony, or shall Treacherously and Perfideously attempt the Alteration and Subversion of our Frame of Government Fundamentally established by His Majesties Gracious Charter Granted to this Colony, by endeavouring the betraying of the same into the hands of any forreign power, he shall be put to death.[4]

The *Laws of the Colony of New Plymouth,* in the revision of 1636, had merely included under "Capitall offences lyable to death," "Treason or rebellion against the person of the King, State or Commonwealth, either of England or these Colonies." But the *General Laws and Liberties of New Plimouth Colony, 1671,* in chapter II, "Capital Laws," expanded the definition in terms like those of the New Haven act:

> 3. Treason against the Person of our Soveraign Lord the King, the State and Common-wealth of England, shall be punished by death.

> 4. That whosoever shall Conspire and Attempt any Invasion, Insurrection, or Publick Rebellion against this Jurisdiction, or the Surprizal of any Town, Plantation, Fortification or Ammunition, therein provided for the safety thereof, or shall Treacherously and Perfidiously Attempt and Endeavour the Alteration and

Subversion of the Fundamental Frame and Constitutions of this Government; every such Person shall be put to Death.[5]

The last provision was in substance included in *The General Laws and Liberties of Massachusetts Bay* (May, 1678), with about the same biblical citations as in the New Haven provision, and in the *Duke of York's Laws* (1665–1675), compiled from the statutes for the government of the other northern English colonies in America by the first English governor, Nicolls, as well as in the criminal code adopted in 1668 by Carteret's Assembly in New Jersey and the *General Laws and Liberties of the Province of New Hampshire,* of 1679.[6]

The bulk of colonial legislation on treason, including the later statutes in the northern colonies, looks to English law for the definition of the offense. Some of these acts adopt the phraseology of the Statute of 25 Edward III, with additions inspired by local problems. The earliest indication of this reliance on the Statute of Edward seems to be the text of "An Act for Treasons" which was considered, but not passed, at the session of the Maryland General Assembly in February–March, 1638. Bacon tells us:

By this Bill the following Offences were to be adjudged Treasons within this Province, *viz.* To compass or conspire the Death of the King, or the Queen his Wife, or of his Son and Heir; or to levy War against his Majesty, or to counterfeit the King's Great or Privy Seal, or his Coin; or to join or adhere to any foreign Prince or State, being a professed Enemy of his Majesty, in any Practice or Attempt against his said Majesty: Or to compass, conspire, or cause the Death of the Lord Proprietary within this Province, or of his Lieut. General for the Time being, (in Absence of his Lordship,) or to join, adhere or confederate with any *Indians,* or any foreign Prince or Governor to the invading of this Province, or disheriting the Lord Proprietary of his Seignory and Dominion therein. All Offences of Treason to be punished by Drawing, Hanging and Quartering of a Man, and Burning of a Woman; the Offender's Blood to be corrupted, and to forfeit all his Lands, Tenements, Goods, &c. to his Lordship. But Punishment of Death to be inflicted on a Lord of a Manor by Beheading.[7]

The Connecticut *Acts and Laws (1702)* added to the special provisions already noted in the laws of that colony the more familiar declarations:

That if any person or persons, shall compass or imagine the Death of our Soveraign Lord the KING, or of our Lady the QUEEN, or of the Heir apparent to the Crown; or if any person shall leavy War against our Lord the KING, or be adherent to the Kings Enemies, giving them aid, and comfort in the Realm, or elsewhere, and thereof be probably attainted of open deed by His Peers, upon the Testimony of two Lawful and Credible Witnesses upon Oath, brought before the offender face to face, at the time of his arraignment; or voluntary confession of the party arraigned. Or if any person or persons shall counterfeit the Kings Great Seal, or privy Seal, and thereof be duely convicted, as aforesaid, then every such person and persons, so as aforesaid Offending, shall be deemed, declared, and adjudged, to be Traitors, and shall suffer pains of Death, and also lose and forfeit as in cases of High Treason.

And be it further Enacted by the Authority aforesaid, That the Tryal of all, and every person and persons whatsoever, accused, indicted and prosecuted for High Treason, and misprission of such Treason, shall be regulated according to Act of Parliament, made in the Seventh year of His present Majesties Reign, Entituled, *An Act for Regulating of Tryals in Cases of Treason and Misprission of Treason;* and the party so accused, indicted and prosecuted, to be allowed the benefits and priviledges, in and by the said Act granted and declared.[8]

Similar legislation had been passed in the Massachusetts Bay Colony in 1692 and 1696, and acts of 1706 and 1744 likewise incorporated the procedural guaranties of the statute of 7 William III into more specific legislation directed against "traiterous correspondence with his Majesty's enemies."[9] In New Hampshire, the Act of May 15, 1714, followed the Connecticut and Massachusetts pattern.[10]

More numerous were provisions which, in varying terms, declared that the offense of treason should be defined, proceeded against and punished as under the laws of England. Although some of these acts in terms seem limited to incorporating the procedural or penalty provisions of the English law, they evidence a general inclination to look to that law for guidance, and none of them contains anything denying the applicability of English concepts of the scope of the offense. Such legislation is found in Delaware, New York, North Carolina, Pennsylvania, Rhode Island, South Carolina, and possibly Virginia. Of the colonies, only Georgia and New Jersey seem not to have adopted legislation of one of these types.[11]

Surveillance exercised by the authorities in the mother country served, further, to enforce awareness of the English law of treason in the definition of the offense in America. Thus, although the Massachusetts act of 1692 already referred to had substantially copied the language of the Statute of Edward III, it was disallowed by the Privy Council, on August 22, 1695, because

> in yᵉ Article of Treason no punishment is inflicted for counterfeiting the Great Seal of England or the seal of yᵉ Province nor is that article agreeable to the statute of the 25th of Edward the third in relation to Treason.[12]

The colonial legislature remedied the objections in the act of 1696. Again, the Commissioners for Trade and Plantations objected to the Pennsylvania Act of November 27, 1700, which declared it an offense punishable by forfeiture of half the offender's property or by one year's imprisonment to compass the death of the proprietary and governor. The Commissioners stated that: "We think this act not proper to be laid before Her Majesty, the proprietary and governor having already the same protection by law as other Her Majesty's subjects." Accordingly, the Queen in Council repealed the act.[13]

In New York, the Act of May 6, 1691, abjuring the royal house of Stuart, had declared it treason "by force of arms or otherwise to disturb the peace good and quiet of this their Majestyes Government as it is now Established." The home authorities found this act objectionably broad and vague, and instructions were sent the governor to procure its repeal. It was, hence, repealed by the Act of June 27, 1704, whose recital reflects an influence upon the colonists to look for their law to England in this regard:

> whereas her most sacred Majesty hath been graciously pleased out of her princely Care for the good and Safety of her Subjects in their Lives and Estates to observe in her Intruccons to the Governor that the meaning of the said Clause hath been of late misinterpreted to the oppression of her Subjects, and is pleased to direct that for preventing the like abuses for the future the said Clause should be repealed the Laws of England having Sufficiently provided for the true purposes thereof.[14]

King v. Bayard, a prosecution in New York in 1702 under the Act of 1691 just noted, is the only pre-Revolutionary case of which we have an extensive record. Though the issues centered on the interpretation of the New York act, which was not couched in familiar English statutory terms, the defense resorted to Coke and the principal English statutes to evolve a theory of restrictive construction of treason legislation.[15] Law libraries in the colonies were almost nonexistent until the end of the 17th century, but from then until the Revolution, English treatises, statute books and law reports became more accessible, and it is reasonable to assume that leading lawyers of the period had opportunity, both in the legal education which some enjoyed in England, and in the books available in the colonies, to familiarize themselves with much that was written on the subject. The *Commonplace Book* of James Wilson contains quite extensive notes on the doctrines of the law of treason, obviously reflecting the use of the English lawbooks.[16]

All of this points to the fact that the several colonies drew on the general concepts of English law for the definition of treason and the incidents of its prosecution. The evidence is too scant, however, to justify any confident verdict as to how detailed was the knowledge of the mother country's law and experience in the matter; and it is consistent with the general history of the colonies' development to believe that local experience was the most substantial contributor to the attitudes of policy and the doctrines to be found here.

The striking characteristic of all of the pre-Revolutionary legislation in the colonies is the evident emphasis on the safety of the state or government, and the subordinate role of any concern for the liberties of the individual. Whereas the outstanding feature of the treason clause placed in the Constitution of the United States is that it is on its face restrictive of the scope of the offense, the emphasis of colonial legislation is almost wholly affirmative. This is not surprising. Relatively weak and remote settlements, necessarily alert to the nearness of hostile empires and Indian tribes, would naturally think first in terms of positive defense against external enemies. The implications of the utility of the law of treason against domestic upset would also be mainly favorable to the official and landed or wealthy mercantile classes which dominated political affairs in the various colonies. Such laws as those passed at very early dates in the colonies north of Maryland would thus seem to have very practical explanations, and not to be designed merely to complete the logical symmetry of paper codes. The practical bases for the positive character of the colonial laws are further evidenced by the tendency for additional legislation to appear at the time of foreign wars or domestic disturbances.[17]

The best evidence that the prevailing policy was concern for the safety of the state or government and not the careful protection of the individual citizen is in the types of conduct which the statutes declared treasonable. It has been noted that broad authority to employ martial law against "insurrection," "rebellion," "mutiny," or "sedition" was commonly conferred in original charters or proprietary grants. The crime of compassing the death of the king—a notable omission in the treason definition finally placed in the Constitution of the United States—was copied from the Statute of Edward III by Connecticut, Maryland, Massachusetts Bay, and New Hampshire; and was in effect adopted by the seven other colonies whose legislation recognized, in one form or another, the applicability of the English law of treason within their limits.

Of course, it might be contended that since the basic English Statute of Edward III has been traditionally praised as setting limits to a dangerously vague common law of treason, the mere adoption of the English laws descending from this beneficent act showed a restrictive intent on the part of colonial legislatures. In view of the practical extension of the vague categories of the Statute of Edward III by the English courts, however, this argument seems somewhat artificial, especially as applied to governments which had reason to be keenly concerned for their safety from external foes. The only plausible reason for adopting English law offered by the statute books is the claim of the "common law" as the "birthright of English subjects" in the acts by which

Delaware and Pennsylvania adopted the English statutes of treason.[18]

Maryland and Pennsylvania went further than other colonies and made it a state offense to compass the death of the proprietor. The Pennsylvania act, as was noted above, was repealed by the Queen in Council, for a reason which reflects a desire to curb the political pretensions of the colony rather than to guard the citizen's liberties. The earlier Maryland act does not seem to have incurred the disapproval of the Crown; but it was in effect for only three years. Its passage seems indicative of a climate of policy.[19]

The offense of levying war against the sovereign is given a broad definition in two ways in the colonial legislation. One of the major accomplishments of judicial construction of the Statute of Edward III in England was the eventual creation of the crime of treason by "constructive levying of war," the concerted effort, by violence, to set aside the laws or the authority of the government or to accomplish objects of general public policy outside the established procedures of governmental action. This was not left wholly to judicial construction, however, in the several early colonial statutes which included in their condemnation of treason the offenses of "insurrection," "publick Rebellion," or of attempting "the Alteration and Subversion of our Frame of Government Fundamentally established by His Majesties Gracious Charter," as well as "rebellion against the person of the King, State or Commonwealth, either of England or these Colonies," the "Endeavour by force of arms or otherwise to disturbe the peace good and quiet of this their Majestyes Government as it is now Established," or the speaking or writing of words questioning the King's dominion.[20]

The New York Act of 1691 was repealed under instructions from the Crown, because its vague terms had been "misinterpreted" to the oppression of the subjects; but even this unusual pronouncement in favor of the liberty of the citizen was immediately balanced in the repealing statute's declaration that the laws of England "sufficiently provided" for the suppression of domestic treason.[21] Most of these acts broadly including domestic disturbance in the crime of treason antedate 1700, but there is no evidence that any were repealed or allowed to expire because they were believed to extend the scope of treason unduly. Moreover, during the 18th century all of the colonies which had passed such early, broad treason acts (except New Jersey), adopted or recognized the applicability of the terms of the Statute of Edward III under which English courts were then reinforcing the concept of "constructive levying of war." Quincy reports charges to the Grand Jury in 1765 and 1766 by the Chief Justice of the Province of Massachusetts Bay, in which the law is declared to be:

> Levying War against the King is High Treason; as where People set about redressing public Wrongs; this, Gentlemen, the Law calls levying War against the King; because it is going in direct Opposition to the King's Authority, who is the Redresser of all Wrongs.[22]

The other respect in which the first colonial legislation expanded the offense of levying war was by including conspiracy to levy war. The English courts had early ruled that such conspiracy did not come within the Statute of Edward III. Again, the American legislation antedates 1700.[23] But, again, it must be pointed out that during the 18th century all of these jurisdictions (except New Jersey) together with others, either copied the terms of the Statute of Edward III into their books, or recognized the applicability of English treason law within their boundaries, including the offense of compassing the king's death, which by now had been construed by the English courts in effect to cover conspiracy to levy war.[24] It would be artificial to maintain that these colonies thereby consciously adopted all of the constructions of the king's courts; but it is equally true that this record cannot be taken to evidence an intent to narrow the scope of the offense.

Certain colonial statutes of the French and Indian Wars, following English models, suggest an extension of the bounds of the offense of adhering to the enemy, and have special interest, because they foreshadow legislation of the same type in the Revolutionary period. The Massachusetts Bay Act of August 31, 1706, "For preventing all traiterous correspondence with the French king, or his subjects, or the Indian enemy or rebels, and supplying them with warlike or other stores," declared it high treason to furnish provisions to the enemy, and also made it treason

> if . . . any person or persons shall, during the continuance of the present war with France, be convicted of holding a traiterous correspondence with any of her majesty's enemies, by letters or otherwise, whereby they shall give them intelligence tending to the damage of her majesty's subjects or interests, or to the benefit or advantage of the enemy.

It was likewise declared high treason

> if any of her majesty's subjects within this province shall . . . during the continuance of the present war with France, without license from her majesty's governour or commander-in-chief of this her majesty's province for the time being, by and with the advice and consent of the council, voluntarily go, repair or embarque in or upon any vessel or vessels, with an intention to go into, reside or inhabit in any of the dominions or territories of the said French king, or amongst any of the Indian enemy or rebels aforesaid. . . .

The Act contained a proviso:

> That nothing in this act contained shall be construed, intended, deemed or taken to extend to bar the necessary relief and supply of any French prisoners of war, or of any flagg of truce, or to the supply of the English prisoners in French or Indian hands; or for secret services made or done, at all times, by the direction of the governour, with the advice of the council; or to bar a present charitable relief to any of the enemy that by adversity may be cast on shoar upon this coast, for the preservation of life; intelligence thereof to be forthwith dispatch'd to the governour.[25]

The broad terms of this statute raise the interesting question, whether to convict under it, a specific intent to betray the colony must be shown. This is the implication, *prima facie,* of the prohibition of "traiterous" correspondence, but the adjective might also be taken to be adequately explained by what follows; and the remainder of the provision in terms condemns a correspondence which in fact conveys information tending to damage the colony or benefit the enemy, without mention of an intent thereby to betray the colony.

The terms of the next section, regarding unlicensed departure for enemy territory, include no innuendo of a showing of specific intent thereby to give aid or comfort to the enemy; an unlicensed departure on private business for profit or to go to family or friends would seem within the ban. Where the penalty of death and forfeiture of property is involved, a court would normally rule as a matter of course that a guilty mind was intended to be an element of the offense; but this argument here begs the question, which is whether in view of the likelihood of peril to the state, the guilty mind does not consist in the intention which puts the actor in so ambiguous a situation, regardless of any further showing of a specific motive to betray. That the act was intended to be taken in a broad sense, is suggested by the proviso, which excludes matters which it would otherwise seem needless to mention. Perhaps the strongest argument against the broad interpretation is that the offense of "traiterous correspondence" is linked in the act with that of selling or delivering provisions to the enemy, an offense which in wartime can hardly be treated as open to innocent explanation.

An act of substantially similar terms was passed June 26, 1744, in the same colony.[26] These should be compared with the series of statutes beginning with the Act of March 29, 1755, which forbade citizens of the province "to hold any correspondence or communication with any inhabitants of Louisburgh or any other of the French settlements in North America, either by land or water," and penalized violation by forfeiture of vessel and cargo, and, for the vessel's master, loss of one ear and 39 lashes and deprivation of the right to hold any office of trust or honor under the province. Since the preamble recited that the statute was designed to prevent knowledge of gathering plans against Louisburgh from reaching the French, it seems particularly likely that its sweeping prohibition was meant to be taken without the requirement of showing a specific intent to betray.[27]

If the colonial legislation thus shows an almost unbroken trend to put the interest in community security first in defining the types of conduct which shall be deemed treasonable, it is equally true, however, that it displays a persistent concern for safeguarding the individual regarding the quantum of proof and the decencies of procedure. Certain early statutes required at least two witnesses to prove any capital offense. From the latter part of the 17th century on, in most of the colonies the two-witness requirement and the procedural guaranties laid down by the Statute of 7 William III in treason trials were expressly enacted by reference to that statute or to the English statutes on treason generally.[28] The witness requirement of course meant simply a requirement of two witnesses without the specification, laid down subsequently in the United States Constitution, that they be to the same overt act. On the other hand, pursuant to the statute of William III, they must be witnesses to the same treasonable offense, and one witness to each of two separate, or at least different types, of treason, would not suffice.

The records of prosecutions or decisions in treason cases in the colonial period are too scanty to be of much help in seeing the trend of policy. In particular, nothing helpful has been found to illuminate the borderline cases of adherence to the enemy. Almost all the cases which had sufficient color and interest to cause the preservation of some record were cases of domestic insurrection—"constructive levying of war." Where political difference rose to the degree of armed resistance that it did in Bacon's Rebellion, in Virginia, in 1675–76, there was clearly treason, if domestic disturbance were to be recognized as within the offense at all; the question of a wise executive clemency in the case is something again.[29] On the other hand, there is evidence that there were cases of abuse by prosecutions for political differences which should not have been deemed to carry such a threat of subversion of the state as to be treasonable. Such a case seems the celebrated *King v. Bayard,* in New York in 1702.[30] But there is a total lack of any specific evidence to show that such incidents were sufficiently numerous or outrageous to form a current of opinion that the scope of treason must be narrowed for the safety of the citizen. None of the restrictive arguments urged at the time of the drafting and ratification of the Federal Constitution is based on an appeal to American colonial experience in this regard.

(b) The Revolution: 1775–1783

As a matter of law, the Revolution called for new legislation on treason, for new political entities had arisen to claim allegiance, betrayal of which was treason.[31] As a matter of fact, the dangers from disaffected persons in the colonies, and in the new states, were so clear and pressing as naturally to produce legislative reactions. Scattered provisions in the new state constitutions banned legislative attainders, abolished corruption of blood as a penalty, limited the pardoning power of the executive, or required trial in the county where the offense was committed; but none spoke of the scope of the offense or the nature of its proof. New statutes in most states undertook to define the offense and prescribe for proof and trial procedure; and about this nucleus clustered other legislation, sometimes elaborating the scope of the crime, sometimes creating ancillary offenses—disloyal utterances, traffic with the enemy, confiscation of property of disaffected persons—which help indicate the views of policy with which the offense was approached. Summary executive action amounting to less than the full penalty for treason finds frequent reflection in the histories of the times; but, as in the earlier period, records of trials for treason are scant and do not contribute as much as the statutory material to outlining the attitudes taken towards the crime.[32]

The Revolution does not break the thread of continuity with traditional English materials defining the scope of treason. When the Continental Congress, on June 24, 1776, adopting the recommendation of its "Committee on Spies," recommended to the colonies that they pass treason legislation, it used the familiar terms of the Statute of Edward III, with a suggestion of the evidentiary requirements of the Statute of 7 William III:

> *Resolved,* That all persons abiding within any of the United Colonies, and deriving protection from the laws of the same, owe allegiance to the said laws, and are members of such colony; and that all persons passing through, visiting, or make [sic] a temporary stay in any of the said colonies, being entitled to the

protection of the laws during the time of such passage, visita-
tion, or temporary stay, owe, during the same time, allegiance
thereto:

That all persons, members of, or owing allegiance to any of the
United Colonies, as before described, who shall levy war against
any of the said colonies within the same, or be adherent to the king
of Great Britain, or others the enemies of the said colonies, or any
of them, within the same, giving to him or them aid and comfort,
are guilty of treason against such colony:

That it be recommended to the legislatures of the several
United Colonies, to pass laws for punishing, in such manner as to
them shall seem fit, such persons before described, as shall be
proveably attainted of open deed, by people of their condition, of
any of the treasons before described.[33]

The committee which had recommended the resolutions
included John Adams, Thomas Jefferson, John Rutledge,
James Wilson and Robert Livingston. The familiar words of
the resolutions apart, it would be incredible that this distinguished group of lawyers and students of the law did not
draft their suggestions with a background of English law in
mind, and at least in the case of Jefferson and Wilson we
know that they had previous familiarity with English materials.[34]

In the course of the next year, the advice of the Continental
Congress was taken by most of the states, which adopted basic
statutes employing the recommended formula. In the minority of states which anticipated the Congressional suggestion, or thereafter adopted substantially differing legislation,
the key definition of the offense was still in terms similar to
the Statute of Edward III.[35] Moreover, the terms of subsidi-
ary legislation punishing disloyal utterances, sometimes as
treason, sometimes as lesser offenses, suggest analogies in test
oath provisions which the colonial laws had adopted from
England.[36]

The few treason cases of the period, reported in the volumes of Dallas, show counsel to be familiar with the basic English statutes and treatises; but it may be significant of the limitations of local law libraries that in his argument in *Respublica v. Carlisle,* in 1778, the Attorney General of Pennsylvania cites *Lord Preston's* case from Foster's treatise and not from the reports. Similarly, Chief Justice McKean's notes of the argument made by James Wilson for the defense in the *Carlisle* case show Wilson as relying on the English statutes and treatises, with no mention of any citation to the reports.[37] But, if American lawyers and statesmen did not have the detailed development of English judge-made law at their finger tips, the evidence and the probabilities nevertheless clearly establish that they drew their ideas of the scope of the offense and the nature of proceedings therein from important English materials.

Continuity with the colonial period also marks the time of the Revolution with respect to the definition of the scope of the offense. The struggle with Great Britain was bitterly fought and the outcome long in doubt, with neighbor divided from neighbor and suspicion prevalent. In this atmosphere, it was to be expected that the dominant emphasis, as in the preceding period, would be on the security of the state rather than the liberty of the individual.

However, the break with England itself produced the first manifest distrust of the abuse of treason trials, and the Revolutionary years show the definite beginnings of the wary policy which was to find expression in the Federal Constitution. In his draft of "Instructions for the Deputies appointed to meet in General Congress on the part of this Colony,"[38] Thomas Jefferson raised the issue of the definition of treason. Noting General Gage's proclamation, in Massachusetts, declaring it treason for the inhabitants to assemble to consider grievances and to form associations in this connection, Jefferson argued that if he considers himself as acting in the character of his Majesty's representative, we would remind him that the statute 25th, Edward the Third has expressed and defined all treasonable offences, and that the legislature of Great Britain had declared, that no offence shall be construed to be treason, but such as is pointed out by that statute, and that this was done to take out of the hands of tyrannical Kings, and of weak and wicked Ministers, that deadly weapon, which constructive treason had furnished them with, and which had drawn the blood of the best and honestest men in the kingdom.[39]

The burden of complaint with regard to the law of treason, so far as the great public debate was concerned, related, however, to an important matter of procedure. Among the grievances recited by the Continental Congress in the preamble to its resolutions declaring the rights of the colonies, adopted October 14, 1774, was the fact that

it has lately been resolved in Parliament, that by force of a statute, made in the thirty-fifth year of the reign of king Henry the eighth, colonists may be transported to England, and tried there upon accusations for treasons, and misprisions, or concealments of treasons committed in the colonies; and by a late statute, such trials have been directed in cases therein mentioned.[40]

Abuse of treason trials was not listed, in explicit terms, by the Declaration of Independence among its charges of oppressive conduct, but both the scope of prosecutions threatened and the unfairness of trials in remote England seem to be protested in the complaint "For transporting us beyond seas to be tried for pretended offenses. . . . "[41]

Jefferson participated in drafting both the treason act which the Congress recommended to the colonies on June 24, 1776, and the Virginia treason statute of October, 1776. There seems to be no record of the policy deliberations of the draftsmen of these measures. It was pointed out in the analysis of the colonial legislation that the mere use of the terms of the Statute of Edward III is ambiguous on the issue of extensive versus restrictive intent.[42] The situation may by this time, however, have been altered, since, as Jefferson's essay of 1774 shows, there was now a political reason to emphasize the tradition which makes the Statute of Edward a restrictive act. Moreover, the new American treason acts included no provision analogous to that of compassing the king's death. This omission was of course logically explainable on the ground that in a republic there was no proper place for an analogous offense, that the state alone, and not the head of the state, was to be given the protection of this dread penalty, and that it was adequately protected by the provisions against levying war or adhering to enemies. There seems to be no contemporary exposition of this theory, however, and its logic is a bit too pat to seem a convincing explanation of the rather haphazard processes of state legislation of that day.[43] It is altogether likely that in most states, the offense of compassing the death of the king was dropped for no more elaborate reason than that there was no longer a king. On the other hand, one cannot make such assumptions about legislation in the drawing of which Thomas Jefferson had a hand. We may draw some further light from the notes which Jefferson wrote to Chancellor Wythe, on November 1, 1778, regarding Jefferson's proposed "bill for proportioning Crimes and Punishments, in cases heretofore Capital." Jefferson proposed a section providing (footnotes are his):

[2]If a man do levy war[3] against the Commonwealth [*in the same*], or be adherent to the enemies of the Commonwealth [*within the same*][4], giving to them aid or comfort in the Commonwealth, or elsewhere, and thereof be convicted of open deed, by the evidence of two sufficient witnesses, or his own voluntary confession, the said cases, and no[5] others, shall be adjudged treasons which

extend to the Commonwealth, and the person so convicted shall suffer death, by hanging, and shall forfeit his lands and goods to the Commonwealth.

In his footnotes, Jefferson explained the policies behind his draftsmanship:

[2]25 E. 3. st. 5 c. 2. 7. W. 3. c. 3 § 2.

[3]Though the crime of an accomplice in treason is not here described, yet, Lord Coke says, the partaking and maintaining a treason herein described, makes him a principal in that treason: it being a rule that in treason all are principals. 3 Inst. 138. 2 Inst. 590. 1 H. 6.5.

[4]These words in the English statute narrow its operation. A man adhering to the enemies of the Commonwealth, in a foreign country, would certainly not be guilty of treason with us, if these words be retained. The convictions of treason of that kind in England have been under that branch of the statute which makes the compassing the king's death treason. Foster 196. 197. But as we omit that branch, we must by other means reach this flagrant case.

[5]The stat. 25 E. 3. directs all other cases of treasons to await the opinion of Parliament. This has the effect of negative words, excluding all other treasons. As we drop that part of the statute, we must, by negative words, prevent an inundation of common law treasons. I strike out the word 'it', therefore, and insert 'the said cases, and no others.' Quaere, how far those negative words may affect the case of accomplices above mentioned? Though if their case was within the statute, so as that it needed not await the opinion of Parliament, it should seem to be also within our act, so as not to be ousted by the negative words.[44]

From this it appears that Jefferson was alert to the fact that the law of "constructive treasons" had grown in important cases under the "compassing" phraseology which the American acts had omitted; and that in his eyes it was not the clauses stating particular types of treasonable conduct, so much as the provision requiring parliamentary action on novel cases, that gave the Statute of Edward III its restrictive character. Foreshadowing his later distrust of judicial lawmaking, Jefferson saw the need of new limiting language, if there were not to be new "common law," *i.e.,* judge-made treasons. Plainly, in 1778 he favored a general policy of limiting the scope of the offense. On the other hand, like the draftsmen of the Federal Constitution, he wished the law to give firm protection to the state within the area embraced by the definition: hence his extended definition of "adhering to the enemy." And his analysis of the liability of accomplices introduces a most important limitation on his general restrictive approach, for he is apparently ready to accept the words of 25 Edward III c. 2 plus at least some of the gloss put upon them by the English judges. In the letter transmitting his draft bill on punishments to Chancellor Wythe, Jefferson explained his general approach in this regard:

> In its style, I have aimed at accuracy, brevity, and simplicity, preserving, however, the very words of the established law, wherever their meaning had been sanctioned by judicial decisions, or rendered technical by usage. . . . And I must pray you to be as watchful over what I have not said, as what is said; for the omissions of this bill have all their positive meaning. I have thought it better to drop, in silence, the laws we mean to discontinue, and let them be swept away by the general negative words of this, than to detail them in clauses of express repeal. . . .[45]

To use words of art is a natural inclination in a professional draftsman; but in this case it obviously makes possible considerable nullification of the policy of limiting the bounds of the crime.

Whether or not his ideas directly or indirectly reached any of the framers at Philadelphia, the trend of Jefferson's thought so plainly resembles that of the restrictive clause inserted in the Federal Constitution as to suggest a kind of thinking which must have been in the air for some time before 1787. But the Revolutionary period gives us more direct testimony on this point, from one of the men who drew the constitutional provision. In 1778, in Philadelphia, spurred by the indignation of patriots, the commonwealth prosecuted for treason several persons who had had various relations with the British during their occupation of that city. James Wilson, leading figure on the American side, was also a leader of the bar, and, moreover, a fundamentally conservative man not in sympathy with the more radical and vociferous wing of the patriotic movement. The accused had been men of some standing, and much contemporary, as well as subsequent, opinion was that they were handled with unjust severity. There is, therefore, room to believe that, as one of the defense counsel in this group of cases, Wilson spoke with more than mere advocate's zeal. Like Jefferson, he now saw a restrictive policy to be deduced from the Statute of Edward III.[46]

None of the decisions in the Pennsylvania treason trials mounted to the level of a legal classic, but the opinions are marked with judicial restraint and it appears that the court was careful of the rights of the defendants. However, in the opinions in the *Malin* and *Roberts* cases—in which alone does the court discuss the scope of the offense—the rulings tend to extend the limits of the crime. In the *Malin* case the defendant, mistaking a corps of American troops for British, went over to them. The Attorney General offered evidence of the defendant's words to prove his mistake and real intent. Sustaining the defense objection to the introduction of such evidence, the court offered the dubious explanation, that there was no "act" of treason, but admitted the evidence for another purpose:

> No evidence of words, relative to the mistake of the *American* troops, can be admitted; for any adherence to them, though contrary to the design of the party, cannot possibly come within the idea of treason. But, as it appears that the prisoner was actually with the enemy, at another time, words indicating his intention to join them are proper testimony, to explain the motives upon which that intention was afterwards carried into effect.[47]

In the *Roberts* case, the court agreed with the defense contention that under the Pennsylvania statute penalizing the "persuading the others to enlist" in the enemy army, a case was not made out where it appeared that the person approached refused so to enlist. However, under the charge of adhering to the enemy by himself enlisting, the court noted that "There is proof of an *overt* act, that the prisoner did *enlist*," and said that the evidence of his unsuccessful attempt to persuade the other to enlist "is proper to show *quo animo* the prisoner himself joined the British forces."[48] Both cases plainly draw a line between proof of the requisite overt act and proof of the intent. The practical effect of such an analysis would seem to be to broaden the types of conduct which may be relied on as the overt act necessary to make out the crime.

Thus the period of the Revolution introduces cautionary notes regarding the scope of "treason" such as were not seen in the colonial era; but the evidences of the new trend are only suggestive and wavering in their implications. The burden of the story remains the security of the state.

The clearest complaint of the Declaration of Independence, it has been seen, was with reference to oppressive trial practice regarding treason, rather than to the breadth of the crime. There is no evidence that the colonial period had left a specific legacy of fears about abuses in treason trials, though there had quite clearly been cases of such abuse. It is, therefore, not surprising to find that none of the new state constitutions, prior to 1790, includes any limitation on the scope of the offense or the type or amount of proof.[49]

The use of the terms of the Statute of Edward III in the basic treason statutes of almost all the states may now fairly be argued to have an extensive significance that we cannot be so sure of in earlier usage. By 1776–1778 the broad pattern of construction of its phrases by the English courts was complete. We have seen evidence that this learning was familiar to American lawyers at least through the standard treatises, and that the most skilled draftsman of the day used the old statutory terms with intent to take them with at least some of the gloss which English judges had put upon them. The Maryland legislature also made this approach explicit in its Act of April 20, 1777, declaring, after it had adopted the well-known language concerning the levying of war and adhering to the enemy, that "the several crimes aforesaid shall receive the same constructions that have been given to such of the said crimes as are enumerated in the statute of Edward the third, commonly called the statute of treasons."[50]

Moreover, none of the state statutes of the Revolution used the sort of negative language which Jefferson, in 1778, or the framers of the Federal Constitution, in 1787, regarded as of critical importance to indicate a cautious hedging about of the offense. In a supplementary treason act of October 22, 1779, the New York legislature provided

> That besides the several Matters by the Law of England, declared to be Evidence and Overt Acts of High Treason, in adhering to the King's Enemies; and which are hereby declared to be Evidence and Overt Acts of High Treason, in adhering to the Enemies of

the People of this State as Sovereign thereof; the following Matters shall be and are hereby declared to be Evidence and Overt Acts, of adhering to the Enemies of the People of this State. . . . [51]

If one looks at the specific categories of conduct condemned as betrayal of the state, the picture is clearly one of a broad effort to safeguard the community with little tenderness for the individual's choices or dissents. Provisions in Pennsylvania, South Carolina and Vermont expressly attacked domestic levy of war in terms reminiscent of the early 17th century acts in the northern colonies.[52] The typical basic treason statutes, it is true, did not undertake to enact *eo nomine* the law of constructive levy of war; but, as has been suggested, at this late date the fair inference is that the main outlines of English judicial construction of Edward III's statute were intended by those who used its words. The threat of the external enemy naturally predominates in this period, but the colonial period had left some tradition of the use of the treason offense against domestic disturbance.

We have seen that conspiracy to levy war was expressly included in a number of 17th century colonial statutes, and have suggested that though this language disappears in the 18th century books, it is replaced by the provisions of the Statute of Edward III, including that against compassing the death of the king, under which the English courts managed to bring conspiracies to levy war. The omission of any terms analogous to the "compassing" clause in the 1776–1778 statutes would seem to bar including conspiracy to levy war within their scope. In view of the obviously inexpert character of much state legislation in this period, one may doubt the extent to which this result would actually be in the minds of local legislators, few of whom were likely to approach their problems with the technical skill of Jefferson. In any case, it is noteworthy that in about half of the states, conspiracy to levy war was expressly included in the treason statutes, for the first time since the 1660's, and that related statutes add what in effect are offenses of conspiring to adhere to the enemy, giving him aid and comfort.[53]

Contact with the enemy was the subject of much explicit attention. Some statutes, clearly requiring a showing of specific intent to betray, penalize the conveying of "intelligence" or the holding of "correspondence" "for betraying this State, or the United States, into the Hands or Power of any foreign Enemy."[54] Others penalize the "carrying on a treasonable and treacherous Correspondence" with an enemy.[55] Less clearcut were those acts declaring those persons guilty of treason who were "adherent to . . . the enemies of this State within the same, or to the Enemies of the United States . . . giving to . . . them Aid or Comfort, or by giving to . . . them Advice or Intelligence either by Letters, Messages, Words, Signs or Tokens, or in any way whatsoever, or by procuring for, or furnishing to . . . them any Kind of Provisions or Warlike Stores. . . ."[56] This language might be interpreted to cover the knowing conveyance of information or supplies, without regard to any showing that the conduct was part of a plot to betray the country. In its context in the basic treason acts of the states concerned, however, and in view of the death penalty attached, such language would probably be construed to require a showing of intent to aid the enemy for the defeat or overthrow of the government. Where the legislatures were content to impose less drastic penalties, however, they quite clearly punished persons for the mere fact of voluntary, unauthorized contact with the enemy. The Maryland Act of April 20, 1777, provided that

> if any subject or inhabitant of this state, shall write or convey any letter, or send or carry any message, to any person employed in the service of Great-Britain against the United States, or any of them, without the leave of the governor of this state, or some one of the general officers of the army of the United States, or shall

knowingly receive or bring any letter or message from any such person, and shall not deliver or communicate the same, as soon as conveniently may be, to the governor, or some one of the judges or justices of the peace within this state, and shall be thereof convicted in any county court of this state, such person shall be fined not exceeding one hundred pounds current money, in the discretion of the court.[57]

And the Maryland Act of December 3, 1777, declared that

if any subject or inhabitant of this state shall go on board any vessel of war or transport belonging to the enemy, or to their camp, or to any city, town, port or place, within any of the United States, in their possession, without permission in writing from the governor and the council of this state, and if any subject or inhabitant of this state shall receive any protection for himself or property from the enemy, or anyone under their authority, such person, on conviction thereof in the general or any county court of this state, shall be fined by the court not exceeding the rate of ten pounds for every hundred pounds of property belonging to such person within this state; and if any person convicted of any of the offences aforesaid shall not have property within this state, valued and rated agreeable to the late assessment act at more than two hundred pounds, the court may fine such person at the rate aforesaid, and also adjudge him to be imprisoned for any term not exceeding one year, or to be whipped not exceeding thirty-nine lashes, or both, in their discretion.[58]

In Massachusetts, the Act of November 8, 1782, provided that

any Person, an Inhabitant of this State, voluntarily passing from this or any of the United States of *America,* to any Post or Place within the Continent of *America* in Possession of the Enemy, without Leave obtained from the Legislature of this State, or the

Supreme Executive in the Recess of the General Court, such Person shall not afterwards be permitted to return again to this State, without Leave first obtained therefor from the Legislature, and shall forfeit all his Estate to the Use of the Commonwealth. . . .

and, further, that if such a person returned without authorization he should be transported back to an enemy-controlled area, and if he return a second time, be imprisoned during the war.[59] In two acts of 1775, Rhode Island first imposed a fine up to £500 or imprisonment up to one year, and subsequently decreed death and forfeiture of all property for any of its inhabitants who should act as pilots aboard any British ship or vessel.[60]

New Jersey legislation aimed at curbing trade with the enemy provides the most interesting legislation imposing severe penalties for contact or attempted contact with the enemy without a showing of a specific intent to betray the state. The Act of October 8, 1778, reciting that "many disaffected Subjects of this State do keep up an Intercourse and Communication with the Subjects or Troops of the King of *Great-Britain,* highly dangerous to the Publick Safety . . . ," provided that any one owing allegiance to the state who should be taken on his "Way to the Lines or Encampments, or to any Place in the Possession of the Subjects or Troops" of the King, "with Intent to go into the same without a License, Permission or Passport" previously obtained from the authorities should be fined £50–£1000, or be imprisoned 3–12 months, or suffer such corporal punishment not extending to life or member as the court should deem fit. A fine up to £2000, or imprisonment to 18 months, or such corporal punishment not extending to life or member as the court should appoint were provided for any such person who should "voluntarily go into the Lines or Encampments, or to any Place in the Possession of the Subjects or Troops of the

King of *Great-Britain,* without a License, Permission or Passport obtained as aforesaid." This act was many times renewed, and more painful or degrading punishments set.[61]

That the broad sweep of the statutes did not require a showing of specific treasonable intent was shown in the extraordinary proviso which a codifying act of June 24, 1782, felt it necessary to include:

> That this Act shall not extend to prevent any commissioned Officer . . . of Troops raised for the Defence of this State, with any Party of Men under his Command, from going into the Lines or Encampments of the Enemy or of their Adherents, or into any Place in their actual Power or Possession, for the Purpose of annoying the Enemy, or of apprehending such Persons as may be found going into or coming out of the said Lines or Places, or of seizing and securing all such Goods, Wares or Merchandize as may be attempted to be conveyed into, or brought out of the said Lines or Places, without legal Permission or Passport first obtained as aforesaid.[62]

A long series of legislation was capped by the Act of December 21, 1782. Reciting that the law was still being evaded, this act provided that all cattle found to the southeastward of a specified road "shall be deemed and taken as intended to supply the Enemy, and liable to Seizure and Condemnation," and required permits for the movement of cattle from out of state anywhere through the county of Bergen. Its second section provided that any live stock, provisions or naval stores conveyed or driven toward the enemy lines in specified counties after dark within five miles of any place in enemy control "shall be deemed and taken as intended for the Enemy, and liable to Seizure and Condemnation," together with the equipment used in conveying them, "any Passport or Permission for the same to the contrary notwithstanding." Section 3 stipulated:

That every Article of Provision or Merchandise, seized in any of the Creeks, Rivers, Bays, Meadows or Upland, in the Counties aforesaid, going towards the Enemy's Lines, or Places aforesaid, and that shall have passed on beyond the inhabited Dwellinghouses adjoining or nearest to the same, it shall be deemed and construed sufficient Evidence to prove that the same were going to the Enemy, and shall be condemned accordingly.

But the most drastic penalty was imposed by Section 5 against persons concerned with the movement of the suspect property:

That . . . if any Person or Persons shall, with Firelocks, or other Weapons of War, be found carrying or conveying, or be aiding and assisting in the Conveyance thereof, of any Article or Thing prohibited by this or the above recited act [the codifying act], such Person or Persons shall be declared guilty of Felony, and on Conviction thereof, shall suffer death accordingly.[63]

In addition to the familiar phrases condemning the levying of war or the adhering to the enemy, the state statutes expressly declared treasonable certain rather clear forms of adherence, such as "joining their Armies," or "inlisting or persuading others to inlist for that Purpose," or "furnishing Enemies with Arms or Ammunition, Provision or any other Articles for such their Aid or Comfort," or "wilfully betraying, or voluntarily yielding or delivering any vessel belonging to this State or the United States to the Enemies of the United States of America." Likewise, the statutes punished as traitors those who

have joined, or shall hereafter join the Enemies of this State, or put themselves under the Power and Protection of the said Enemies, who shall come into this State and rob or plunder any Person or Persons of their Goods and Effects, or shall burn any

Dwelling House or other Building, or be aiding or assisting therein . . .

or such persons as maliciously, "with an intention to obstruct the service," dissuade others from enlisting in the army or navy of the United States, or with like malice,

> spread such false Rumours concerning the *American* Forces, or the Forces of the Enemy, as will tend to alienate the Affections of the People from the Government, or to terrify or discourage the good Subjects of this State, or to dispose them to favour the Pretensions of the Enemy . . .

or those who "shall take a Commission or Commissions from the King of Great Britain, or any under his Authority, or other the Enemies of this State, or the United States of America."[64]

These types of provision do not represent notable extensions of the general categories of treason, and, indeed, to the contrary, it has been suggested that the Pennsylvania Act of February 11, 1777, which tacks such specifications of treasonable acts onto the traditional provision against adherence to the enemy thereby implies an intention to limit the scope of that offense. Connecticut, North Carolina, and Vermont enacted similarly phrased statutes; obviously three of these were copies, though the evidence does not show clearly which was the original. Of the other states, however, nine passed basic treason acts containing the familiar, broad, adherence clause without limiting specifications; and Connecticut also had such an act on its books, enacted after its more limited statute and apparently not repealed by any of the re-enactments of the more limited statute. The Pennsylvania-type act cannot, thus, be taken as representative of the basic treason legislation in the Revolutionary period. Moreover, such restrictive argument as may be drawn from its phrasing, viewed in isolation, carries little conviction as evidence of a prevailing climate of policy when that statute is put in the context of the severe test oath legislation, sedition and confiscation acts and like measures which stud the revolutionary statute books in all of the states. The abundance of such enactments suggests that legislative attention was at this time directed with overwhelming urgency towards the security of the new governments.[65]

Less clearcut, perhaps, are the New Jersey Acts of December 11, 1778, and October 3, 1782, which declared that those who had "voluntarily gone to, taken Refuge or continued with, or endeavored to continue with the Enemy aforesaid, and aid them by Counsel or otherwise" were guilty of high treason, and fixed penalties of forfeiture of estate and death.[66] "Aid by Counsel" might be the same as conveying intelligence of military value, but the phrase was not necessarily that narrow and might include a wide range of dealing or conferring. Whatever be thought of this, the concept of treasonable adherence to the enemy was certainly given an extremely sweeping application in the legislation which imposed penalties ranging from heavy fines or jail sentences to the death sentence and complete forfeiture of property for the mere utterance of opinions denying the independent authority of the new states and asserting the continued sovereignty of the King. Typical of these acts was that passed as late as March 30, 1781, by New York:

> WHEREAS, altho' adhering to the Enemies of this State, is by Law, High Treason against the People of this State; yet in Order more effectually to prevent an Adherence to the King of Great Britain, it is deemed requisite that farther Provision should be made by law;
>
> *Be it therefore enacted* . . . That if any Person being a Citizen or Subject of this State, or of any of the United States of America, and abiding or residing within this State, shall maliciously, advisedly and directly, by preaching, teaching, speaking, writing, or

printing, declare or maintain, that the King of Great Britain hath, or of Right ought to have, any Authority, or Dominion, in or over this State, or the Inhabitants thereof, or shall maliciously and advisedly seduce or persuade, or attempt to persuade or seduce any Inhabitant of this State, to renounce his or her Allegiance to this State, or to acknowledge Allegiance or Subjection to the King or Crown of Great Britain, or shall maliciously and advisedly declare or affirm, that he or she doth owe Allegiance to the King or Crown of Great Britain, and be convicted thereof, shall be adjudged guilty of Felony, and shall suffer the Pains and Penalties prescribed by Law in Cases of Felony without Benefit of Clergy. . . .

Provided, nevertheless, That it shall and may be lawful for the Court before whom such Offender shall be convicted, if such Court shall deem it proper, instead of giving Judgment of Death, to order and direct that such Offender shall be sent, as soon as conveniently may be, to serve for the Term of three Years, on board of any Ship of War, belonging to this State, or to the United States, or to an Ally of the United States; and if any Offender so ordered by any such Court, to be sent to serve on board any such Ship of War for the Term aforesaid, shall desert from such Service and be found within this State, or any other of the United States, the Person so deserting shall be liable to be punished as a Person attainted of Felony without Benefit of Clergy. . . .[67]

This type of legislation obviously breathes the spirit of hot partisanship, but the New York act is particularly interesting because it suggests that there may have been something more than sheer emotion behind so drastic a punishment of the mere expression of a political allegiance. The preamble emphasizes the need more effectually to prevent persons adhering to the enemy. In other words, the requisite overt act may be defined as conduct possibly many steps removed from an immediate threat to the state where the offending conduct is regarded as creating dangerously fertile ground for the commission of more tangible acts of betrayal. That the mere utterance of a political opinion is being penalized in these cases becomes even clearer in a statute such as that in Virginia, which declared the utterance of the opinion, or action upon it, to be equally offensive, providing a fine not exceeding £20,000 and imprisonment not exceeding five years

> if any person residing or being within this commonwealth shall . . . by any word, open deed, or act, advisedly and willingly maintain and defend the authority, jurisdiction, or power, of the king or parliament of Great Britain, heretofore claimed and exercised within this colony, or shall attribute any such authority, jurisdiction, or power, to the king or parliament of Great Britain.[68]

Apart from their *prima facie* meaning, the terms of such statutes are obviously capable of being applied to sweep in all manner of incautious political talk in a time of stress. The readiness displayed to put the offense of treason to liberal use for the security of the new states is comparable to any but the most extreme instances of extension of the crime by statute or construction in England.

The broad extent of "treason" during the Revolution is demonstrated, finally, in the severe acts imposing forfeiture of estate, banishment, or, in some circumstances, the death penalty, upon persons who had withdrawn to enemy-controlled areas after the beginning of hostilities. In later and calmer years, judges looking with obvious disfavor on this harsh legislation and eager to apply strict construction to limit the extent of forfeitures thereunder, denied that these were "treason" acts. Those who left the newly independent states for British territory had not hitherto owed allegiance to the states, since the states had not previously existed as independent entities to claim allegiance. Those who withdrew were simply exercising a right recognized in international law to choose the country of their abode; and the states which took their property were simply exercising the basic right of any sovereign to determine the conditions on which "aliens" might hold property within his domain.[69] The theory found some contemporary expression, as in the Rhode Island Act of October, 1779, which declared that a person who had withdrawn to British-controlled areas and had not returned and been received as a subject in the state, "shall be held, taken, deemed and judged to have voluntarily renounced all civil and political relation to each and every of the said United States, and be considered as an Alien."[70]

But even in this Act, the preamble's recital of the state's grievance against its former residents indicates that the taking of property under the act was viewed as a penal action rather than a colorless exercise of sovereign authority to define property rights. It was there asserted that

all countries have a Right to the personal Services of its [sic] Inhabitants, the greatest Exertions of whom, in their different Capacities, are especially requisite for the Defence and Protection of their Lives, Liberties and Properties, during the actual Invasion of Enemies; and a Refusal or withdrawing the same being against the Rights of human Society, and the being voluntarily adherent to public Enemies, by giving them Aid or Comfort, or the seeking of their Protection, amount to a total Renunciation of all former Rights, Privileges and Inheritances whatever: And whereas . . . sundry of said Inhabitants, regardless of their Ties and Obligations aforesaid, have left their Habitations, joined and been adherent to the Enemies aforesaid, thereby giving them Aid and Comfort, or continued to reside in Places invaded by or in the Power of said Enemies, and have voluntarily aided or abetted them. . . .

And the New Jersey Act of December 11, 1778, did not hesitate to declare "treason" to be the basis for the confiscation it ordained:

> each and every Inhabitant of this State, seized or possessed of, interested in, or entitled unto, any Estate Real or Personal within the same, who hath since [April 19, 1775, and before October 4, 1776] . . . aided and assisted the Enemies thereof, or of the United States, by joining their Armies within this State, or elsewhere, or who hath voluntarily gone to, taken Refuge or continued with, or endeavoured to continue with the Enemy aforesaid, and aid them by Counsel or otherwise, and who hath not since returned and become a Subject in Allegiance to the present Government, by taking the Oaths or Affirmations prescribed in the Act [of September 19, 1776] . . . when required, each and every such Person is hereby declared to be guilty of High Treason against this State; and on Conviction thereof by Inquisition found and . . . final Judgment thereon entered in Favour of the State, as herein after is declared, such Conviction shall amount to a full and absolute Forfeiture of such Person's Estate, both Real and Personal whatsoever within this State, to and for the Use and Benefit of the same: Provided always, That such Conviction shall not extend to affect the Person of any such Offender, but shall operate against his or her Estate only. . . .[71]

Viewed in the history of the times, and, more particularly, in the context of other legislation abounding in the same statute books, it is clear that the Rhode Island preamble and the New Jersey declaration expressed the practical animus behind the confiscatory acts.

A few of the confiscation acts made the taking depend on a finding that the former owner had actively aided the enemy, in addition to withdrawing to the enemy's territory.[72] Other banishing or confiscatory provisions are ambiguous, reciting that the action is based on the fact that the former owner has "joined" the enemy.[73] But another class of statute, including about as many as the two previous classes together, stated as at least an alternative basis for confiscation, the mere finding that the former owner had in fact withdrawn to territory in enemy control, or had remained in an area which the enemy took over, or, being absent in English territory when hostilities began, had not returned. So far as these provisions in these acts were concerned, there was no need to show any further overt act of aid or comfort to the enemy, nor any specific intent to betray the state.[74] Later judges evidently so interpreted the scope of these statutes.[75]

That this interpretation is not out of line with the temper of opinion in which this sort of legislation was being passed is indicated by the history of one part of the New York confiscation acts. The Act of October 9, 1780, imposed a tax upon any person whose minor son had joined the enemy since the Declaration of Independence, if the son at the time of joining the enemy was resident with his parents, and had not since returned voluntarily to reside in some part of the state not under enemy control. Being thus bluntly put, the act apparently imposed the tax regardless of any cooperating treasonable intent on the part of the parent. It might have been argued that such an intent element was supplied by a presumption of parental control of a minor son's actions in these circumstances. That this interpretation of the early statute is wrong was evidenced, however, by the Act of March 15, 1781, which, reciting that sons of parents themselves loyal to the American cause may have gone over to the enemy without parental knowledge or consent, provided opportunity for the parent to appear and show that the tax was thus unjustly levied on him.[76]

Severe as were most of the foregoing acts, they yet dealt out only banishment or forfeiture of property. There were in several states, however, statutes which reinforced initial judgments of banishment, based on withdrawal to enemy-controlled areas or refusal to swear allegiance to the state, by providing the death penalty if the individual should thereafter be found within the state.[77]

This analysis of the scope of the offense of treason during the Revolutionary period began by pointing out that, in contrast to the colonial era, there were some significant signs of the growth of an opinion that "treason" must be more carefully defined and limited. Taken in the context of the period as a whole, however, this note of skepticism was still subordinate to a broad and impulsive use of "treason" as the means by which to ward off what were viewed as extreme dangers to the security of the states.

There is little to be said regarding the procedural incidents of treason trials as set out in the laws of the Revolutionary period. Almost all the basic treason acts either required "the testimony of two lawful and credible witnesses" (without linking this to the proof of overt acts), or in substance adopted the language of the Act of 7 William III.[78] There is no innovation, and certainly no hint of the type of two-witness requirement later inserted in the United States Constitution. Where provisions regarding the quantum of proof were omitted—which was especially true of acts creating supplementary and novel definitions of treasonable offenses—the obviously haphazard quality of legislative drafting makes it seem more likely due to inadvertence than to policy.[79]

NOTES

1. Treason was declared to exist "In case where a man doth compass or imagine the death of our Lord the King, the Lady his Consort, or of their eldest son and heir; or if a man violate the King's Consort or the King's eldest daughter being unmarried, or the consort of the King's eldest son and heir. And if a man levy war against our said Lord the King in his realm, or be

adherent to the enemies of our Lord the King in the realm, giving to them aid and support in his realm or elsewhere; and thereof be attainted upon due proof of open deed by people of their condition." 25 Edw. III, Stat. 5, c. 2 (1350). Translated from the original French by Luder in 5 Howell's State Trials (1810) 971–77.

2. 5 Thorpe, The Federal and State Constitutions, Colonial Charters, and Other Organic Laws (1909) 2770; *cf.* 3 Thorpe, *op. cit.* 1833, 1866 (Massachusetts Bay); 5 Thorpe, *op. cit.* 3049, 3056, 3065, 3074 (Pennsylvania).

3. Laws of New Haven Colony (1656; Hartford ed., 1858) *24.

4. The Book of the General Laws (Connecticut) (1673; reprint, 1865) 9.

5. Brigham, The Compact with the Charter and Laws of the Colony of New Plymouth (1836) 42, 244.

6. The Charters and General Laws of the Colony and Province of Massachusetts Bay (1814) c. XVIII, § 12; 1 Colonial Laws of New York (1664–1775) (1894) 20; Leaming and Spicer, Grants, Concessions, and Original Constitutions (1664–1702) of the Province of New-Jersey (1758) 80; 1 Laws of New Hampshire (Batchellor ed. 1904) 12. The Duke of York's Laws were also applied in the area which became Pennsylvania, before 1682. See George, Nead and McCamant, Charter to William Penn and Laws of the Province of Pennsylvania (1879) iv, 15. *Cf.* the terms of the oath included in the instructions from the General Court of New Plymouth Colony to Thomas Prence, commissioned for erecting an orderly government among the inhabitants of the Kennebeck: "You shalbe true and faithfull to the State of England as it is now established and whereas you choose att present to Reside within the Goverment of New Plymouth you shall not doe or cause to be done any acte or actes directly or indirectly by land or water that shall or may tend to the destruction or overthrow of the whole or parte of this government that shallbee orderly erected or established; but shall contrary wise hinder oppose and discover such entents and purposes as tend thereunto to those that are in place for the time being that the Government may be enformed thereof with all convenient speed. . . . " Brigham, *op. cit. supra* note 5, at 322.

Another unconventional early definition of treason was laid down in Act I of the Virginia Grand Assembly, session of Oct. 10, 1649. Reciting that evilly disposed persons were defending the legality of the proceedings against Charles I and deducing that the existing government of the commonwealth was without legal authority, this act provided that any stranger or inhabitant who should "by reasoning, discourse or argument" defend or maintain the proceedings against the late king, "and being proved by competent witnes, shall be adjudged an accessory *post factum,* to the death of the aforesaid King, and shall be proceeded against for the same, according to the knowne lawes of England," and—apparently adding a different offense of seditious speech—that whoever by irreverent words should go about to blast the memory of the King should suffer such punishment as found suitable by the Governor and Council. Moreover, the Act provided, whoever by words or speeches endeavors to insinuate any doubt regarding the right "of his

Majesty that now is" to the colony and all others of his dominions, as King, "such words and speeches shall be adjudged high treason." See 1 Hening, Statutes at Large (1823) 359, 360–61. But, "The submission of Virginia to the commonwealth soon afterward (1652) made this drastic law a dead letter . . . . " Scott, Criminal Law in Colonial Virginia (1930) 155. Regarding the similarities in the early legislation of the colonies north of Maryland, see Journal of the Courts of Common Right and Chancery of East New Jersey, 1683–1702 (Edsall ed., 1937) 113, 116.

7. Bacon, Laws of Maryland at Large (1637–1763) (1765), Assembly of Feb. 25–Mar. 19, 1638, No. 22. Bacon notes that at the previous General Assembly of Jan. 25–Mar. 24, 1637, the freemen, having rejected a "Body of Laws" drawn in England and transmitted by the proprietor to be passed in the colony, submitted to him a number of bills including No. 36 "A Bill for Treasons." These were never enacted, however, and copies of them have been lost.

Chancellor Kilty notes: "In the year 1642, an act was passed [Act of Aug. 1, 1642, c. 19, renewed until 1645 by Act of Sept. 13, 1642, c. 45], ordaining punishment for certain greater capital offences, in which were comprised all offences done within the province, which are declared treasons by statute of 25 Edw. 3, Ch. 2, and all offences of conspiring the death or destruction, or of attempting any violence against the person of the lord proprietary, &c. or of holding any private intelligence with a declared enemy of the province, or of rising in arms or mutinying against the lord proprietor, &c. This act was at first of very short duration; but it was re-enacted at another session in the same year, and expired in 1645.

"An act was passed in 1649 (Ch. 4,) for the punishment of certain offences against the peace and safety of the province, which related only to mutinous and seditious speeches, practices or attempts, with or without force.

"No other act respecting treason was passed in the province, and the necessity of enacting that of 1642, arose probably from the opinion at first entertained, that in criminal cases, the statutes of England did not extend to the province; and to the change of that opinion may be attributed, the circumstance of no further acts being passed on this subject." Kilty, A Report of All Such English Statutes, etc. (1811) 217–20. The Chancellor's remarks are part of a note to his recommendation that the Statute of Edward III be included in the list of English statutes drawn up by him at the request of the legislature, to be declared applicable in the State of Maryland.

8. Acts and Laws (1702) of His Majesties Colony of Connecticut. (1702; reprint, 1901) 13–14. This revision, however, also continued the "Capital Laws" provision of 1673 (note 4 *supra*); and both types of treason provision appear in Acts and Laws (1715), (1743), (1750), (1769). The "Capital Laws" provision disappears with the first post-Revolutionary revision, in 1781.

9. Oct. 29, 1692, c. 19, 1 Acts and Resolves of the Province of Massachusetts Bay (1869–1909) 55 (disallowed by the Privy Council, Aug. 22, 1695, *id.* at 56; see note 12 *infra*); Dec. 8, 1696, c. 12, *id.* at 255; Aug. 31, 1706, c. 8, *id.* at 595; June 26, 1744, c. 6, *3 op. cit.* 152; Mar. 29, 1755, c. 34, *3 op. cit.*

814; *cf.* May, 1678, The Charters and General Laws of the Colony and Province of Massachusetts Bay (1814) c. XVIII. See note 28 *infra*.

10. Acts and Laws Passed by the General Court or Assembly of His Majesties Province of New Hampshire in New England (1716; reprint, 1885) 46. Despite its repeal by the Crown, Aug. 27, 1718, this act is continued in the compilations of 1726 and 1765 (same title as above), but is lacking in the compilation of 1771, with no explanation given. See 2 Laws of New Hampshire (Batchellor ed. 1904) 141.

11. Delaware: 1719, Laws, c. XXII, in 1 Laws of the State of Delaware (1700–1797) (1797) 64; and 1742, Laws, c. LXXXIV, *id.* at 225. New York: June 27, 1704, 1 Colonial Laws (1664–1775) (1894) 575; Dec. 24, 1767, 4 *op. cit.* 953, 953n. North Carolina: 1711, Laws, c. I, 25 State Records of North Carolina (Clark ed. 1904–06) 152; 1715, Laws, c. XXXI, 23 *op. cit.* 38; 1715, Laws, c. LXVI, 23 *op. cit.* 94 (repealed, 1749, Laws, c. VI, 23 *op. cit.* 332); 1749, Laws, c. I, 23 *op. cit.* 317. Pennsylvania: May 31, 1718, c. CCXXXVI, 3 Statutes at Large (1682–1801) (1896–1915) 199. Rhode Island: "An ACT, regulating sundry Proceedings in the several Courts in this Colony" (noted as 1700, 1716, 1718, 1729, 1734, 1736, 1746, 1749, 1750 and 1760), in Acts and Laws of the English Colony of Rhode-Island and Providence-Plantations, in New-England, in America (1767) 55; see, "An Act for punishing Criminal Offences," 1728, Acts and Laws, in Acts and Laws of His Majesty's Colony of Rhode Island and Providence-Plantations, in America, 1663–1729 (1730) 169. South Carolina: Dec. 12, 1712, No. 333, 1 Laws of Province (1736) 236; see Grimké, Public Laws of the State of South-Carolina (1790) 34. Virginia: The applicability of English law seems fairly implied from references in Act I of the Grand Assembly Session of Oct. 10, 1649 (note 6 *supra*); and Act I of the Feb. 1676–7 session and other legislation of that session regarding Bacon's Rebellion, 2 Hening, Statutes at Large (1823) 366 ff.; Nov., 1714, c. I, 4 *op. cit.* 51. See Digest of the Laws of the State of Georgia (1755–1798) (1800) 46.

The failure of a colonial legislature to enact a law on treason might be argued to mean simply that prosecutions must be conducted under the prevailing law of the mother country. This was the opinion of the Attorney General and Solicitor General regarding the proper procedure against alleged traitors in New Hampshire in 1775, the New Hampshire treason act having been disallowed by Order in Council in 1718. See Archbold's Pleading, Evidence & Practice in Criminal Cases (31st ed., 1943) 1058n. (a), quoted in the opinion of the Court of Criminal Appeal in Rex v. Casement, [1917] 1 K. B. 98, 143. On the other hand, there is no indication that because of this residual applicability of the English law in the colonies, the latter were ever held to be totally disabled from passing legislation on treason; and the contrary implication is to be drawn from the fact that such colonial acts as were disallowed were voided for more particularly specified reasons. The applicability of English statutes in the colonies in the absence of adoption by local authority has of course been a much mooted point, and it seems unlikely that Americans would have agreed with the opinion of the English law officers in the significant year 1775. *Cf.* Batchellor, *Introduction* to 2 Laws of New Hampshire (1904) xvii–xviii.

12. See note 9 *supra.* The Act of Dec. 8, 1696, was probably passed to meet the objections raised by the Privy Council. (See note 9 *supra.*) Apart from adding the offense of counterfeiting the Great Seal, the 1696 Act made it treasonable to compass the death of the heir apparent, or to give aid and comfort to an enemy "in the realm or elsewhere." Other changes seem to involve terminology only.

13. 2 Statutes at Large (1682–1801) (1896–1915) 52, and n., appl. I, sect. II, 465.

14. 1 Colonial Laws (1664–1775) (1894) 223, 575; 1 Labaree, Royal Instructions to British Colonial Governors 1670–1776 (1935) 157; *cf.* Labaree, *op. cit.* 159 (repeal of Virginia legislation regarding Bacon's Rebellion). The Act thus disapproved in 1704 had, however, originally been confirmed by the King in Council, May 11, 1697. *Ibid.* See also Russell, Review of American Colonial Legislation by the King in Council (1915) 29, 104; Washburne, Imperial Control of the Administration of Justice in the Thirteen American Colonies, 1684–1776 (1923) 48.

As has been noted, the Duke of York's Laws, with the familiar "Capital Laws" provisions against treason (see notes 4, 5, 6 *supra*), were included in the New Hampshire Act of Mar. 16, 1679. Batchellor noted that the authorities are in disagreement whether these laws were not subsequently disallowed by the Committee of Lords for Trade and Plantations. 1 Laws of New Hampshire (1904) 10. At any rate the copy which he reproduces, from the English archives, bears marginal notations indicating disapproval of the provisions on the ground that the matters dealt with were "provided for" and hence that the provisions should be "set aside." No explanatory ruling has been found in connection with the action of the Crown, Aug. 27, 1718, in repealing the New Hampshire treason act of May 15, 1714. See note 10 *supra.*

The acts of attainder and partial pardon passed by the Virginia assembly in the session of Feb. 1676–77 in consequence of Bacon's Rebellion were disapproved in general terms by the committee of the Privy Council because the narrowness of the pardon conflicted with the King's proclamation of amnesty and because the laws were deemed to exceed the legislative powers of the colonial government, and instructions to procure their repeal were, accordingly, given the new governor. See Russell, *op. cit. supra* at 29–30; 1 Labaree, *op. cit. supra* at 159. The data are not explicit enough, perhaps, to count this as an example of royal check on colonial definition of the offense; it may, rather, constitute a curb on improper execution of the laws. *Cf.* note 29 *infra.*

15. See *The Trial of Colonel Nicholas Bayard in the Province of New-York for High-Treason, 1702,* in 14 Howell's State Trials (1812) 471, 478, 495, 499, 506; 10 Lawson, American State Trials (1918) 518, 533, 535; Goebel and Naughton, Law Enforcement in Colonial New York (1944) xxiii, xxv. Though the record in Bayard's trial reflects familiarity with English trial procedure in treason cases, it may be suggestive of the limits of the material

available that the able argument on the scope of the offense is drawn from
English statutes and from Coke, without citation of reported decisions.

The best account of the history of treason prosecutions in a given colony is
in Scott, Criminal Law in Colonial Virginia (1930) 154–71 (Virginia). *Cf.*
Kilty, *op. cit. supra* note 7, 217–20 (Maryland). See also Chitwood, *Justice in
Colonial Virginia* in 23 Johns Hopkins University Studies in Historical and
Political Science Nos. 7–8 (1905) 20–21; Chumbley, Colonial Justice in
Virginia (1938) 71, 126; Records of the Particular Court of Connecticut
(1639–1663) (1928) 248; Hilkey, Legal Development in Colonial Mas-
sachusetts, 1630–1686 (1910) 97; Prince, An Examination of Peter's "Blue-
Laws" (1898) 100–101.

16. See Aumann, The Changing American Legal System (1940) c. III;
Goebel and Naughton, *loc. cit. supra* note 15; Hamlin, Legal Education in
Colonial New York (1939) c. 5; *cf.,* however, Morris, Studies in the History of
American Law (1930) 44 ff., 67; Warren, A History of the American Bar
(1911) c. VIII.

17. For legislation reflecting tensions of the French and Indian Wars, see,
in Connecticut: 1743, Acts and Laws (1743; reprint, 1918) 520; Maryland:
May 25, 1705, c. V, and Apr. 15, 1707, c. I, Bacon, Laws of Maryland at
Large (1765); Massachusetts: Mar. 20, 1699–1700, c. 21, and Aug. 31, 1706,
c. 8, June 26, 1744, c. 6, and Mar. 29, 1755, c. 34, 1 Acts and Resolves of the
Province of Massachusetts Bay 401, 595, 3 *id.* at 152, 814; New York: Dec. 23,
1755, 4 Colonial Laws (1664–1775) (1894) 8; Pennsylvania: July 8, 1763, c.
DI, 6 Statutes at Large (1682–1801) 297; Virginia: April, 1757, c. II, 7
Hening, Statutes at Large (1820) 87. Legislative reflections of domestic
disturbances include, in Maryland: c. XXIV of the session of Apr. 6–29,
1650, Act of Nov. 15, 1678, c. XVIII, Bacon, *op. cit. supra;* New Jersey:
Declaration of the Proprietors, Dec. 6, 1672, Leaming and Spicer, *op. cit.
supra* note 6, at 35; Acts and Proceedings of the Legislature of West-Jersey,
Nov. 21–28, 1681, par. XXI, *op. cit.* 433; Acts of 1703, c. III, in 1 Nevill, Acts
of the General Assembly of the Province of New-Jersey (1703–1761) (1752)
5; New York: May 6, 1691, 1 Colonial Laws, 1664–1775 (1894) 223, and Mar.
9, 1774, 5 *op. cit.* 647, 654; North Carolina: 1711, Laws, c. I and 1715, Laws,
c. XXXI, 25 State Records, *op. cit. supra* note 11, at 152 and 23 *op. cit.* 38, 94,
332; Virginia: Feb. 1676–7, Act I, 2 Hening, *op. cit. supra* at 366, and April,
1684, Act II, 3 Hening, *op. cit.* 10. Legislation reflecting fundamental
upheavals in the mother country includes, in Maryland: June 3, 1715, c.
XXX, and Aug. 10, 1716, c. V, Bacon, Laws of Maryland at Large (1765);
New Jersey: 1722, c. XXXIII, 1 Nevill, *op. cit. supra;* New York: Sept. 21,
1744, 3 Colonial Laws, 1664–1775 (1894) 424; Rhode Island: 1756 and 1766,
Acts and Laws (1767), *op. cit. supra* note 11, at 6, "for the more effectual
securing to his Majesty the Allegiance of his Subjects." Not all of these laws
define offenses as "treason," but such as do not do so are sufficiently related to
treason acts in the purpose of state security and severity of penalties to be
relevant evidence of the prevailing climate of policy.

18. See notes 7–11 *supra,* and also May, 1678, The General Laws and

Liberties of Massachusetts Bay, c. XVIII, § 20, The Charters and General Laws, *op. cit. supra* note 6; and, in North Carolina, 1711, Laws, c. I, 25 State Records, *op. cit. supra* note 11, at 152, and 1715, Laws, c. XXXI, 23 *op. cit.* 38, 94, 332. The Delaware act is 1719, c. XXII, Laws of the State of Delaware, (1700–1797) (1797) 64; the Pennsylvania statute is May 31, 1718, c. CCXXXVI (note 11 *supra*). *Cf.* the remark of Chancellor Kilty, quoted note 28 *infra,* reflecting the common attitude after 1789.

19. The Pennsylvania Act of Nov. 27, 1700, c. XLVII (note 13 *supra*) enacted: "That if any person within this province or territories thereof shall compass, devise or endeavor the death, destruction or any bodily harm tending to the death or destruction, maim or wounding, imprisonment or restraint of the person of the proprietary and governor, in order to deprive or depose him of or from his government, or do stir up or assist any to invade this province or territories, such person being legally convicted thereof by the testimony of two or more credible witnesses proving the same, or by due course of law, shall forfeit half his estate real and personal, or suffer imprisonment during one whole year."

The alternative penalties seem oddly disproportionate, but the borrowing of the terms of the Statute of Edward III regarding compassing, the reference to the security of the colony, the inclusion of a two-witness requirement, and the possible severity of the forfeiture make this in substance a treason act, though not expressly declared so. The act spells out forms of "compassing" which had to be developed by the constructions of the judges in England. Does this imply a knowledge of the English doctrinal history? The Maryland Act of Aug. 1, 1642, we have only in Chancellor Kilty's description (note 7 *supra*). It expressly coupled the offense against the proprietor with enactment of the treasons defined by the Statute of Edward III.

20. In addition to the legislation cited in notes 3–6 *supra,* see the Maryland Acts of May 25, 1705 and Apr. 15, 1707, note 17 *supra;* the New York Act of May 6, 1691, note 14 *supra;* in Virginia, Act I of the session of Oct. 10, 1649, note 6 *supra. Cf.* Nov. 15, 1678, Bacon, Laws of Maryland at Large, (1765), c. XVIII; Dec. 22, 1690, No. 53, 2 Statutes at Large of South Carolina (1837) 44.

The unconventional terms of several other acts are worth noting. Among the Orders Made by the Court at Exeter [New Hampshire], previous to the Union with Massachusetts in 1643 — *i.e.,* in the period of town government prior to incorporation of the area into the Massachusetts colony — was that of Feb. 9, 1640, 1 Laws of New Hampshire (Batchellor ed. 1904) 740, which provided "That if any person or persons shall plot or practise either by combination or otherwise, the betrayinge of the contry or any principal part thereof into the hands of any foreign State, Spanish, Dutch or French, contrary to the allegiance we profess and owe to our dread sovereign lord King Charles his heirs and successors, it being his majesties pleasure to protect us his loyal subjects, shall be punished with death. If any person or persons shall plot or practise treacherye, treason, or rebellion, or shall revile his majesty the Lord's Anointed, contrary to the allegiance we professe and owe to our dread sovereign Lord King Charles his heirs and successors (ut supra) shall be punished with death. Numb. 16; Exo. 22, 28; 1 Kings 2, 8, 9, 44."

Chapter XIV of the Concessions and Agreements of the Proprietors, Freeholders and Inhabitants of the Province of West New-Jersey in America, Mar. 3, 1676 (Leaming and Spicer, *op. cit. supra* note 6, at 393–94) is perhaps the most unusual act on domestic treason to be found in the colonies, creating a special offense on the part of members of the legislature. After reciting the obligation of the Assembly not to make laws contrary to fundamental rights defined in c. XIII, c. XIV declared: "But if it so happen that any Person or Persons of the said free Assembly, shall therein designedly, willfully, and maliciously, move or excite any to move, any Matter or Thing whatsoever, that contradicts or any ways Subverts, any Fundamentals of the said Laws in the Constitution of the Government of this Province, it being proved by seven honest and reputable Persons, he or they shall be proceeded against as Traitors to the said Government."

Among the Virginia laws of the session of April, 1684, Act II is reminiscent of English decisions which found a constructive levying of war in concerted plans to burn all brothels, destroy all dissenting chapels, and the like. Reciting that evilly disposed persons, about May 1, 1682 and thereafter, tumultuously and mutinously assembled to cut up and destroy all tobacco plants and with force and arms in a traitorous and rebellious manner entered the plantations of many good subjects for this purpose, "to the hazarding and subvertion of the whole government, and ruine and destruction of his majesties good subjects," had not the authorities timely intervened so that some notorious actors had been convicted and executed, the Act declared its purpose to be to state the law "to the end and purpose, that none of his majesties subjects may be at any time hereafter seduced by the specious pretenses of any persons, that such tumultuous and mutinous assemblyes, to cut up or destroy tobacco plants or any other the crop or labours of the inhabitants of the said collony, are but riots and trespasses. . . . "

Accordingly, it provided "That if any person or persons whatsoever, to the number of eight or above, being assembled together, shall at any time after the first day of June now next ensuing, intend, goe about, practice or put in use with force, unlawfully to cut, pull up or destroy any tobacco plants, either in beds or hills, growing within the said collony, or to destroy the same, either cureing or cured, either before the same is in hogs-heads or afterwards, or to pull downe, burne or destroy the houses or other places where any such tobacco shall be, or to pull downe the fences or enclosures of any tobacco plants, with intent to cut up or destroy the same, (and such person or persons being commanded or required in his majesties name by the governour or other commander in chief, or any one of the councell, or one or more of the justices of the peace of the said collony, commanding and requireing such persons to disperse themselves, and peaceably to depart to their habitations) shall continue together by the space of four houres after such proclamation made, at or nigh the place where such persons shall be soe assembled; that then every such persons soe willingly assembled, in forceable manner, to doe any of the acts before mentioned and soe continuing together as aforesaid, and being thereof lawfully convicted, shall be deemed, declared and adjudged to be traytors, and shall suffer paines of death, and alsoe loose and forfeite as in cases of high treason."

The 1682 plant-cutting disturbances had arisen out of the effort of certain planters by this method to enforce crop restriction to cure the distress of low tobacco prices, after earlier attempts to restrict plantings by law had failed. Relying explicitly upon the English authority on constructive levying of war, Governor Culpeper caused several prosecutions for treason to be brought, as a result of which one person was acquitted and three convicted. Of the latter, one was reprieved because of his youth and the other two hanged and their estates seized. Thereafter the act of 1684 was passed, in order — as it declares — to remove the general impression that such disturbances were mere riots. There seem to have been no trials for treason under this act. See Scott, *op. cit. supra* note 6, at 159–61.

Cf. the usual provision of militia laws against seditious or mutinous conduct, of which the Massachusetts Act of Mar. 20, 1699–1700, c. 21 (1 Acts and Resolves of the Province, *op. cit. supra* note 9, at 401) is typical: "That every person that shall be in his majestie's service, being mustered and in pay as an officer or souldier, who shall at any time during the continuance of this act excite, cause or joyn in any mutiny or sedition in the army, fortress or garrison whereto such officer or souldier belongs, or shall desert his majesty's service in the army, fortress or garrison, shall suffer death, or such other punishment as by a court martial shall be inflicted."

21. See note 14 *supra. Cf.* Quincy, Reports of Cases Argued and Adjudged in the Superior Court of Judicature of the Province of Massachusetts Bay between 1761 and 1772 (1865) 176, 221.

22. *Ibid.*

23. See legislation cited in notes 3–6 *supra;* the Maryland Acts of May 25, 1705 and Apr. 15, 1707 (note 17 *supra*); the Exeter Order of Feb. 9, 1640 (note 20 *supra*); the New York Act of May 6, 1691 (note 14 *supra*); the Pennsylvania Act of Nov. 27, 1700 (note 19 *supra*).

24. See 8 Holdsworth, History of English Law (2d ed. 1937) 313, 314, 318.

25. 1 Acts and Resolves of the Province, *op. cit. supra* note 9, at 595; 3 *op. cit.* 152.

26. See p. 80 *supra.*

27. 3 Acts and Resolves of the Province, *op. cit. supra* note 9, at 814; *cf.* Act of June 14, 1755, c. 6, *id.* at 865, and Act of Feb. 25, 1757, c. 25, *id.* at 1027.

28. The earliest act requiring two or more witnesses for capital offenses in general seems to be Laws of New Haven Colony (1656; Hartford ed., 1858) *17; "That no man shall be put to death, for any offence, or misdemeanour in any case, without the testimony of two witnesses at least, or that which is Equivalent thereunto, provided, and to prevent, or suppresse much inconvenience, which may grow, either to the publick, or to particular Persons, by a

mistake herein, it is Ordered, and declared, by the Authority aforesaid, that two, or three single witnesses, being of competent age, of sound understanding, and of good Reputation, and witnessing to the case in question (whither it concerne the publick peace, and welfare, or any one, and the same particular person) shall be accounted (the party concerned, having no just exception against them) sufficient proofe, though they did not together see, or heare, and so witnesse to the same individuall, any particular Act, in reference to those circumstances of time, and place."

None of the General Laws of Connecticut, however, adopted this provision. *The General Laws and Liberties of New Plimouth Colony* (1671), c. I, "The Generall Fundamentals," Brigham, *op. cit. supra* note 5, at 242, provided "6. That no Man be Sentenced to Death without Testimonies of two witnesses at least, or that which is equivalent thereunto, and that two or three Witnesses being of competent Age, Understanding and of good Reputation, Testifying to the case in question, shall be accounted and accepted as full Testimony in any case, though they did not together see or hear, and so Witness to the same individual Act, in reference to circumstances of time and place; Provided the Bench and Jury be satisfied with such Testimony."

In New Jersey, the Act of May 30, 1668 (Leaming and Spicer, *op. cit. supra* note 6, at 84), stated that "Concerning taking away of a Man's Life, It is Enacted . . . that no Man's Life shall be taken away under any Pretence but by Virtue of some Law established in this Province, that it be proved by this Mouth of two or three sufficient Witnesses." A similar declaration regarding all crimes was contained in c. XX of the Concessions and Agreements of the Proprietors, etc., Mar. 3, 1676. *Id.* at 397.

Statutes providing generally for conviction of treason of persons "provably attainted of open deed upon the testimony of two lawful and credible witnesses upon oath," or expressly providing that trials in treason cases should be regulated according to the Act of 7 William III, are cited in notes 8–11 *supra*. See also Pennsylvania Act of Nov. 27, 1700 (note 19 *supra*). Chancellor Kilty notes, regarding indictments brought in Maryland in 1706 and 1707 for feloniously and traitorously receiving one Richard Clarke, outlawed on a charge of conspiracy to overthrow the government, that "the record in the first [case] states, that the prisoner (when brought to be tried) had, before that time, had a copy of the indictment, and a copy of a panel of jurors delivered to him, according to the form of the statute. This was the statute 7 W. 3, Ch. 3, and in the last case the prisoner declared, that he was ready; that he wanted no process for witnesses, &c., that he released, or rather declared, that he had a copy of the indictment and panel, and forewent any advantage for the trial before due time fixed by the statute 7 king William for regulating trials in high treason, and on misprision of treason. That statute having been thus recognized furnishes strong evidence if it were necessary that the one now under consideration [25 Edw. III, Stat. 5] was in part adopted also, being essential to the safety of the inhabitants, as defining what offenses only should be treason." Kilty, *op. cit. supra* note 7, at 217–20.

29. See note 14 *supra,* and Scott, *op. cit. supra* note 6, at 156–59. See 1 Morison and Commager, The Growth of the American Republic (1942) 80: "Berkeley rounded up the leaders and had thirty-seven of them executed for treason. 'That old fool has hanged more men in that naked country than I have done for the murder of my father,' exclaimed Charles II."

30. See note 15 *supra.* Executive action against persons guilty of what amounted probably to "constructive levying of war" is reflected in c. XXIV of the Laws of the Maryland General Assembly of Apr. 6–29, 1650, Bacon, Laws of Maryland at Large (1765) and in Kilty's account of the prosecutions of 1706 and 1707 (see note 28 *supra*); in New Jersey, by the Declaration of the Proprietors, Dec. 6, 1672, III (Leaming and Spicer, *op. cit. supra* note 6, at 36), par. XXXVII of the Acts in Assembly of Nov. 5, 1675 (*Laws in Carteret's Time,* Leaming and Spicer, *op. cit. supra* at 110–11) par. XXI of the Acts and Laws of the Assembly of Nov. 21, 1681 (*Laws Passed in West-Jersey,* Leaming and Spicer, *op. cit. supra* at 433) and 1703, Laws, c. III (1 Nevill, *op. cit supra* note 17); and in New York, in addition to the Act of May 6, 1691, by the Act of Mar. 9, 1774 (5 Colonial Laws of New York (1664–1775) (1894) 647, 654).

31. *Cf.* Kent, Ch. J., in Jackson v. Catlin, 2 Johns. 248, 260 (N. Y. 1807); see note 69 *infra.*

32. As to the reality of the danger from disaffected persons, see Paltsits, Minutes of the Commissioners for detecting and defeating Conspiracies in the State of New York, 1778–1781 (1909) *passim.* That the reason for the paucity of civil trials for treason was not any lack of a problem, but rather the resort to summary administrative or court martial handling of cases, see *ibid.* and Van Tyne, The Loyalists in the American Revolution (1929) 271, 272. Further examples will be found in Davis, The Confiscation of John Chandler's Estate (1903) c. III; De Mond, The Loyalists in North Carolina During the Revolution (1940) *passim;* Harrell, Loyalism in Virginia (1926) *passim; Sequestration, Confiscation and Sale of Estates,* 6, State Papers of Vermont (Nye ed. 1941) *passim.*

33. 5 Journals of the Continental Congress (1906) 475; 6 Force, American Archives, 4th ser. (1846) 1720. The composition of the committee which recommended the resolutions is stated in Adams, *Life of John Adams,* in 1 Works of John Adams (1856) 224–25.

34. See "Instructions for the Deputies appointed to meet in General Congress on the part of this Colony," Aug., 1774, 1 The Writings of Thomas Jefferson (Library ed., 1903) 13, 211, 215; Wilson, Commonplace Book (MS., Pa. Hist. Soc. 1767).

35. The following states substantially adopted the Congress' recommendation: Delaware: Feb. 22, 1777 (General Assembly session of Oct. 28, 1776, c. LXXXVIII, 359), bound with Laws of the Government of New-Castle, Kent and Sussex, upon Delaware (1763) (see Act of June 26, 1778, 4); the 1777 Act was limited by its terms to the duration of the present war, and was apparently allowed to lapse, leaving in effect the general adoption of the English law, by 1719, Delaware Laws, c. XXII, 64 (see note 11 *supra*), limited by 1792, Delaware Constitution, Art. V, § 4, copied from the

provision of the United States Constitution. See 2 Laws of the State of Delaware, *op. cit. supra* note 11, at 595. Massachusetts: Feb. 1, 1777, c. 32, 5 Acts and Resolves of the Province, *op. cit. supra* note 9, at 615. New Hampshire: Jan. 17, 1777, Acts and Laws (1776–80) of the State of New Hampshire in America (1780) 63. New Jersey: Oct. 4, 1776, c. V, in Wilson, Acts of Council and Assembly from Establishment of Present Government to Dec. 24, 1783 (1784) 4. New York: Resolution of the Convention of Representatives of the State of New York, July 16, 1776, 1 Force, American Archives, 5th ser. (1846) 446–47. North Carolina: Ordinance of Dec. 23, 1776 (Ordinances of Convention — 1776), 23 State Records, *op. cit. supra* note 11, at 997; see also 1777, Laws (1st Sess.) c. III, and 1777, Laws (2d Sess.), c. VI, 24 *op. cit.* 9, 84. Pennsylvania: Sept. 5, 1776, c. DCCXXXII, 9 Statutes at Large (1903), *op. cit. supra* note 11, at 18; see Feb. 11, 1777, c. DCCXL, *id.* at 45. Rhode Island: May, 1777, Laws 30. Though not copying the full form of the act recommended by Congress, c. III of the Virginia statutes, Oct. 1776 (9 Hening, *op. cit. supra* note 11, at 168), should be counted among the acts stemming from the Congressional advice, since we know that Thomas Jefferson at least participated in the writing of the act after he had left the Continental Congress to take his seat in the Virginia House of Delegates. The index of the Clerk of the House of Delegates, for the Journal for 1776 notes, under date of Oct. 28, 1776, "TREASON / Leave for bill Declaring what shall be treason, with resolutions of General Congress / Referred to a committee (messrs. Bullitt, Griffin, Lee, Curle, Henry, and Jefferson) to prepare." (Reference through the courtesy of Mr. William J. Van Schreeven, Head Archivist, Virginia State Library, Richmond). See 1 Randall, Life of Thomas Jefferson (1858) 203, 205; Kean, *Thomas Jefferson As A Legislator* (1887) 11 Va. L. J. 705, 714.

Statutes differing in greater degree from the recommendation of the Continental Congress, whether or not antedating that suggestion, are the Connecticut Act of Oct., 1776 in Acts and Laws (1784) 251; *cf.* 1781, Acts and Laws, *id.* at 569. Maryland: Apr. 20, 1777, c. XX, in 1 The Laws of Maryland (1799, 1800). South Carolina: Apr. 11, 1776, No. 1017, 4 Statutes at Large, *op. cit. supra* note 20 at 343. *Cf.* Vermont, 1779, Acts and Laws, 6. Georgia does not appear to have enacted any general treason act, though numerous separate acts of attainder were passed. See 19 Colonial Records of the State of Georgia (1911) Part II, 673; *cf.* Marbury and Crawford, Digest of the Laws of the State of Georgia (1755–1800) (1802) 62–111.

Force, American Archives (1846), gives data regarding several of the state acts: 4th ser., v. V, 1604 (Connecticut), v. VI, 1500 (Maryland), v. VI, 1648 and 5th ser., v. I, 412 (New Jersey); 5th ser., v. I, 446 (New York), 549 (Rhode Island), 1210 (Pennsylvania).

Lists of test oath laws and of the "principal" laws directed against the Loyalists in the American Revolution are contained in Van Tyne, The Loyalists in the American Revolution (1929) app. B and C, 318, 327.

36. Compare, *e.g.,* New York Act of Sept. 21, 1744, 3 Colonial Laws, *op. cit. supra* note 6, at 424, and Rhode Island, 1756, 1766, Acts, in Acts and Laws

(1767), *op. cit. supra* note 11, at 6, with Massachusetts, May 1, 1776, c. 21, 5 Acts and Resolves of the Province, *op. cit. supra* note 9, at 479; New York Act of Mar. 30, 1781, c. XLVIII, in Laws of the State of New York (1782) 189; Rhode Island, July, 1776, Laws, 133.

37. See notes of arguments in Respublica v. Malin, 1 Dall. 33 (Pa. Ct. of Oyer & Terminer, 1778); Respublica v. Carlisle, *id.* at 35, 36; Respublica v. Roberts, *id.* at 39. In the "Notes of C. J. McKean in case of Ab'm Carlisle, 1778," 7 Pennsylvania Archives (Hazard ed. 1853) 44–52, Wilson cites Blackstone, Hale, and Hawkins, and the statutes of 25 Edw. III, 1 Edw. VI, 1 & 2 Ph. & M., c. 10, 7 Wm. III, c. 3, and 7 Anne, c. 21. Hazard states (*op. cit. supra* at 52, n.), that Mr. Chief Justice McKean's notes on the arguments in the *Roberts* case could not be found.

38. Aug., 1774.

39. 1 Writings, *op. cit. supra* note 34, at 211, 215. As Secretary of State, in his letter of Apr. 24, 1792, to Messrs. Carmichael and Short, giving instructions regarding negotiations with Spain, Jefferson explained why this country would not wish to agree to surrender political refugees: "Treason, . . . when real, merits the highest punishment. But most codes extend their definitions of treason to acts not really against one's country. They do not distinguish between acts against the *government,* and acts against the *oppressions of the government;* the latter are virtues; yet they have furnished more victims to the executioner than the former; real treasons are rare; oppressions frequent. The unsuccessful strugglers against tyranny, have been the chief martyrs of treason laws in all countries." 8 *op. cit.* 332; *cf.* the Notes on Virginia (1782), 2 *op. cit.* 216. With his disappointment at the failure to convict Burr fresh in mind, President Jefferson emphasized the need for reexamining the adequacy of the extent of the offense rather than its limitations, in his Seventh Annual Message (1807), 3 *op. cit.* 451–52.

40. 1 Journals of the Continental Congress (1920) 63, 65. See the more elaborate statement of this complaint in the "propositions offered by J. Duane, to the Committee for stating Rights, Grievances and the Means of Redress. In Congress at Philadelphia, between 7th and 22d September, 1774," 1 Burnett, Letters of Members of the Continental Congress (1921) 43, 44, n.36.

41. This was a highly practical point in the fears and resentments of colonial leaders. See letter of Joseph Hewes to James Iredell, Philadelphia, Oct. 31, 1774, 1 Burnett, *op. cit. supra* note 40, at 83; 1 Van Tyne, The Founding of the American Republic (1922) 301–305.

42. See pp. 76–77 *supra.*

43. Substantially the argument outlined is offered in 2 Swift, A System of the Laws of the State of Connecticut (1796) 297–98; Rawle, A View of the Constitution of the United States (2d ed. 1829) 141.

44. 1 Writings, *op. cit. supra* note 34, at 216, 218, 220–221. Jefferson's proposed revision of the criminal code failed of enactment by one vote in 1785; legislation of similar type was finally obtained in 1796. 1 *op. cit.* 257. See Kean, *op. cit. supra* note 35, at 714.

45. 1 Writings, *op. cit. supra* note 34, at 216. In the "Note" which Jefferson later wrote on his achievements in the legislature, he commented, regarding his proposed revision of the criminal code, that "The text . . . had been studiously drawn in the technical terms of the law, so as to give no occasion for new questions by new expressions." 1 *op. cit.* 257.

46. According to the notes of his argument in *Respublica v. Carlisle,* taken by Mr. Chief Justice McKean, Wilson contended: "Treason at common law indefinite & not ascertained, 1 Hawk fo., 34; 4 Blackstone pa. 75; 1 Hale fo, 81. By 25th Edwd , 3, ch. 2, it is ascertained and fixed; the Parliament who enacted this act are called the *Benedictum Parliamentum,* the only rule ever since in England, except that by the 7th William, the prosecution must be within 3 years. . . . " And the Chief Justice notes the following brisk exchange between prosecution and defense:

"Mr. Sergeant, Attorney General, What was treason at common law, the arbitrary proceedings in arbitrary reigns are nothing to the present question.'

4. Blackstone 352 & 3; Laws of Pennsylvania very different & more beneficial. . . . '

Replication by Mr. Wilson, If the Statutes are not extended here, we shall be all afloat as if we were before the 25th Edwd 3, ch. 3,' " See note 37 *supra.* See also Konkle, James Wilson and The Constitution (1907) 19; Loyd, The Early Courts of Pennsylvania (1910) 126; Nevins, The American States During and After the Revolution 1775–1789 (1924) 256; Alexander, *James Wilson, Nation-Builder* (1907) 19 Green Bag 1, 98, 107. Alexander suggests that the harsh suppression and penalizing of the Jacobite rebellion of 1745–1746, in the Scotland of Wilson's youth, was probably a significant element in shaping his political attitudes." *Id.* at 4.

47. 1 Dall. 33 (Pa. Ct. of Oyer & Terminer, 1778). The court's ruling on the first point seems clearly unsound, and is contrary to the great weight of authority in the American treason cases.

48. 1 Dall. at 39.

49. Treasons must be tried in the county where committed: Georgia, Const., 1777, XXXIX. The governor may reprieve, but only the legislature may pardon, in cases of treason: Georgia, Const., 1789, II, 7; Pennsylvania, Const., 1776, § 20 of the Plan of Frame of Government. No person shall be attainted of treason or felony by the legislature; there shall be no corruption of blood or forfeiture of estates, save those of the offender: Maryland, Const., 1776, XVI, XXIV; Massachusetts, Const., 1780, Part I, XXV; New York, Const., 1777, XLI; Pennsylvania, Const., 1790, IX, 18, 19; Vermont, Const., 1786, c. II, par. XVII. See Thorpe, *op. cit. supra* note 2.

50. Apr. 20, 1777, c. XX, 1 The Laws of Maryland (1799, 1800).

51. Laws of the State of New York (1782), c. XXV, 85. The penalty was forfeiture of property. The additional acts specified as "adhering to the Enemies of the STATE" were voluntarily withdrawing to British-controlled areas, or breaking paroles and going to or remaining in British-controlled areas.

52. The Pennsylvania Act of Dec. 3, 1782, c. M, 11 Statutes at Large (1906), *op. cit. supra* note 11, at 14, recited facts indicating social and economic tension between the settled and propertied eastern portion of the state and the frontier areas, pointing out that despite straitened finances the commonwealth had spent much in defense of the frontier, and that large debts were owed the late proprietaries, to which each county should contribute its share, "and the unlocated lands within this state are, and always have been considered a valuable fund towards paying and discharging the said debt." It then declared it high treason, to be punished by death and forfeiture of all property, if anyone "shall erect or form, or shall endeavor to erect or form any new and independent government within the boundaries of this commonwealth. . . . " *Id.* at 15. U.S. Const. Art. IV, § 3 (no new state may be created within the territory of an existing state without the consent of the latter) might now be deemed to confirm the authority of a state to regard such an endeavor as treason. *Cf.* the Pennsylvania Act of Mar. 10, 1787, c. MCCLXX, 12 Statutes at Large, *op. cit. supra* note 11, at 378 (co-operation with Massachusetts by offering reward for apprehension of Daniel Shays). There appears to be no reported decision under the statute of 1782. See (1893) 15 Crim. Law Mag. 191, 192; *cf.* an exchange of comment, apparently involving this act, in the debate over the Sedition Act of 1798, between Representatives Otis (Mass.) and Gallatin (Pa.). 8 Annals of Cong. 2148, 2149 (1851).

In South Carolina, see Apr. 11, 1776, No. 1017, 4 Statutes at Large, *op. cit. supra* note 20, at 343. 1779, Vermont Acts and Laws 6, interestingly, recognizes the possible difference between disaffection to the organized community and to the particular government at any given time (" . . . shall levy War against the State, or Government thereof. . . . "). 1779, Vermont Acts and Laws 73, enacted the old "Invasion, Insurrection, or public Rebellion" clause which had not been seen since the mid-17th century. *Cf.* notes 3–6 *supra*.

53. Conspiracy to levy war is included in the basic treason statutes of Massachusetts, New Hampshire, Rhode Island and Vermont. (See note 35 *supra*.) It is stated as one basis for the confiscation of property in the Massachusetts Act of May 1, 1779, c. 49, 5 Acts and Resolves of the Province, *op. cit. supra* note 9, at 968; and in Oct., 1779, Rhode Island Laws 24. To be "in any way concerned in forming any Combination, Plot, or Conspiracy, for betraying this State, or the United States of America, into the Hands or Power of any foreign Enemy" is declared treason, as a separate offense, in North Carolina, 1777, Laws, (1st Sess., c. III), 24 State Records, *op. cit. supra* note 11, at 9; Pennsylvania, Act of Feb. 11, 1777, c. DCCXL, 9 Statutes at Large, *op. cit. supra* note 11, at 45; South Carolina, Apr. 11, 1776, No. 1017, 4 Statutes at Large, *op. cit. supra* note 20, at 343; Vermont, 1779, Acts and Laws 6. Conspiracy to deliver to the enemy in war time any vessel belonging to the United States, the state or a subject thereof, was declared a felony to be punished by death in Maryland, Dec. 3, 1777, c. I, 1 The Laws of Maryland (1799, 1800); and the Pennsylvania Act of Sept. 22, 1780, c. CMXV, 10 Statutes at Large, *op. cit. supra* at 220, is substantially similar. But *cf.* Connecticut, Acts and Laws (1784) 66.

54. See, in note 35 *supra,* the acts of Connecticut, Maryland, North Carolina, Pennsylvania (1777), South Carolina and Vermont; *cf.* Massachusetts, May 1, 1776, c. 21, 5 Acts and Resolves of the Province, *op. cit. supra* note 9, at 479.

55. See Connecticut (1784) and Pennsylvania (1777) acts, note 35 *supra,* and Rhode Island, Oct., 1775, Acts 160.

56. See New Jersey and North Carolina (1776) acts, note 35 *supra,* and Virginia, Ordinances of the Convention, Dec., 1775, c. VII, 9 Hening, *op. cit. supra* note 11, at 101.

57. 1 The Laws of Maryland, *op. cit. supra* note 35, c. XX. Note that this act singles out as conduct especially dangerous the mere fact of correspondence with one in the service of the enemy. July, 1780, Rhode Island Laws, (1st Sess.) 15, provided that anyone bringing a letter from or carrying it to a place in possession of the enemy, without previous inspection thereof by the authorities "shall be proceeded against as an Offender."

58. 1 The Laws of Maryland, *op. cit. supra* note 35, c. XX.

59. Nov. 8, 1782, c. 32, Acts and Laws of the Commonwealth of Massachusetts (1782–1783) 89.

60. Aug., 1775, Acts, 88; Oct., 1775, 160. See also Massachusetts, May 1, 1776, c. 21, 5 Acts and Resolves of the Province, *op. cit. supra* note 9, at 479.

61. Acts of Council and Assembly, *op. cit. supra* note 35, app. no. V. A fine up to £1000 or imprisonment up to 12 months for the first offense, and death for the second, were provided for anyone who, having a pass to enter enemy territory, took with him more provisions than necessary for his sustenance; and a fine of £500, with the death penalty for a second offense, was set for anyone "who shall send or convey, or be in any Manner aiding or assisting in sending or conveying Provisions or other Necessaries of any Kind into the Lines or Encampments, or into any Place in the Possession of the Subjects or Troops of the King of *Great-Britain,* without being duly authorized as aforesaid." This act was supplemented and amended by Acts of Dec. 11, 1778, c. CXXIII, *id.* at 75; Dec. 25, 1779, c. CLXXXIV, *id.* at 117; Dec. 22, 1780, c. CCXXXIV, *id.* at 155; June 28, 1781, c. CCLXXIII, *id.* at 214; Oct. 6, 1781, c. CCLXXXIII, *id.* at 219; June 24, 1782, c. CCCXVII, *id.* at 287. The death penalty was removed and pillorying, imprisonment, compulsory naval service or banishment substituted by the Act of Dec. 22, 1780, *supra.* The codifying act, of June 24, 1782, *supra,* also removed the death penalty for second offenders, but substituted forfeiture of all property.

62. c. CCCXVII, Acts of Council and Assembly, *op. cit. supra* note 35.

63. Acts of Council and Assembly, *op. cit. supra* note 35.

64. Numerous examples of these various phrasings will be found in the statutes cited in note 35 *supra.*

65. The restrictive argument is drawn from the phrasing of the Pennsylvania act in the brief of the defendant on reargument in *United States v. Cramer* (U.S. Sup. Ct., October Term, 1944), in the thesis that the specifications of treasonable acts indicated an intention to limit the crime to accomplished aid and comfort, barring as "treason" anything which might be deemed merely an attempt. The statute's terms offer some support to this

argument. *Cf.* Respublica v. Roberts, 1 Dall. 39 (Pa. Ct. of Oyer and Terminer, 1778). But, as is suggested in the text, the support is not great when the act is viewed in relation to the general legislative history of the time. Indeed, the preamble of the Pennsylvania statute itself bears witness to the prevailing temper, when it justifies the act by a broad assertion of the need for preventing danger to the state: "Whereas it is absolutely necessary for the safety of every state to prevent as much as possible all treasonable and dangerous practices that may be carried on by the internal enemies thereof and to provide punishments in some degree adequate thereto, in order to deter all persons from the perpetration of such horried and dangerous crimes. . . . "

Similar acts are Connecticut Acts and Laws (1784) 251; 1777, Acts of Assembly of North Carolina (1st Sess.) c. III, 11 and (2d Sess.) c. VI, 41; and 1779, Vermont Acts and Laws 6. The familiar, general clause on adherence to enemies is contained in Feb. 21, 1781, Connecticut Acts and Laws 569, and in the basic treason statutes of Delaware, Maryland, Massachusetts, New Hampshire, New Jersey, New York, Rhode Island and Virginia, while a substantially similar clause forms a part of the fundamental treason act of South Carolina. See note 35 *supra*. In practically every one of these states there are additional provisions, spelling out what amount to acts of aid and comfort; but these are not so framed as to suggest any limitation on the general provision. The Ordinance of Dec. 23, 1776 in North Carolina, and the act of Sept. 5, 1776, in Pennsylvania, contained the general adherence clause; but these acts would probably be deemed repealed by implication by the subsequent statutes. See note 35 *supra*. The Massachusetts act of May 1, 1776, c. 22, is somewhat similar to the Pennsylvania act of Feb. 11, 1777; but is complemented, if not repealed, by the act of Feb. 1, 1777, c. 32, following the model suggested by the Continental Congress.

One might argue that the fact that in some of these cases the legislatures provided penalties much less severe than the sentence of death and forfeiture of estate familiar in high treason, suggests that the legislators were in practice indicating a policy restricting the offense of "high treason" by creating lesser felonies and even misdemeanors for conduct which might have been subjected to the harsher punishments. However, many of these acts explicitly treat the offenses as "treason" or betrayal, and there seems no authority that the severity of punishment is the criterion of what is "treason," the essence of which seems to consist in a betrayal of allegiance. The provision of the United States Constitution, conferring on Congress the authority to fix the penalty for treason, within the limitations there set, implies that it is not the severity of penalty which defines the offense.

A narrower argument restrictive of the scope of the crime might be drawn from the Massachusetts Act of Feb. 1, 1777, c. 32, 5 Acts and Resolves of the Province, *op. cit. supra* note 9, at 615; and May, 1777, Rhode Island, Acts, (2d Sess.) 30, which provide "That Concealment or keeping secret, of any Treason, be deemed and taken *only* Misprision of treason. . . . " [Emphasis supplied.] The result of this negative language is apparently that what otherwise might well be treated as a form of treason by giving aid or comfort to the enemy must be prosecuted as the lesser offense. However, in all the other states, the crime of misprision is created without the use of such restrictive words, so that discretion is apparently left to the prosecutor as to the severity of the penalty which he might seek in a case of concealment.

66. Acts of Council and Assembly, *op. cit. supra* note 35.

67. 1781 (4th Sess.) c. XLVIII, Laws of the State of New-York 189. Equally severe are Connecticut Acts and Laws, (1781) 569; and Apr. 6, 1781, 4 Laws of New Hampshire (Batchellor ed. 1904) 384.

68. Oct., 1776, Laws, c. V, 9 Hening, *op. cit. supra* note 11, at 170. The bulk of this type of legislation imposed penalties of fine, imprisonment, or civil disabilities. Connecticut: Acts and Laws (1781) 569 (alternative penalty). New Hampshire: Act of Apr. 6, 1781 (note 67 *supra*) (alternative penalty). Rhode Island: July, 1776, Acts 133. Virginia: May, 1780, Laws, c. XVI, 10 Hening, *op. cit. supra* at 268. See also the acts of Delaware (1777), Maryland (1777), New Jersey (1776), and North Carolina (1776), cited in note 35 *supra*. *Cf.* the usual test oath acts, imposing penalties for refusal to swear, ranging from banishment to civil disabilities: *e.g.*, Delaware, Act of May 18, 1778; Maryland, Dec. 3, 1777, 1 The Laws of Maryland (1799, 1800), c. XX; New Jersey, June 5, 1777, Acts of Council and Assembly, *op. cit. supra* note 35, c. XXXIII; Virginia, May, 1777, Laws, c. III, 9 Hening, *op. cit. supra* at 281.

69. See Inglis v. Trustees of the Sailor's Snug Harbor, 3 Pet. 99, 121, 168 (U. S. 1830); Dana, C. J., in Martin v. Commonwealth, 1 Mass. 347, 397 (1805); Sedgwick, J., *id.* at 384; Kent, Ch. J., in Jackson v. Catlin, 2 Johns. 248, 260 (N. Y. 1807); Wells v. Martin, 2 Bay 20 (S. C. 1796); Mongin v. Baker and Stevens, 1 Bay 73 (S. C. 1789); *cf.* Collins v. Kincaid, 2 Bay 536 (S. C. 1804). But *cf.* Cooper v. Telfair, 4 Dall. 14, 18, 19 (U. S. 1800); Richardson, C. J., in Thompson v. Carr. 5 N. H. 510, 515 (1831); argument of counsel in M'Neil v. Bright, 4 Mass. 282, 297 (1808); Camp v. Lockwood, 1 Dall. 393 (Pa. Ct. Com. Pleas of Phil. Co., 1788).

70. 1779, Acts 24.

71. Acts of Council and Assembly, *op. cit. supra* note 35, c. CXXII, 67. See Kempe's Lessee v. Kennedy, 14 Fed. Cas. 281, No. 7686 (C. C. D. J. 1808), 5 Cranch 173 (U. S. 1809). The New Jersey act is not the less significant, because it limits its penalties to those who had not merely withdrawn, but had also aided the "enemy," since such aid would not be "treason" unless given by one whom the state regarded as owing it allegiance.

72. Massachusetts: Apr. 30, 1779, c. 48, 5 Acts and Resolves of the Province, *op. cit. supra* note 9, at 966. New Jersey: Act of Dec. 11, 1778 (see note 71 *supra*). New York: Oct. 22, 1779, Laws of the State of New-York 85. Pennsylvania: Mar. 6, 1778, c. DCCLXXXIV, 9 Statutes at Large, *op. cit. supra* note 11, at 201. South Carolina: Feb. 26, 1782, No. 1155, 4 Statutes at Large, *op. cit. supra* note 20 at 523.

73. Massachusetts: Oct. 16, 1778, c. 24, 5 Acts and Resolves of the Province, *op. cit. supra* note 9, at 912; *cf.* May 10, 1777, c. 48, *op. cit.* 648. New

Hampshire: Nov. 19, 1778, Acts and Laws, *op. cit. supra* note 35, at 128. New
Jersey: Dec. 11, 1778, Acts of Council and Assembly, *op. cit. supra* note 35, c.
CXXII, 67; Oct. 3, 1782, c. CCCXVIII, *op. cit.;* see Kempe's Lessee v.
Kennedy, 14 Fed. Cas. 281, No. 7686 (C. C. D. N. J. 1808), 5 Cranch 173 (U.S.
1809). North Carolina: 1777, Laws (2d Sess.) c. XVII, 24 State Records, *op.
cit. supra* note 11, at 123. South Carolina: Mar. 17, 1783, No. 1189, 4 Statutes
at Large, *op. cit. supra* note 20, at 568. *Quaere,* regarding Rhode Island, Oct.,
1779, Acts 24. See note 70 *supra. Cf.* New York: Act of May 12, 1784, c.
LXVI, *op. cit. supra* note 36, and Laws of the State of New York (1778–1789)
(1789) (misprision). New York Council of Revision objected to this last act in
an opinion of the same date: "Because by the first enacting clause, the
voluntarily remaining with the fleets and armies of the King of *Great Britain*
is made an offence highly penal; whereas by the known laws of all nations,
persons who remain with their possessions when the country is over-run by a
conquering army, are at least excused, if not justified; and should our laws be
made to retrospect in a manner so directly contrary to the received opinions
of all civilized nations, and even the known principles of common justice, it
will be highly derogatory to the honor of the state, and fill the minds of our
fellow citizens with the apprehension of suffering in future some heavy
punishment for that conduct which at present is perfectly innocent." See
Street, The Council of Revision of the State of New York (1859) 254; Law of
the Legislature of the State of New York in Force Against the Loyalists etc.
(1786) app. no. 2, 171. The law was enacted, however, notwithstanding the
Council's objection. *Cf.* Street, *op. cit. supra* at 219, 246.

74. Maryland: Apr. 20, 1777, c. XX, in 1 The Laws of Maryland (1799,
1800); Feb. 2, 1781, *ibid.;* Massachusetts: May 1, 1779, c. 49, 5 Acts and
Resolves of the Province, *op. cit. supra* at 968. New Hampshire: Mar.
25, 1782, 4 Laws of New Hampshire, *op. cit. supra* note 6, at 456. New York:
Oct. 22, 1779, c. XXV, Laws of the State of New York, 85; *cf.* July 1, 1780, c.
LXXVI, *id.* at 143; and acts cited in note 76 *infra.* North Carolina: Act of
1777 (note 73 *supra*). Rhode Island: Oct., 1779, Acts 24. South Carolina: Feb.
26, 1782, No. 1155 (note 72 *supra*).

75. See opinions cited in note 69 *supra.*

76. Oct. 9, 1780, c. XIV, and Mar. 15, 1781, c. XXVIII, Laws of the State
of New York, *op. cit. supra* note 36, at 160, 176.

77. Massachusetts: Oct. 16, 1778, c. 24, 5 Acts and Resolves of the
Province, *op. cit. supra* note 9, at 912. New Hampshire: Nov. 19, 1778, Acts
and Laws, *op. cit. supra* note 35, at 128. North Carolina: 1777, Laws (1st Sess.)
c. III and (2d Sess.) c. VI, 24 State Records, *op. cit. supra* note 11, at 9, 84.
Rhode Island: July, 1780, Acts (1st Sess.) 19. South Carolina: Feb. 13, 1777,
No. 1051, 1 Statutes at Large, *op. cit. supra* note 20, at 135; 4 *op. cit.* 424; Oct.
9, 1778, No. 1101, *id.* at 450. Vermont: 1779, Acts and Laws 71.

78. See statutes cited in note 35 *supra.*

79. The 1776 acts in Connecticut, North Carolina, Pennsylvania and South
Carolina, note 35 *supra,* lacked two-witness clauses. That this was due to

inadvertence rather than a judgment of policy is suggested by the appearance of such clauses in the more carefully fashioned acts of 1777 in North Carolina and Pennsylvania. Two witness provisions were included in some of the legislation setting forth novel or supplementary definitions of treasonable offenses. See, *e.g.,* the disloyal utterances provisions of Delaware Act of Feb. 22, 1777; North Carolina, 1777, Laws, c. III and Pennsylvania Act of Feb. 11, 1777, c DCCXL, note 35 *supra. Cf.* Maryland Act of Dec. 3, 1777, 1 The Laws of Maryland (1799, 1800) c. XX, par. XXXIX (misprision).

4

Treason and the Constitution

(a) General Policy: A Restrictive Definition

Grievances over oppressive prosecutions for treason or other offenses did not form one of the causes which brought the Federal Convention together in 1787. But once the outlines of a really strong government were sketched, the political liberalism which marked this conservative body made it logical to consider necessary curbs upon abuse of the new power created. The basic policy of the treason clause written into the Constitution emerges from all the evidence available as a restrictive one. Everyone took for granted that, since a new sovereignty was being created, its authority must be given protection. The matter which dominated all references to the subject, however, was not the establishment of this protection, but its careful limitation to the minimum necessary to safeguard the community.

This restrictive emphasis stands out with special sharpness, because the story begins on a more positive note. In the summer of 1786 there were stirrings in the Continental Congress for amendments to strengthen the Articles of

Confederation. On August 7, 1786, a committee named in July to report amendments brought forth several proposals, of which Charles Pinckney was apparently the principal author. Article 19 of these amendments proposed to grant to Congress the sole and exclusive power of defining and punishing treason.[1] No limitations were suggested.

The other fact which provides background for the story of the treason clause occurred in the autumn of 1786 when mobs of western Massachusetts farmers, taking Daniel Shays for their leader, resorted to force to halt the debt proceedings and mortgage foreclosures against which they had so far fruitlessly sought legislative relief. Shays' Rebellion sent a shudder of shocked alarm through moderate and conservative elements in the country at large; the Continental Congress took secret measures to provide federal troops to support the energetic action of the Massachusetts executive and militia in successful suppression of the outbreak; and additional, powerful impetus was given the movement for creating a stronger central government. Records of the Continental Congress, of the Federal Convention and of the debate over ratification of the Constitution furnish ample evidence of how vividly the threat of Shays' Rebellion was in the minds of proponents of the new government. The adopted Constitution contained specific authorization for the central government to support or initiate action against further insurrection.[2] With positive provision for the safety of the state thus to the fore in congressional proposals for changing the frame of government, and the example of Massachusetts strong in the minds of men looking for assurances of orderly and secure economic and social development, the limitations of the treason clause must reflect deeply held notions of individual security against official oppression.[3]

The positive emphasis is still apparent at the beginning of the Convention. The Pinckney plan for the new government, defining the powers of the federal legislature in terms obviously drawn from the 1786 proposals to the Continental Congress, provided

> 15. S. & H. D. in C. ass. shall institute Offices and appoint Officers for the Departments of for. Affairs, War, Treasury and Admiralty—
>   They shall have the exclusive Power of declaring what shall be Treason and Misp. of Treason agt. U. S.[4]

Hamilton's plan of government, apparently leaving the creation of treasonable offenses to general powers conferred on the central government, provided that the Executive should have power to pardon in cases of treason only with the approbation of the Senate. Both the Executive and Senate, holding office during good behavior, were a step removed from the electorate, which was to choose the Electors who would select Senators and a "Governour." It is not surprising that Hamilton's only reference to treason should seek to enforce a strong hand against disaffected persons.[5]

The first evidence of concern to set limits to the offense is in a draft of the "New Jersey Resolutions." Paterson's notebook includes a Resolution "that it is necessary to define what offences, committed in any State, shall be deemed high treason against the United States." This proposal is crossed out in Paterson's record book, and is not included in Madison's report of the New Jersey plan.[6] In any event, its place in a body of "small state" resolutions suggests that delimitation of central government as compared to state authority, rather than protection of the individual, was the moving force; and this hypothesis is consistent with the lengthy discussion in the Convention over the relative boundaries of federal and state power over treason. On the policy of protecting the individual, there was no small state-large state division in the Convention, and, indeed, some of the most vigorous advocacy of limitations was by Virginia delegates.

Save for these references in papers laid before the Convention, there was no mention of treason until the Committee of Detail submitted its draft constitution to the Convention in August, 1787. The treason clause was the creation of this Committee. No specific instructions on the subject were included in the resolutions sent to the Committee, and its authority to deal with the matter must be derived from the omnibus resolution providing that the "national legislature" be empowered "to legislate in all cases to which the separate States are incompetent."[7]

In this, as in most other matters, we have little direct evidence of the deliberations of Ellsworth (Connecticut), Gorham (Massachusetts), Randolph (Virginia), Rutledge (South Carolina), and Wilson (Pennsylvania), in the Committee of Detail. What we have, however, marks the beginning of concentration on limiting the scope of the offense. A draft in Wilson's handwriting contains the simple authorization of the Pinckney plan, for Congress "to declare what shall be Treason against the United States," with the addition, in Rutledge's hand, of the limitation of the punishment, "not to work Corruption of Blood or Forfeit except during the Life of the Party." However, a document in the handwriting of Randolph (with each item checked or crossed out, indicating use of the paper in preparation of subsequent drafts), narrows the definition of legislative power to the authority "To declare it to be treason to levy war against, or adhere to the enemies of the U.S." And in the draft constitution reported by the Committee, August 6, 1787, Article VII, Section 2 provided that

treason against the United States shall consist only in levying war against the United States, or any of them; and in adhering to the

enemies of the United States, or any of them. The Legislature of
the United States shall have power to declare the punishment of
treason. No person shall be convicted of treason, unless on the
testimony of two witnesses. No attainder of treason shall work
corruption of blood nor forfeiture, except during the life of the
person attainted.[8]

At one stroke, the basis of the restrictive policy had been laid:
all authority is taken from any other agency to define the
extent of the crime; the decision is taken that there shall be no
analogy to the ancient offense of compassing the king's death;
a stipulation on quantum of proof is given constitutional
sanction. But, the language on adherence is not qualified by
the traditional "aid or comfort" phrase, nor is there explicit
recognition of the overt act as an element of the offense,
and of course, therefore, no linking of the two-witness requirement to the overt act. Acts of treason against a state
are made treason against the United States, a provision finally
eliminated.

The treason clause was discussed at some length by the
Convention, in Committee of the Whole, August 20, 1787, in
a debate which serves to underline the framers' preoccupation with limiting the scope of the crime. This is apparent, in
the first place, from the discussion of the general terms of the
clause. Surprisingly, Madison opened the discussion with a
plea for less restrictive language:

> Mr. Madison thought the definition too narrow. It did not appear
> to go as far as the Stat. of Edwd. III. He did not see why more
> latitude might not be left to the Legislature. It wd. be as safe as in
> the hands of State legislatures; and it was inconvenient to bar a
> discretion which experience might enlighten, and which might be
> applied to good purposes as well as be abused.[9]

Mason, on the other hand, was in favor of following the

language of the Statute of Edward III. That he believed the old terms were valuable to limit the definition of the crime is suggested by the fact that later in the discussion he moved to add to the clause concerning adherence to the enemy the familiar terms of aid and comfort—"as restrictive of 'adhering to their Enemies &c'—the latter he thought would be otherwise too indefinite—." Further discussion over the extent to which the Committee of Detail had enlarged or narrowed the scope of the language of Edward III's statute shows that the old English law was at least prominently in the minds of the Convention.

In the midst of the debate concerning relative state and federal power to create the offense, King introduced the only note of skepticism as to the importance of limiting the definition of treason when he observed "that the controversy relating to Treason might be of less magnitude than was supposed; as the legislature might punish capitally under other names than Treason." Taken in its general implications, this was clearly not the view of Gouverneur Morris and Randolph, who moved to postpone further consideration of the suggested treason clause in order to take up a substitute which declared:

> Whereas it is essential to the preservation of liberty to define precisely and exclusively what shall constitute the crime of Treason, it is therefore ordained, declared & established, that if a man do levy war agst. the U.S. within their territories, or be adherent to the enemies of the U. S. within the said territories, giving them aid and comfort within their territories or elsewhere, and thereof be provably attainted of open deed by the People of his condition, he shall be adjudged guilty of Treason.

Despite its preamble, this proposal seems less confining than that of the Committee of Detail; but it is clear that its proponents offered it out of a desire to set closer limits to the crime. Their motion was defeated, but before the day was out the two principal additions of the Morris-Randolph draft ("aid and comfort" and the requirement of an overt act) were inserted in the draft which lay before the Committee of the Whole.

In addition to the implications of such discussion of the general language used in the section, distrust of the possible scope of the offense is reflected particularly in the amendment made to the clause concerning adherence to enemies. There was initially some confusion over just what was broad, and what was narrow terminology here. Randolph introduced the subject by saying that he "thought the clause defective in adopting the words in adhering only. The British Stat: adds. 'giving them aid and comfort' which had a more extensive meaning." Ellsworth "considered the definition as the same in fact with that of the Statute," and, in replying to him, Gouverneur Morris reflected some confusion over the breadth of the terms involved, saying that "'adhering' does not go so far as 'giving aid and Comfort' or the latter words may be restrictive of 'adhering' . . . in either case the Statute is not pursued." Wilson thought the words added no limitation: he held "'giving aid and comfort' to be explanatory, not operative words; and that it was better to omit them." Dickinson then objected from the viewpoint of one concerned to limit the definition: he thought "the addition of 'giving aid and comfort' unnecessary & improper; being too vague and extending too far." Dr. Johnson apparently felt the added words would limit, by explaining, the basic terms in the provision, since he "considered 'giving aid and comfort' as explanatory of 'adhering.'" Randolph and Morris then moved to consider the draft quoted above before considering the draft by the Committee of Detail. The restrictive purpose indicated by their proposed substitute seems rather inconsistent with their earlier indications that they regarded the "aid and comfort" phrase as possibly extending the area of the offense, for it was, nevertheless, employed in their own proposal. However, after all of this confusion, the final action of the day was taken on a clearly restrictive note.

> Col. Mason moved to insert the words "giving (them) aid comfort". as restrictive of "adhering to their Enemies &c"—the latter he thought would be otherwise too indefinite—This motion was agreed to (Conn: Del: & Georgia only being in the Negative).

Mason was, therefore, consistent with his opinion, at the outset, in favor of "pursuing the Stat: of Edwd. III."

Finally, a fundamentally restrictive attitude also marks the treatment of the requirements of an overt act and of two witnesses to establish the offense. The draft by the Committee of Detail did not refer to the proof of an overt act. The Journal of August 20 notes that a motion was adopted to insert the words "some overt act of" at the beginning of the draft clause, so that the clause would read, "Treason against the United States shall consist only in some overt act of levying war against the United States, etc. . . ." Subsequently, the Committee of the Whole inserted "to the same overt act" after "witnesses," and it was then voted to strike the reference to overt acts which had been placed at the beginning of the section. Curiously, Madison's "Notes" contain no direct reference to these various votes; but the inference seems fair that there was a definite intention to require the showing of an overt act as an independent element of the offense, and that the first insertion, which made this plain, was stricken probably for artistic reasons, after the reference to an overt act had been linked with the requirement of two witnesses. [10]

The interpretation of the proceedings is somewhat clouded by the fact that the final exchange of comment on the language involving "overt act" emphasized solely the strengthening of the evidentiary guaranty against perjury.

When it was moved to insert "to the same overt act" after the two-witness requirement, Madison notes that "Docr Franklin wished this amendment to take place—prosecutions for treason were generally virulent; and perjury too easily made use of against innocence." And James Wilson observed that "much may be said on both sides. Treason may sometimes be practised in such a manner as to render proof extremely difficult—as in a traitorous correspondence with an Enemy." The vote was 8–3 in favor of inserting the overt-act phrase in connection with the requirement of two witnesses. Though this may seem to subordinate the overt-act phrase, the inference seems a fair one, from the record as a whole, that it was thought important to stipulate expressly that an overt act should constitute a distinct element of proof of the offense.

As much time was devoted on August 20 to discussing the problem of treason in the federal system—the extent to which the central government and the states might, respectively, undertake to define the offense—as was given to debate on all the other points considered. However, the debate on the general phrasing and elements of the offense, so far as it went, seems clearly to establish a general agreement on the wisdom of limiting the scope of the offense in all doubtful cases.[11] The only respects in which the Convention may be said to have rejected opportunities to confine the scope of the offense were in rejecting the suggestions that the states be denied any authority to define treason against themselves, and that participation in a civil war, between a state and the nation, be excepted. The debate seems, however, to have turned on judgments of what would constitute an equitable and workable plan in this regard for a federal system; and to have involved no conscious departure from the policy of safeguarding the individual from oppressive extensions of the nature of "treason."[12]

The only member of the Convention of whose views we have any substantial evidence, apart from the record of the

Convention discussion, is James Wilson. He is a key figure, however, as a member of the Committee of Detail, which took the responsibility for taking a restrictive rather than an extensive approach to the definition of the offense. The crisp statement and logical progression of the clause as it came from the Committee of Detail strongly suggests the hand of Wilson, probably the ablest lawyer on the committee.[13] We have seen that Wilson had long been familiar with basic English materials on the law of treason. In 1778 he had joined the defense in the Pennsylvania treason trials when that was a highly unpopular thing to do, and had stoutly upheld the wisdom of avoiding the creation of novel treasons by staying close to the familiar terms of the Statute of Edward III. His participation in the Convention discussion of August 20 is not very illuminating, it is true. He was against inclusion of the "aid and comfort" phrase, significantly, however, on grounds of draftsmanship and not of policy. Regarding the two-witness requirements, he recognized the dangers of putting an impractical burden on the prosecution; but when the question was put to the vote, the Pennsylvania delegation was recorded as unanimous for the limitation. His papers contain an undated memorandum headed "Reasons for adopting the Constitution," and among the seventeen points which he thought significant enough to list was[14]

the accurate Description of Treason—its [one word and part of another crossed out: apparently "mild Puni," probably "mild Punishment"] Consequences confined to the Cri [Criminal?]; consid. Art. 3. s. 3./ Mont. 6.12.c. 7. ss. 18. [apparently a reference to Montesquieu].

The inferences, that Wilson took particular interest in the treason clause, and that he believed its virtue lay in its fundamentally restrictive character, are borne out by his detailed praise of it in the Pennsylvania ratifying convention.

Twice, of his own motion, and without any criticism of the
provision having been voiced by an alert and suspicious
opposition, Wilson cited the clause as an ornament of the
proposed Constitution.[15] He placed such emphasis on the
constitutional provision that he devoted an entire lecture to it
in his law lectures delivered at the College of Philadelphia, in
1790 and 1791. He stressed as the whole point of his analysis
the virtues of setting careful bounds to the crime:

> It is the observation of the celebrated Montesquieu, that if the
> crime of treason be indeterminate, this alone is sufficient to make
> any government degenerate into arbitrary power.[16]

Praising as the most important part of the Statute of
Edward III the provision that the Parliament, and not the
judges, should pass on novel cases claimed to be treason,
Wilson argued the superiority of American law in placing this
restrictive principle beyond even legislative encroachment:

> In this manner, the citizens of the Union are secured effectually
> from even legislative tyranny: and in this instance, as in many
> others, the happiest and most approved example of other times
> has not only been imitated, but excelled.[17]

Such continuing concentration on a clause which, whatever its
merits, is certainly not one of the more conspicuously discussed parts of the Constitution, strongly suggests pride of
authorship. At any rate, there can be no doubt as to the
central conclusion of policy which Wilson would derive from
the clause for the guidance of legislators and judges.

If we turn from the Philadelphia Convention and its
members to the great debate which surged throughout the
country over the ratification of the Constitution, the story is
the same. The Constitution was everywhere under attack,
because it contained no bill of rights, and created a strong

government with broad powers, which the imagination of its opponents foresaw could be turned in many ways to destroy the liberties of the citizen. In this situation, it is of the highest significance that without material exception the treason clause was adduced only by proponents of the Constitution, as a prideful argument for the protection with which that document surrounded the individual; and that there was no real effort made at any time, so far as the record shows, to claim that the new government could oppress its people under the guise of prosecutions for treason. [18]

The closest approach to a clash over the treason clause in the state ratifying conventions took place in Virginia. Replying to a speech of Patrick Henry in which the spectre of "the most grievous oppressions" had been raised, George Nicholas took the initiative in citing the treason clause:

> Treason consists in levying war against the United States, or in adhering to their enemies, giving them aid and comfort. The punishment of this well-defined crime is to be declared by Congress; no oppression, therefore, can arise on this ground. This security does away the objection that the most grievous oppressions might happen under color of punishing crimes against the general government. The limitation of the forfeiture to the life of the criminal is also an additional privilege. [19]

It is noteworthy that when the Virginia convention reached the treason section in its turn in a section-by-section discussion of the Constitution, the record shows no mention of the provision, though there had been a very lengthy argument over the preceding parts of Article III.

The fight in North Carolina was a particularly hot one, and concluded with a refusal either to ratify or reject the proposed Constitution, but rather a stipulation that North Carolina would ratify if certain rights were declared and ambiguous passages clarified. Since the opposition was alert to point out every aspect in which they saw the danger of political oppression of the individual under the new government, it is again significant that when the convention reached the treason clause in its section-by-section consideration of the document, the record states merely, "3d section [Article III] read without any observation."

Subsequently, what began as apparent criticism of the treason clause ended in weak professions of mistaken meaning on the part of opposition leaders.[20] In many states, advocates of the Constitution cited the treason clause as a valued part of the document, and the opposition maintained silence.[21] The only respect in which the debates over ratification may be said to have suggested a broader concept of "treason" in consequence of the provisions of the Federal Constitution was the inference which might be drawn that any circumstances which would call into play the guaranty extended to every state of a republican form of government would probably involve treasonable conduct on the part of those threatening the state government. But at most this seems to involve no more than application of familiar precedents concerning the constructive levying of war.

(b) The Content of the Restrictive Definition

A close examination of the evidence makes it possible to suggest in certain respects a more precise statement of what the strict construction policy of the treason clause involves. In the first place, though the most obvious emphasis in discussion was upon limiting the power of the legislature to extend the scope of "treason," there can be no doubt that the restrictive policy was intended likewise to limit judges and to curb the creation of novel treasons by construction. This was certainly Wilson's intent. As defense counsel in the treason cases of 1778 he had strongly urged that courts should construe strictly the terms of treason statutes and take care not to extend the crimes there defined. In his December 7 speech to the Pennsylvania ratifying convention, he chose as an example of the perils of a loose extension of the offense one of the most cited instances of the "constructive" (*i.e.,* judge-made) treasons of English law.[22] In his law lectures, in 1790, he emphasized that the great advance made by the Statute of Edward III was to curb the power of the judges by reserving to Parliament the right to decide whether novel cases should be deemed treason, and his praise for the provision in the Constitution was that it improved the English situation by broadening the limitation to cover the legislature as well.[23] There would seem significance in the fact that the Committee of Style shifted the treason clause out of Article I into Article III in the final shaping of the document; the matter of the scope of the offense had been so clearly taken from Congress that it was logical to place the remaining admonition of policy in the part of the document dealing with the courts, which must still administer the clause.[24] In 1792, Mr. Justice Iredell, who had cited the treason clause in support of the Constitution in the North Carolina convention, viewed it as preventing the punishment of "constructive acts of treason."[25]

Though the restrictive policy was taken to limit judges as well as legislators, the treason clause used words of the Statute of Edward III upon which English judges had had much to say over centuries. Despite the condemnation of "constructive" treasons, in political polemics, it was also assumed that "levying war" or "adhering to enemies" would be construed in the light of previous application of these terms. Wilson, indeed, found in the judicial gloss upon the words of Edward III's statute one of the sources of protection against oppression. Though the Statute had been "like a rock, strong by nature," he noted that it had been "fortified, as successive occasions required, by the able and honest assistance of art" so as to stand "impregnable by all the rude and boisterous assaults, which have been made upon it, at different quarters, by ministers and by judges." [26]

It is quite evident, moreover—nor, in view of the prominence of Shays' Rebellion in the minds of the Constitution's proponents, is this surprising—that it was assumed that to some ill-defined extent the constructive levying of war would be covered by the treason clause. [27] The evidence thus poses a most difficult problem, which it does not resolve. The omission from the constitutional clause of any provision analogous to that in English law which punished compassing the death of the king removed the foundation on which the English judges had built much of the reprobated structure of "constructive" treasons. It is a fair inference, in view of the vigor with which the restrictive policy of the Constitution emerges from the evidence, that it would violate that policy to import into our law English doctrine peculiarly based on the omitted clause of the Statute of Edward III. Even so, there were in English history ingenious constructions under those clauses of the Statute which the Constitution did adopt, and if the full gloss is to be taken with the clauses, the limiting value attributed to the use of the familiar words might be considerably depreciated. The problem is made the more difficult, because in England indictments often contained counts under both the charges of compassing the king's death and levying war against him, or adhering to his enemies; and broad rulings of the courts did not draw distinctions as to the relative scope of these different charges. All that can be said is that, so far as the contemporary materials are concerned, their weight is clearly in favor of resolving doubts on the side of precise definition of the offense. Obviously this is the point of Wilson's law lectures. [28]

It seems possible, finally, to cast some light on the particular type of oppression which the proponents of the treason clause feared under loose definitions of the offense. Aside from what may be implied in Dr. Franklin's reference to the "virulence" of prosecutions for treason as creating the danger of perjured evidence, the data suggest that the fear most in mind was of abuse of "treason" for the building or upholding of domestic political faction, rather than its vindictive use under wartime hysteria against "enemies." This is not the same thing as to draw a line between the offenses of levying war and adhering to enemies, and to apply a policy of strict construction only to the former. Though limited to wartime, the latter offense might obviously then be put to oppressive use against political foes or restless classes by the familiar technique of holding them to the "natural consequences" of their conduct.[29]

What is suggested is that the historic policy restrictive of the scope of "treason" under the Constitution was most consciously based on the fear of extension of the offense to penalize types of conduct familiar in the normal processes of the struggle for domestic political or economic power. The sale of provisions to an enemy in wartime, or the conveying of intelligence to him, or the proffer of counsel and assistance to his agents, are types of conduct quite distinct from activities of a sort to which political opponents or economic groups would normally resort in their efforts to influence public policy. There is less danger that charges of this type could, in view of the sharply defined character of the conduct in question, be used to suppress free competition for the power to direct the policies of the republic. It is not that the offense of adhering to enemies is, *in toto,* exempt from the restrictive policy of the Constitution, but that that policy was formed with attention directed at only certain types of the conduct which might constitute adherence.[30]

There is little that is helpful in developing this point in the Convention discussion. It is worth recalling, however, that when the proposal to require "two witnesses to the same overt act" was laid before the Committee of the Whole, following

Franklin's expression of fear over the "virulence" of prosecutions for treason and the ease with which perjury was used against innocence, James Wilson commented that "much may be said on both sides. Treason may sometimes be practised in such a manner, as to render proof extremely difficult—as in a traitorous correspondence with an Enemy."[31] Wilson apparently voted in favor of the more strict two-witness requirement, but this vote on the evidentiary safeguard does not necessarily limit the implications of his suggestion of a stronger hand in defining the offense of trafficking with the enemy. In the debate in the Pennsylvania ratifying convention, it is a reasonable implication that Wilson is concerned for suppression of essentially political conduct, when he exclaims: "Crimes against the state! and against the officers of the state! History informs us that more wrong may be done on this subject than on any other whatsoever."[32] When he cited a case to illustrate the excesses of the English law of "constructive" treason, it was one in which the charge had been domestic disloyalty to the king, "compassing the death of the king." Moreover, he argued that there was no special reason to fear governmental oppression where the government did not have separate interests from the people—which would be the case as regards protection against actual dealings with the enemy—and then adduced the treason clause to show that "Whenever the general government can be a party against a citizen, the trial is guarded and secured in the Constitution itself." In this context, his caution that "if we have recourse to the history of the different governments that have hitherto subsisted, we shall find that a very great part of their tyranny over the people has arisen from the extension of the definition of treason" is properly read as aimed at cases where the government and people might have separate interests: *i.e.,* where the real issue was the control of domestic power.[33]

The abuses which the pamphleteers believed defeated by the Constitution's treason clause seem most likely to have been the suppression of political opposition or the legitimate expression of views on the conduct of public policy. The danger pointed to by Madison in *The Federalist* was that "new-fangled and artificial treasons have been the great engines by which violent factions, the natural offspring of free government, have usually wreaked their alternate malignity on each other."[34] References in other discussions to the protection offered by the treason clause against the "avarice and rapacity of government," to its "truly republican" character and its "pre-eminence in the scale of political security" likewise imply primary attention to the use of the offense against normal activities of political opposition and opinion.[35]

In 1808, Rufus King, who had figured prominently in the work of the Federal Convention, wrote to Pickering commenting on the bill introduced by Senator Giles to correct the gaps in the law which, it was conceived, had permitted Burr to escape conviction. King's remarks are, of course, prompted by his ardent anti-Jeffersonian position, but his opinion of the history of the policy informing the treason clause so tallies with the contemporary evidence as to deserve note:

> The limitation which the Constitution establishes on the subject of Treason, proceeded from a principle, which will readily be approved by every man who is acquainted with the vindictive spirit that, at different times in the History of England, has animated the ascendant faction against their political adversaries. If the proposed law on the subject of Treason neither enlarges nor lessens its constitutional definition, the law is unnecessary; if it does the one or the other, it is unconstitutional. In the unfortunate periods, during which a country is torn by contending factions, the Treason Laws should not be altered. Neither ought they to be changed just at the time when the Govt. is angry or disappointed

in the failure to convict such as are believed to have committed
Treason. . . .[36]

The materials for the period of the Constitution cast little
light on detailed problems of the elements of treason. Aside
from the references to the Statute of Edward III, there is no
mention in the Convention's discussion of the idea that use of
the word "treason" of itself imported any particular doctrines, though obviously it was used to express the central
concept of betrayal of allegiance. The idea of "allegiance"
itself receives no exposition, however. "Treason" also bears
the implication that a specific intent to betray must be shown,
and, though there is no direct evidence on the point, the
whole emphasis on a policy of strict construction in defining
the offense reinforces the normal implication of the language.
Though the constitutional provision is phrased somewhat
backhandedly on the point, it is clear from the development
of the section that the overt act is intended as a distinct
element of proof of the offense in addition to intent. This
would seem at least clearly to rule out treason prosecutions
for the mere holding of dissident opinions.[37] An effort, by
violence, to resist the general execution of the laws, however,
would apparently be viewed by the proponents of the treason
clause as sufficient to make out a levying of war.[38] "Traitorous" correspondence with the enemy would establish adherence to him.[39] Beyond these scant items, the constitutional
record gives us no specific help.
The sequence of amendments by which the evidentiary
clause was strengthened clearly shows a strongly felt policy to
be involved. What that policy aimed at seems quite simple.
Franklin feared that the government would procure perjured
witnesses, and evidently felt that the requirement as written
would make this task more difficult. This explanation was the
accepted basis of the clause. If any more specific history

explains the reason for placing the evidentiary requirement in the Constitution, there seems no evidence of it.

In the Act of April 30, 1790,[40] Congress substantially restated the language of the constitutional provision and, exercising its power to fix the penalty, decreed death. There is no record of any discussion concerning this first federal treason statute which casts light on contemporary views of the constitutional provision.[41] Contemporary treatises drew their statements on the specific incidents of treason from English decisions and the early 19th century American decisions, but found no further enlightenment in the constitutional materials. All emphasize, however, the fundamentally restrictive policy represented in the constitutional provision.[42]

(c) The Treason Clause as a Limitation on Governmental Power

If certain conduct is not within the scope of the constitutional definition, either because it is not treason under any historic definition, or because it is one of the historic branches of the crime which the framers omitted from their delimitation, does this mean simply that the actor may not be indicted for treason as such, though his conduct may subject him to another charge; or does it mean that he may not be charged with any offense, the gravamen of which is the allegedly subversive character of that conduct? Does the treason clause merely define a particular crime, or does it express a policy exempting certain types of activity from the risk of criminal prosecution?

Obviously, the clause is at least an exclusive definition of a crime called "treason," forbidding any agency of government from increasing the categories of conduct which may be prosecuted under that name.[43] Nor may the scope of the offense be extended by including under the heads of adherence to enemies or levying of war conduct lacking historic elements of those crimes, or by taking a "liberal" view of the evidence deemed relevant to establish the elements of such treasons. [44] Legislation purporting to declare that particular situations constitute levying of war, or adherence to enemies, would probably be unconstitutional. The treason clause pointedly restricts congressional authority to the determination of penalties for the crime, and its position in Article III underlines the implication that problems of application are solely for the courts. [45] But this may, in the last analysis, be a matter of form, since under its broad power to fix penalties, Congress could hardly be denied the right to set different grades of punishment and, necessarily, to specify the varieties of treasonable conduct to which the respective penalties should apply. [46]

Some dicta assert that the scope of treason as defined by the Constitution may not be "diminished," any more than it can be expanded. [47] What this means is not specified. Perhaps it means that the Congress could not bar the prosecution of alleged traitors by legislation purporting to legalize conduct treasonable under the constitutional definition. Perhaps it is meant to assert that Congress may not reduce treasonable conduct to the grade of a misdemeanor. [48] Neither proposition seems to have much substance in view of the grant to Congress of the power "to declare the Punishment of Treason," limited only against severity and not against lenience by the prohibition on "Corruption of Blood or Forfeiture except during the Life of the Person attainted." [49] Likewise, the unrestricted pardon power of the President would seem to negative an interpretation limiting executive authority to "diminish" the crime. Indeed, the Philadelphia Convention rejected a proposal to require congressional concurrence in presidential pardons in treason cases. [50]

One sense in which the scope of the constitutional defini-

tion should not be capable of being "diminished" is with
respect to the requirement that there be "the Testimony of
two Witnesses to the same overt Act." Though the record of
the Philadelphia Convention contains but a brief reference to
the insertion of this stringent requirement, it is enough to
show that this provision was insisted on out of a highly
practical view of the dangers of political abuse of treason
prosecutions.[51] Judges have carefully sought to give the
provision full substance in trials for treason.[52]

On the other hand, where the defendant is charged with
conduct involving all the elements of treason within the
constitutional definition, and the gravamen of the accusation
against him is an effort to subvert the government, or aid its
enemies, it would seem in disregard of the policy of the
Constitution to permit him to be tried under another charge
than "treason." However, the decision in Ex parte *Quirin*[53]
casts considerable doubt on the validity of this analysis. One
of the saboteurs landed on the eastern coast of the United
States from German submarines in the spring of 1942 was an
American citizen. The Supreme Court considered and rejected the argument that he must be prosecuted for treason, and
not for an offense against the laws of war. The Court's
analysis went not to the historic scope of military jurisdiction
(which might be deemed to limit the general application of
civil process), but to the scope of the crime of treason:

> The argument leaves out of account the nature of the offense
> which the Government charges and which the Act of Congress, by
> incorporating the law of war, punishes. It is that each petitioner, in
> circumstances which gave him the status of an enemy belligerent,
> passed our military and naval lines and defenses or went behind
> those lines, in civilian dress and with hostile purpose. The offense
> was complete when with that purpose they entered—or, having so
> entered, they remained upon—our territory in time of war
> without uniform or other appropriate means of identification. For

that reason, even when committed by a citizen, the offense is
distinct from the crime of treason defined in Article III, s. 3 of the
Constitution, since the absence of uniform essential to one is
irrelevant to the other. *Cf. Morgan* v. *Devine,* 237 U. S. 632;
Albrecht v. *United States,* 273 U. S. 1, 11–12.[54]

The decisions cited as analogies by the Court are the now
standard authorities holding that the double jeopardy clause
of the Constitution is not violated by conviction for two or
more offenses which are in substance part of the same
criminal transaction, but which involve different elements in
the allegation.[55] It is not a convincing technique of interpretation to apply to a constitutional guaranty having its own
history of policy a formal test developed under a different
clause of the Constitution, with no demonstration that the
policies behind the respective clauses are so similar as to be
fulfilled by the same criterion. The double jeopardy clause is
historically a guaranty against abuse of the law enforcement
machinery as such, without reference to abuses peculiar to
any one of the major types of crime. When the Constitution
singles out the offense of treason as subject to special abuse,
citation of a highly technical rule developed by judicial
construction out of the general guaranty is in itself little
evidence that the peculiar dangers against which the special
guaranty was erected have been avoided.[56] Though the type
of offense charged against the American citizen in the saboteur group is a very clear case of treason, it is also within the
category of charge the abuse of which was feared by the
framers. The "absence of uniform" noted as the essentially
distinct element of the offense under the law of war made the
defendant's conduct more dangerous simply because it enabled him to appear as what he was—one of the body of
citizens. And it was citizens that the limitations of the treason
clause were intended to protect.

There are respects in which the treason clause might have

practical meaning as a restriction on official agencies, even if it does no more than limit the kinds of conduct which may be prosecuted under the name of treason. The barbarous or oppressive penalties which were once a distinguishing mark of the crime have been abolished, but treason is still a capital crime; and thus it may be of consequence whether the prosecutor can make out a case under that heading, or is restricted to a lesser penalty under another charge. This is likely to be a consideration only in most unusual cases, however; the history has been one of decreasing penalties, not simply as a matter of humane policy, but because juries are reluctant to convict on a capital charge.[57] There is the possibility that Congress might be restrained by the constitutional ban on cruel or unusual punishments from imposing the highest penalties for certain conduct, unless it were held to mount to the level of treason.[58]

A more tangible reason why it may be more than a matter of words whether an indictment charges treason rather than another crime is the peculiar intimidation and stigma carried by the mere accusation of treason. Federalist treason prosecutions arising out of the Whiskey Rebellion and designed to tar the "Democratic clubs" with the imputation of treason; Democratic accusations of treason against the Hartford Convention, which helped make that venture the last blow to the tottering Federalist party structure; the effort to employ treason prosecutions to make examples against widespread opposition to the Jeffersonian Embargo and the Fugitive Slave Law; the use of treason indictments against leaders of the Homestead Strike to break rank and file morale—all show that American history is not without demonstrations of the use of the treason charge as an instrument to turn public opinion and promote fear and loss of confidence among the opposition.[59] Apart from such considerations, which give "treason" a separate significance even though a defendant's conduct may be punishable under some other head, it may of course be that the defendant will not be subject to any criminal liability at all, if his case cannot be fitted within the bounds of "treason." This may be true at any given time because of a gap in the statutes.[60] And there might be cases in which whether legislative proscription of certain conduct could be justified, unless treason was involved, would present a substantial issue under the due process clause; for that offense may involve conduct which is commonplace and legitimate except as it is linked with a treasonable design.[61]

These are more or less plausible reasons why, as an exclusive definition of a particular crime, the treason clause may have more than merely taxonomic significance. But the treason clause is the product of history and not of analytical jurisprudence. There is some evidence that the characteristic severity of the punishment for treason has furnished a ground for the desire for a careful definition.[62] And it is plain that in 1787 men appreciated the potentialities of "treason" as a political epithet.[63] But among the suggestions which may be advanced to explain the practical significance of the clause as an exclusive definition of a particular crime, these alone have any definite link to the historical record, and that not well-defined. The highly practical concern of the Philadelphia Convention over the careful framing of the treason clause, however, and the pride with which proponents of the Constitution subsequently pointed to this item of the framers' handiwork as in substance a part of an American "Bill of Rights," imply a belief that more was being done than to state what might be prosecuted under the label of "treason."

On the face of the clause, it might be argued that "treason" is a generic term for efforts to subvert the government, and that therefore there can be no crimes, the gravamen of which is such a subversive intent, outside the bounds of the constitutional definition.[64] Both in its general usage and in English legal history, "treason" has at one time or another embraced about everything which could fairly be called subversive activity, and a good deal that could not be.[65] But this is not necessarily to say that subversive conduct was not also covered by other heads of the criminal law; and in fact there seems to have been no period after the Statute of Edward III when English law did not include offenses separate from treason though in substance dealing with what was, at least at the time, regarded as seditious activity or belief.[66] The term is broadly inclusive, but not necessarily exclusive, in itself. Nor did the term acquire such an exclusive meaning in American colonial or state statute books prior to 1787, for these abound with penalties for activity obviously punished because deemed of a subversive nature, but not denominated "treason."[67] There is no evidence that the word was used in the Constitution with intent to exclude the creation of all possible varieties and degrees of subversive crime except the levying of war and adherence to enemies.[68]

The Act of April 30, 1790, "for the Punishment of certain Crimes against the United States," would imply a contrary construction, since in addition to restating the constitutionally defined crime of treason and declaring the death penalty therefor, it defined and punished the offenses of misprision of treason; "piracy" in the form of the commission by any citizen of "any act of hostility against the United States . . . upon the high sea, under colour of any commission from any foreign prince, or state," or being accessory to such piracy, before or after the fact, or confederating with pirates; and rescue by force of any person committed for or found guilty of treason.[69] In the lengthy, hard-fought debates over the Sedition Act of July 14, 1798, none of the Act's opponents seems to have argued that the treason clause barred the creation of any new crimes aimed at subversive conduct; and in fact they conceded the validity of the first section of the Act, which punished conspiracies to oppose the laws of the United States and attempts to raise forcible resistance to them.[70] There is, thus, some support in history for the result

if not for all of the rationalization in Marshall's dictum in Ex
parte *Bollman,* that

> crimes so atrocious as those which have for their object the
> subversion by violence of those laws and those institutions which
> have been ordained in order to secure the peace and happiness of
> society, are not to escape punishment because they have not
> ripened into treason. The wisdom of the legislature is competent
> to provide for the case; and the framers of our constitution, who
> not only defined and limited the crime, but with jealous circum-
> spection attempted to protect their limitation by providing that no
> person should be convicted of it, unless on the testimony of two
> witnesses to the same overt act, or on confession in open court,
> must have conceived it more safe that punishment in such cases
> should be ordained by general laws, formed upon deliberation,
> under the influence of no resentments, and without knowing on
> whom they were to operate, than that it should be inflicted under
> the influence of those passions which the occasion seldom fails to
> excite, and which a flexible definition of the crime, or a construc-
> tion which would render it flexible, might bring into operation. It
> is, therefore, more safe as well as more consonant to the principles
> of our constitution, that the crime of treason should not be
> extended by construction to doubtful cases; and that crimes not
> clearly within the constitutional definition, should receive such
> punishment as the legislature in its wisdom may provide. [71]

But the record does suggest that the clause was intended to
guarantee nonviolent political processes against prosecution
under any theory or charge, the burden of which was the
allegedly seditious character of the conduct in question. The
most obviously restrictive feature of the constitutional definition is its omission of any provision analogous to that branch
of the Statute of Edward III which punished treason by
compassing the death of the king. In a narrow sense, this
provision perhaps had no proper analogue in a republic. [72]

However, to interpret the silence of the treason clause in this way alone does justice neither to the technical proficiency of the Philadelphia draftsmen nor to the practical statecraft and knowledge of English political history among the framers and proponents of the Constitution. The charge of compassing the king's death had been the principal instrument by which "treason" had been used to suppress a wide range of political opposition, from acts obviously dangerous to order and likely in fact to lead to the king's death to the mere speaking or writing of views restrictive of the royal authority.[73] Resort to treason trials as a weapon of political combat was the abuse; the judicial technique was that of "inferring an intention to kill from overt acts which were only remotely connected, if they were connected at all, with a formed intention to kill the king"—in short, "constructive treason."[74] As Holdsworth's description implies, this had involved more than devitalizing the mental element of the crime, by raising a treasonable intent upon tenuous innuendos. The process had also involved the emasculation of the overt act requirement of the Statute of Edward III, for, if "treason" were to be used effectively to suppress political opposition, it could not be limited to the relatively rare cases of resort to violence or the imminent threat thereof. It must be extended to cover the expression and advocacy of beliefs and ideas, and at the high point of this process it was in fact extended to punish the possession of an unpublished writing.[75]

In the great English treatises from which American lawyers took their knowledge and ideas of the English law, the outstanding note of political liberalism in the discussion of treason was the detailed condemnation of the doctrine that "mere" spoken or written expression of ideas, not amounting to a direct persuasion or consulting to kill the king, could constitute the crime.[76] It is true that the same treatises contain uncritical expositions of the law of criminal libel as it stood in the full, vague sweep of the 17th century decisions.[77]

The 18th century in England, however, saw the great court struggles, led by Erskine, to limit the practical scope of criminal libel; and, though this battle did not reach its successful climax until shortly after the adoption of the United States Constitution (in Fox's Libel Act, 1792), the evidence is that "in the years before the First Amendment freedom of speech was conceived as giving a wide and genuine protection for all sorts of discussion of public matters."[78]

Against this total background, it is significant that the fear of factional abuse of treason trials, and reprobation of "constructive treason," are the most consistently and clearly expressed grounds of policy in contemporary discussion of the treason clause.[79] They continue to dominate the courts' exposition of the policies determining the scope of levying war and adhering to enemies.[80] The object of these abuses had been primarily the suppression of peaceful political activity. Plainly Article III, Section 3 was viewed as completely barring prosecutions of such conduct as "treason," and such has been the opinion of the courts.[81]

But the terms in which the treason clause was praised by proponents of the Constitution imply that it has the more fundamental effect of protecting nonviolent political activity from any suppression by resort to criminal prosecutions. Indeed, it would be hard to believe that Madison, the author of the First Amendment and of the Report on the Virginia Resolutions in opposition to the Sedition Act of 1798, would have agreed that the expression of ideas might be criminally punished, if only the label were shifted from "treason" ("compassing the death of the king") to some other tag.[82]

The mention of Madison, however, naturally suggests the question why the First Amendment was thought necessary, if peaceful political contest was understood to be protected by the restrictive implications of the treason clause. It must be remembered that the evidence suggests only that Section 3 of

Article III was thought of as a political guaranty, whereas the
tradition expressed in the First Amendment is a much
broader one.[83] It must be remembered, also, that the Bill of
Rights was added to the Constitution out of an abundance of
caution, as a concession to the substantial opposition in many
of the ratifying conventions based on fear of the implications
that might lurk in the new document. The freedom of
political criticism was a prominent concern of this opposition.
Proponents of the Constitution uniformly insisted that a bill
of rights was unnecessary in a government wholly of delegated powers.[84] Even in the absence of direct evidence, it
would be fair to infer from their proud citations of the
treason clause as a guaranty of individual liberty, that they
would claim that provision as a general safeguard against
abusive prosecutions. The claim was in fact made in both the
Virginia and the North Carolina conventions, which were
the scenes of two of the hottest fights over ratification. In the
former, Patrick Henry voiced fears of the use of other
charges than treason to suppress political criticism, and
George Nicholas, citing the careful definition of treason,
declared that, "This security does away the objection that the
most grievous oppressions might happen under color of
punishing crimes against the general government."[85]

The issue of free speech was made still more explicit,
however, in the North Carolina convention. Lenoir had
expressed the fear that, exercising its supreme power in its
"ten miles square" citadel, the new government would arbitrarily suppress its critics, and Spaight, in reply, had pointed
to the exclusive definition of treason. At this point, the record
notes, "Mr. Lenoir rose, and said he meant misprision of
treason,"—*i.e.*, a distinct, if related crime. Spaight answered,
shortly, that "The same reasons hold against that, too. . . ."[86]

The narrow view taken in these debates regarding the
powers of Congress in the field of criminal legislation—*i.e.*,
that Congress could not punish any crimes other than those it

was specifically authorized to punish—has not prevailed in the evolution of the Constitution.[87] And it may be argued that in these discussions it was this forsaken theory of the general limits of federal power, rather than any broadly restrictive force of the treason clause, which was claimed as the guaranty against political prosecutions. The aspect of this argument, however, which deprives it of winning conviction, is that it is actually no more than the contention which was advanced against the necessity of the First Amendment, or any other parts of the Bill of Rights. As Hartley suggested in Pennsylvania, the treason clause, like the stipulations regarding habeas corpus and trial by jury in criminal cases, may have been inserted out of an abundance of caution, because of the fundamental character of the issues involved.[88] This fact itself would urge caution in construing away any of the substantial effect which the obviously restrictive policy of the clause might fairly be given. Certainly the rather abstract question, whether the First Amendment merely declares limitations implicit in the theory on which the federal government was created, or imposes additional restrictions on its powers, did not affect the practical significance of that guaranty in the minds of its proponents, nor has it had apparent effect upon later developments under the Amendment.[89]

A further implication concerning the restrictive scope of the treason clause arises from the history of that provision of the Constitution which, as finally adopted in Article IV, Section 4, provides that "The United States shall guarantee to every State in this Union a Republican Form of Government. . . ." This provision is obviously closely related in function to the treason clause, being in effect a stipulation for executive action, as the latter regulates judicial prosecutions, against certain subversive attempts.[90] Significantly, the discussion of the guaranty clause at the Philadelphia Convention shows that its phrasing was reworked in order to make clear the framers' intention that, in effect, only a threat amounting to treason should suffice to bring the guaranty into operation. At one stage, it was proposed that the guaranty read: "That a Republican Constitution and its existing laws ought to be guaranteed to each State by the U. States."[91] Gouverneur Morris objected: he was very unwilling that some existing laws be guaranteed. Wilson replied that "The object is merely to secure the States agst dangerous commotions, insurrections and rebellions." Mason, Randolph, and Gorham spoke further in support of the suggested provision, but all emphasized that the policy involved was directed against violent efforts to overturn state governments, which would inevitably imperil the new nation itself.[92] Wilson finally moved the form of words adopted, and before this approving vote Houston again emphasized the objection to the broad scope of the original phrasing, observing that it would be unwise to guarantee perpetuation of existing constitutions, some of which he thought needed change.[93] It seems plain that the terms of the guaranty clause were changed in order to exclude interference thereunder with peaceful political processes, subject perhaps to the one limitation—if it is such—that even by peaceful means no state might adopt a monarchical or other fundamentally nonrepublican form of government.[94] The history of the guaranty clause thus suggests the scope of the policy probably represented also by the stringent limitations of the closely related treason section.

Doubt may be cast on the validity of this interpretation of the treason clause as a general prohibition of the penalizing of peaceful political activity, by the relatively minor role which the clause played in the attacks on the Sedition Act of 1798.[95] Attack was centered on that section which declared any speech or writing against the President or Congress "with the intent to defame" or to bring them "into contempt or disrepute" a misdemeanor, punishable by fine or imprisonment.[96] It is not especially surprising that the Republicans relied mainly on the First Amendment as the expression of the constitutional policy deemed violated by the Sedition Act. It is the most explicit statement of that policy, and it carried a great moral weight, since its adoption had been an important practical condition of the ratification of the Constitution. It is probably not unimportant that the First Amendment represented a principle particularly dear to both of the chief behind-scenes managers of the opposition—to Madison, its author, and to Jefferson, draftsman of the Virginia Act for establishing religious freedom. The treason clause for some reason failed to strike Madison's imagination in the Philadelphia Convention, though he subsequently advanced it in praise of the Constitution, in *The Federalist.*[97]

The treason clause was, however, introduced into the debate in a manner somewhat similar to that in the discussions over ratifying the Constitution. The Federal Government was wholly one of delegated powers; the only fields of federal criminal legislation were those specified; one of these was treason, which, Albert Gallatin pointed out in the House, "they had a right to punish, but not to define, it being expressly defined by the Constitution itself."[98] But such references do not carry the connotation of those remarks in the ratification debate which suggest that the treason clause was viewed as summing up the law pertaining to subversive activities against the Federal Government. The treason clause was not thus relied on in the arguments of the Virginia or Kentucky Resolutions, nor in Madison's detailed report to the Virginia House of Delegates on the communications from other states regarding the Virginia Resolutions.[99]

But the restrictive potentialities of the treason clause did not pass wholly without mention in the great debate over the Sedition Act, and this reference is of weight, for the speaker is "the intellectual leader of the young Republicans," John Taylor of Caroline.[100] In the debate in the Virginia House of Delegates, Lee pointed out that the Virginia Convention, which framed the first state constitution containing a guaranty of free speech, had found it not inconsistent also to enact the Ordinance of 1776 which imposed a fine up to £20,000, or imprisonment up to five years, for any resident who should "by any word, open deed, or act, advisedly and willingly maintain and defend the authority, jurisdiction, or power of the King or Parliament of Great Britain," or who should "maliciously and advisedly endeavor to excite the people to resist the government of the Commonwealth as by law established, or persuade them to return to a dependence upon the crown of Great Britain."[101] Taylor saw the answer to this alleged legislative construction of the scope of free speech in the restrictive effect of the treason clause of the Federal Constitution:

> The [Virginia] law evidently considers sedition as but one species constituting that genus called treason, which was made up of many parts. It therefore accurately expresses the idea of Virginia of the word "treason"; and shows how she understood it, as used in the Constitution. By that treason is limited to two items, with the punishment of which only the General Government is intrusted. Hence it was evident that Virginia could not have conceived that Congress could proceed constitutionally to that species of treason called sedition; and if this was not the true construction, what security was derived from the restriction in the Constitution relative to treason? Congress might designate the acts there specified by that term, and they might apply other terms to all other acts, from correcting which that clause of the Constitution intended to prohibit them; by doing which, as in the case of sedition, they might go on to erect a code of laws to punish acts heretofore called treasonable, under other names, by fine, confiscation, banishment, or imprisonment, until social intercourse shall be hunted by informers out of our country; and yet all might be said to be constitutionally done, if principles could be evaded by words.[102]

Several years later, replying to John Adams' attempt to justify the punishing of seditious libels on the President, Taylor further indicated his conception of the treason clause as a general guaranty against the use of criminal prosecutions to curb free discussion of public matters, and of the First Amendment as in this aspect a cumulative protection, added out of abundance of caution:

> The opinions in several state constitutions, in favour of mental emancipation, being so construed as to expose mind to legislative fetters, the good sense of mankind had in this, as in many other instances, preceded precept in exploding errour. Political prosecutions for opinion had become as obsolete as those for witchcraft, before the general constitution obeyed public opinion, by declaring their inconsistency with free government; and before the sedition law endeavoured to drive political science into a retrocession of centuries, for the sake of reviving them.
>
> The third section of the third article of the general constitution had been deeply rooted in the natural right of free utterance, before the publick solicitude required its farther security by the first amendment. The utterance of any opinions could not constitute treason. Irreverence expressed for our constitution and government; falsehood or reasoning to bring them into contempt and overturn them; were not thought politically criminal. Instead of being condemned to punishment, they are shielded against prosecution. . . . [103]

For all practical purposes, the issue of the treason clause as a guaranty of free speech and political processes was not mooted after the Sedition Act controversy until similar questions were made acute by legislation during and immediately after the First World War. [104] In *Frohwerk v. United States,* [105] a prosecution based on the publication in a German-language newspaper in Missouri of several articles on the constitutionality and merits of the draft and the war objectives of the United States, the defense raised the treason clause as one basis for the claim of the unconstitutionality of the Espionage Act of June 15, 1917. Mr. Justice Holmes, speaking for a unanimous Court, stated the essence of the defense contention and disposed of it with a curtness which does not do justice to its merits:

> Some reference was made in the proceedings and in argument to the provision in the Constitution concerning treason, and it was suggested on the one hand that some of the matters dealt with in the Act of 1917 were treasonable and punishable as treason or not at all, and on the other that the acts complained of not being treason could not be punished. These suggestions seem to us to need no more than to be stated.[106]

If, on the one hand, certain conduct amounts to treason, Mr. Justice Holmes does not explain why the two-witness requirement of Article III, Section 3 is not violated if the crime may be prosecuted apart from the treason clause merely by giving it another name.[107] Where, on the other hand, the conduct in question consists of the expression of ideas, or even the advocacy of action, concerning the wisdom of public policies, an a priori assertion does not answer the implications of the history heretofore examined. The most likely reason for the inadequate treatment of the treason clause issue in the *Frohwerk* opinion is the totally inadequate presentation of it in the briefs, for neither side presented any data to the Court.[108] That an adequate presentation of the issue might have elicited a much different appraisal of its merits is suggested by subsequent comment of Mr. Justice Brandeis, dissenting in *Schaefer v. United States*,[109] a prosecution under the first Espionage Act for utterances on which an unsuccessful treason trial had already been based:

To prosecute men for such publications reminds of the days when men were hanged for constructive treason. And, indeed, the jury may well have believed from the charge that the Espionage Act had in effect restored the crime of constructive treason.[110]

Mr. Justice Holmes concurred in this dissent. The treason clauses of the federal and state constitutions were raised unsuccessfully as a constitutional defense against other prosecutions for utterances, brought both under the federal Espionage Acts and the state "criminal syndicalism" legislation which flourished in the early '20's. No decision discusses the historic basis for the claim, nor does any opinion offer convincing argument against it. The California court, of course, misunderstood the elementary history of the treason clause when it said that the definitions of the federal and state constitutions

> are merely for the purpose of limiting the number of offenses which can be punishable as treason under the common law, and in no wise limit the power of the legislature to provide for the punishment of acts inimical to the public welfare which theretofore might have been punished as constructive treason.[111]

The most reasoned opinion is that of the Sixth Circuit Court of Appeals, in *Wimmer v. United States*,[112] a conviction under the second Espionage Act for utterances charged as supporting or favoring the cause of a country at war with the United States. The court said,

> ... Wimmer's first position is that the act is unconstitutional, because it punishes treasonable conduct, without proof of the overt act and without the two witnesses thereto required by the Constitution. As we understand the argument, it is, in substance, that adhering to and giving aid and comfort to the enemy is treason, according to the constitutional definition; that to support

the cause of the enemy, or oppose that of the United States, against the prohibition of the Espionage Act, is adhering to and giving aid and comfort to the enemy, and is therefore treason; and hence that it cannot be punished unless shown by the degree of proof required by the Constitution. . . .

If we had to do with a case where the conduct which was prosecuted consisted of acts, we would have to consider the line of reasoning upon which Wimmer depends. That Congress has power to take hold of an act which is, in fact, treason, and to say that it shall be severely punished, without the proof which is required to establish treason, and to justify this result because the conduct is given another name, is a proposition which we have no occasion to affirm or deny. Here the only conduct alleged or proved, as making out the offense, consisted of oral statements— words only. It is well settled that one cannot, by mere words, be guilty of treason. . . . and thus the fallacy of Wimmer's contention becomes apparent. It is a mistake to say that the intent is the thing which makes the treason, and that where the disloyal intent is there treason is. The requirement that there shall be two witnesses is purely evidential, but when the requirement is extended to proof of the overt act, it becomes clear that there must be an overt act to constitute the crime, and the act is incorporated into the definition. Thus we find, in the constitutionally defined crime, two elements, the intent and the act; neither is dominant. Intent minus act is not treason, any more than act minus intent is. Since it was declared by Chief Justice Marshall in the Bollman Case, 4 Cranch, 75, 2 L. Ed. 554, it has never been doubted that Congress may punish, under the ordinary rules of prosecution and without trenching upon the constitutional limitation as to treason, acts which are of a seditious nature and tend toward treason, but which are not of the direct character and superdangerous degree which would meet the constitutional test and make them treason; and even more must this be true of words.

Further distinction is found in the very words of the constitutional definition. Treason is "adhering to their enemies, giving

them aid and comfort." Both adherence and giving aid are
necessary. To "favor or support" is, very likely, to "adhere"; but it
does not carry the idea of giving aid and comfort, unless by a
rather remote implication. Hence it may well be said that adherence by words only is an offense quite distinct from treason.[113]

The true depth of the issue raised by the treason clause was
not seen either by defense counsel or by the court. The court
is correct in pointing out that no question of the two-witness
guaranty is involved where the conduct in question is not
treasonable in substance; and the American authority is
consistent to the effect that the "mere" expression of ideas or
beliefs is not treason.[114] The opinion is historically sound in
linking this latter position to the requirement of an "overt act"
as a distinct element of the crime.[115] But the court too easily
dismisses the other half of the problem. Marshall's dictum in
the *Bollman* case has, indeed, been accepted, and other
evidence supports its conclusion that the treason clause does
not exclude the creation of all other types of subversive
crime.[116] It does not necessarily follow from this general
proposition, however, that the treason clause does not forbid
resort to the criminal law in certain types of allegedly subversive conduct; and historical evidence, ignored by the Circuit
Court of Appeals, strongly suggests that the treason clause
was in fact understood to guarantee nonviolent political
controversy against suppression under the charge of treason
or any other criminal charge based on its supposed subversive
character.[117] The argument that since "'treason' requires
more than mere words to constitute the offense," an offense
based on utterances cannot be within any limits set by the
treason clause,[118] merely begs the question, as some minority
judges have in effect pointed out.[119]
It may be argued that, whatever the historic meaning of the
treason clause as a guaranty of free discussion of public
issues, the matter is of no present practical significance,

because the development of judicial doctrine under the First
and Fourteenth Amendments affords a completely adequate
basis for the protection of such values.[120] This is true, so far
as it goes; and, indeed, since Article III, Section 3 of the
Federal Constitution does not limit the creation by state
legislatures of offenses against state sovereignty, the Fourteenth Amendment affords a broader guaranty than could
the federal treason clause.[121] Even on this level of analysis,
however, the treason clause of the Federal Constitution, and
the similar provisions copied from it by many state constitutions, are guaranties of somewhat different scope than the
typical declarations in favor of free speech. The treason
clauses are clearly limitations upon all the agencies of government, instead of being addressed directly to the legislative
branch only. The literal copying of the federal clause imports
its history into state constitutions in a more clear-cut fashion
than may be true of free speech guaranties which often differ
considerably in declarations of policy from the terms of the
First Amendment. All of this, however, is on a relatively
formal level. Of more substantial importance is the proper
understanding of the historic scope of the treason clause as
evidence of the constitutional policy in favor of free expression and advocacy of ideas and beliefs. The broad sweep of
the First Amendment offers little more than an authorization
and command to develop a free speech policy. The content of
that policy cannot be deemed so precisely defined and firmly
based as to deny significance to some tangible evidence of
what seemed wise and practical to the men who created this
government.

Thus the historic background of the treason clause furnishes specific evidence rather than a priori reasoning for assign-
ing a higher value to the free and nonviolent play of
controversy over public issues than to the broad prevention of
possible danger to security of social institutions. Especially
does it underline the importance of preventing use of the

criminal law as an instrument of competition for political power. Further, it validates the most practical judicial test yet devised to set the standard for permissible intervention by the state. For in its historic context, the requirement of the overt act as a distinct element of "treason" amounts, so far as the expression of ideas or beliefs is involved, to the requirement of a showing of a "clear and present danger that they will bring about the substantive evils that Congress has a right to prevent."[122] And, out of a knowledge of a long and cruel history of abuses of arbitrary power, the history of the law of treason insists on the reality of this distinction with a curt finality found nowhere else: "words may make an Heretick, but not a Traytor."[123] The "clear and present danger" test is still fighting ground. The historic background of the treason clause furnishes a basis never yet adequately examined, for a reconsideration of the constitutionality of such legislation as the federal Espionage Act and state legislation against "criminal syndicalism" insofar as these are directed primarily against utterances. Certainly, as a command levelled directly at judges as well as legislators, the restrictive definition of treason carries an admonition of policy concerning the application of such statutes which has not yet been presented with its due weight of persuasion.

NOTES

1. See 31 Journals of the Continental Congress (1934) 497; Burnett, The Continental Congress (1941) 664.

2. Massachusetts legislation and executive pronouncements declared the rebellion to be "treason." See, in Acts and Resolves of Massachusetts (reprinted under c. 104, Resolves of 1889), the Acts of Feb. 16 and 20, 1787 (1786, c. 56, 59) 176, 187; Resolves of Feb. 4, Mar. 10, and June 15, 1787, and June 10 and 19, 1788, *id.* at 423, 515, 677, 212; Governor's Messages of Sept. 28, 1786 and Feb. 3, 1787, *id.* at 928, 960. See 32, 33 Journals of the Continental Congress (1934) 24, 38–89, 85, 93–105, 110–111, 176n., 719–22,

724, 729; and numerous letters cited under heading "Shays' Rebellion" in 8 Burnett, Letters of Members of the Continental Congress (1936). *Cf.* Congressional reactions to the mutiny of the soldiers demanding back pay, in Philadelphia, 1783. 5 Elliott, The Debates in the Several State Conventions on the Adoption of the Federal Constitution (2d ed. 1845) 66, 92, 93 (hereinafter cited Elliott); *cf.* 7 Burnett, *op. cit. supra* (1934) 499. Regarding the Congressional provision of troops to support Massachusetts, see 5 Elliott 94–95, 99; *cf. id.* at 108. As to the influence of the rebellion on the movement for the Constitution, see The Federalist (Lodge ed. 1908) Nos. 25, 74 (Hamilton), and 43 (Madison); 3 Elliott 82, 101, 180, 274 (Virginia Convention); 4 *id.* at 20, 96, 112, 220 (North Carolina), 282, 327 (South Carolina). See U.S. Const., Art. I, §§ 8, 9, Art. IV, § 4.

3. On the eve of the Federal Convention, the New York Act of Feb. 16, 1787, 2 Laws of the State of New York (1778–1789) (1789) 55, declared "That if any Person do levy War against the People of this State, within this State, or be adherent to the Enemies of the People of this State, or of the United States of *America,* within this State, giving to them Aid and Comfort in this State, or elsewhere, and be thereof, by good Proof, attainted of open Deed, such Offences, and none other, shall be adjudged Treason against the People of the State of *New-York.*"

A two-witness requirement in the terms of the Statute of 7 William III was also provided. The declaration that "none other" than the two named offenses should constitute treason was without precedent in state treason legislation. No clue to the origin of this language has been found in the available records of the legislature. (See Journal of the New York Assembly, 10th sess., 1787, at 9, 10, 14, 38, 40, 41, 45, 50, 54; Journal of the New York Senate, 10th sess., 1787, at 24, 25, 27, 29, 33; a further check of records available in Albany, made through the courtesy of Miss Frances D. Lyon, Law Librarian of the New York State Library, revealed no additional information.) There is no evidence that the act came to the attention of the Federal Convention. The *Journal* (p. 9) notes that the bill which became the Act of Feb. 16, 1787, was laid before the house by Mr. Jones, pursuant to the law for revising the laws of the state. Previously, the *Journal* notes (p. 5), it had been "Ordered that Mr. [Alexander] Hamilton, Mr. [Samuel] Jones, Mr. [John] Ray, Mr. J. [John] Livingston, Mr. C. [Caleb] Smith, or any 3 or more of them, be a Committee to inspect what laws are expired, or near expiring, and that they, from time to time report to the House which of them they judge necessary to be revived or continued, and likewise what new laws they shall conceive necessary to be made for the benefit of the State." There is no evidence that Hamilton urged a restrictive policy on treason in the Philadelphia Convention, though in *The Federalist,* he cites the treason clause as one item to answer the criticism that the Constitution lacked a proper bill of rights. See note 18 *infra.*

4. 2 Farrand, The Records of the Federal Convention of 1787 (1911) 136 (hereinafter cited Farrand). This is from the document which Farrand accepts as the best evidence of Pinckney's plan. In the version which Pinckney

sent John Quincy Adams, in December, 1818 when the latter was preparing the Journal of the Convention for publication, the treason section is similar to that in the Constitution. 3 *id.* at 598, 608. Since the general emphasis of the Pinckney plan seems to be on defining the federal relationship, it is likely that the grant of "exclusive" power to declare treasons was intended to exclude state legislative power, rather than to distinguish legislative-made from judge-made law.

5. See 1 Farrand 292.

6. *Id.* at 242–45. The resolution on treason, crossed out in Paterson's notebook, appeared in the copy of these resolutions, printed Feb. 15, 1788, in the Maryland Gazette and Baltimore Advertiser. Farrand thinks it "altogether probable" that the printer obtained the document from Luther Martin, who had stated in his *Genuine Information* that he had a copy of the New Jersey plan. 3 *id.* at 614.

7. See 2 Curtis, History of the Constitution of the United States (1861) 384; Meigs, Growth of the Constitution (1900) 252–54. Farrand, The Framing of the Constitution of the United States (1913) 48, advances the suggestion of the source of the committee's authority to draft the treason clause.

8. 2 Farrand 144, 168, 182; 4 Farrand, The Records of the Federal Convention of 1787 (rev. ed. 1937) 45.

9. Unless otherwise noted, all of the following incidents of the discussion of Aug. 20 will be found in 2 Farrand 345–50.

Note that Madison's argument bears out the conclusion reached in the examination of the colonial and state materials, that no notable legacy of protest against abuse of treason prosecutions had resulted; see Ch. 3, *supra*, at pp. 82, 86. Compare Madison's strictures on the too limited character of the offense with his comments in a letter of Oct. 18, 1787, to Washington, regarding Mason's objections to the Constitution. 3 Farrand 130; 5 Writings of James Madison (Hunt ed. 1904) 11, 13–14. Madison declares that it is proper, Mason's criticism to the contrary notwithstanding, that the Constitution does not "secure" the common law: "Since the Revolution every State has made great inroads & with great propriety in many instances on this *monarchical* code. . . . What could the Convention have done? If they had in general terms declared the Common law to be in force, they would have broken in upon the legal Code of every State in the most material points; they w^d have done more, they would have brought over from G. B. a thousand heterogeneous & antirepublican doctrines, and even the *ecclesiastical Hierarchy itself*, for that is a part of the Common law."

10. See 2 Farrand 337–39. This harmonizes with the statement of Dickinson, who "wished to know what was meant by the 'testimony of two witnesses,' whether they were to be witnesses to the same overt act or to different overt acts. He thought also that proof of an overt-act ought to be expressed as essential to the case." Dr. Johnson also "considered . . . that something should be inserted in the definition concerning overt-acts."

11. The other point in connection with treason which led to considerable discussion was the proposal to deprive the President of the power to pardon in such cases. This debate yields no help on the definition of the scope of the offense, save as it further indicates the general understanding that fundamental domestic disturbances were embraced within "treason." 2 Farrand 626–27. The concern manifested in this discussion of the pardon power, lest the President abuse it to protect his accomplices in an effort to take unconstitutional power to himself, seems the only instance in which the positive concern for the safety of the state qualified the Convention's general preoccupation with protection of the individual.

12. See 2 *id.* at 345, 348–49; 3 *id.* at 223.

13. *Cf.* Nott, The Mystery of the Pinckney Draught (1908) 187. Wilson speaks most positively in the discussions of the treason clause in the role of draftsman-technician. See 2 Farrand 346, 348–49.

14. 2 Papers of James Wilson, 1775–1792 (MSS. Pa. Hist. Soc.) 60. On p. 59 is a list of "Objections," none of which refers specifically to treason. No. 26 on this list, however, is: "Crimes shall be tried by Jury: therefore Congress may declare Crimes."

15. See 2 Elliott 469, 487; McMaster and Stone, Pennsylvania and the Federal Constitution (1888) 351–53; 3 Farrand 163, CL.

16. *Lectures on Law,* delivered in the College of Philadelphia 1790 and 1791, 3 Works of Hon. James Wilson (Bird Wilson ed. 1804) c. V, 95–106. (As a check on the completeness of the search of the Wilson papers, this study has enjoyed the counsel of the late Burton Alva Konkle, of Swarthmore, Pa., long a student of Wilson's career.)

17. 3 Works of Hon. James Wilson (Bird Wilson ed. 1804) 104.

18. Madison sets the tone of debate, in *The Federalist:* "As treason may be committed against the United States, the authority of the United States ought to be enabled to punish it. But as new-fangled and artificial treasons have been the great engines by which violent factions, the natural offspring of free government, have usually wreaked their alternate malignity on each other, the convention have, with great judgment, opposed a barrier to this peculiar danger, by inserting a constitutional definition of the crime, fixing the proof necessary for conviction of it, and restraining the Congress, even in punishing it, from extending the consequences of guilt beyond the person of its author." No. 43, at 269, 463. Madison here takes an advocate's position in interesting contrast to his opinion on the floor of the convention in favor of broader discretion for the legislature. However, this does not affect the relevance of his argument in *The Federalist,* as reflecting the prevailing thought by which the treason clause was believed justified. *Cf.* his warning, in his first speech in the Virginia ratifying convention, that in republics the turbulence, violence and abuse of power of majorities have more frequently than any other cause produced despotism. 3 Elliott 87.

In another number of *The Federalist,* Hamilton lists the treason section among several provisions protecting the liberties of the individual, in answer to the criticism of the absence of a bill of rights. No. 84, at 533, 534. In Massachusetts, "Cassius" (James Sullivan) asserted, of the treason clause: "This section is truly republican in every sense of the expression, and is of itself fully adequate to proving that the members of the federal convention were actuated by principles the most liberal and free—This single section alone is sufficient to enroll their proceedings on the records of immortal fame.

"Contrast this section with the laws of England, in regard to treason, and, notwithstanding the boasted rights of the subject in that isle, we shall find our own in this, as well as almost every other particular, far to exceed them." *Letters of Cassius,* X, 42, in Essays on the Constitution of the United States (Ford ed. 1892).

In North Carolina, "Marcus" (James Iredell) answered the objections which George Mason of Virginia had carried from the Convention to the hustings. Mason had raised the fear that under the "necessary and proper" clause in the enumeration of the powers of Congress, new crimes and unusual punishments might be created. Iredell pointed out that "in the case of treason, which usually in every country exposes men most to the avarice and rapacity of government, care is taken that the innocent family of the offender shall not suffer for the treason of their relation. This is the crime with respect to which a jealousy is of the most importance, and accordingly it is defined with great plainness and accuracy, and the temptations to abusive prosecutions guarded against as much as possible. . . ." Pamphlets on the Constitution of the United States (Ford ed. 1888) 360; 2 McRee, Life and Correspondence of James Iredell (1858) 199, 207. *Cf.* the numerous charges to federal grand juries, by Mr. Justice Iredell, in McRee.

19. 3 Elliott 102–103. Subsequently, without directly attacking the treason clause, Henry complained of the failure to forbid cruel and unusual punishments: "Congress, from their general powers, may fully go into business of human legislation. They may legislate, in criminal cases, from treason to the lowest offence—petty larceny. They may define crimes and prescribe punishments. In the definition of crimes, I trust they will be directed by what wise representatives ought to be governed by. But when we come to punishments, no latitude ought to be left, nor dependence put on the virtue of representatives."

The constitutionalist leaders were not men to let a point slip by, especially so flagrant a slip. Nicholas promptly corrected Henry: "But the gentleman says that . . . we are not free from torture. Treason against the United States is defined in the Constitution, and the forfeiture limited to the life of the person attainted. Congress have power to define and punish piracies and felonies committed on the high seas, and offences against the laws of nations; but they cannot define or prescribe the punishment of any other crime whatever, without violating the Constitution. . . ."

Randolph also caught up Henry on the point: "The honorable gentlemen observe that Congress might define punishments, from petty larceny to high treason. This is an unfortunate quotation for the gentlemen, because treason is expressly defined in the 3d section of the 3d article, and they can add no feature to it. They have not cognizance over any other crime except piracies, felonies committed on the high seas, and offences against the law of nations." 3 Elliott 447, 451, 466.

20. See 4 Elliott 176, 203, 205, 209. *Cf.* Iredell's reply to Lenoir, *id.* at 219, 220.

21. See remarks of General Brooks in the Massachusetts Convention, in Debates, Resolutions and other Proceedings of the Convention of the Commonwealth of Massachusetts (1856) 201; remarks of Messrs. Hartley and M'Kean, in the Pennsylvania Convention, McMaster and Stone, *op. cit. supra* note 15, at 291, 375.

22. "Some very remarkable instances [of the extension of the definition of treason] have occurred, even in so free a country as England. . . . A person possessed a favorite buck, and, on finding it killed, wished the horns in the belly of the person who killed it. This happened to be the king; the injured complainant was tried, and convicted of treason for wishing the king's death." Quoted in 2 Elliott 487.

23. On the issue of whether by acting as city gatekeeper by appointment of the British, Carlisle had, within the meaning of the Pennsylvania act, taken a "commission" from the enemy, Wilson cited Blackstone for the strict construction of penal statutes. 7 Pennsylvania Archives (Hazard ed. 1853) 50. In addition to the quotations on p. 136 *supra,* see the references to the "uncertain and ambiguous" state of the common law of treason, and to Hale's praise for "the great wisdom and care of the parliament, to keep judges within the bounds and express limits of this statute, and not to suffer them to run out, upon their own opinions, into constructive treasons, though in cases which seem to have a parity of reason." *Lectures on Law,* 3 Works, *op. cit. supra* note 16, at 96, 97.

24. *Cf.* Warren, The Making of the Constitution (1928) 489–90.

25. Charge Delivered to the Grand Jury for the District of Massachusetts, in the Circuit Court of the United States, Boston, Oct. 12, 1792, 2 McRee, *op. cit. supra* note 18, at 368. *Cf.* Marshall, C. J., in Marbury v. Madison, 1 Cranch 137, 179 (U. S. 1803). Iredell was not yet displaying the extreme Federalist position which marked his charges to juries in later years, and his emphasis on the limitation of judge-made treason may fairly be taken to reflect a prevailing attitude of 1789. *Cf.* his remarks in answer to Mason's objections to the Constitution, note 18 *supra.*

26. *Lectures on Law,* 3 Works, *op. cit. supra* note 16, at 99–100. These qualities had now been borrowed for the strengthening of the Constitution: "This single sentence comprehends our whole of national treason; and, as I mentioned before, is transcribed from a part of the statute of Edward the third. By those who proposed the national constitution, this was done, that, in a subject so essentially interesting to each and to all, not a single expression should be introduced, but such as could show in its favour, that it was recommended by the mature experience, and ascertained by the legal interpretation, of numerous revolving centuries." *Id.* at 100.

See, to the same effect, 2 Story, Commentaries on the Constitution of the United States (2d ed. 1851) 540.

27. See, *e.g.,* discussions in the Federal Convention and the ratifying debates regarding the proposal to limit the President's power to pardon in cases of treason, 2 Farrand 637, 639; 3 *id.* at 127, 158, 218; 4 *op. cit.* (rev. ed. 1937) at 59, 60. See also references to the guaranty of a republican form of government for the states and protection against insurrection: 2 *id.* at 47–49; The Federalist (Lodge ed. 1908) Nos. 25, 74 (Hamilton); 2 Elliott 430, 520–21; 3 *id.* at 497, 498; 4 *id.* at 20, 96, 112, 195, 220; *cf.* terms of amendments proposed in ratifying conventions, 1 *id.* at 325, 326 (disarming citizens), 327, 328, 334, 335; 2 *id.* at 542, 546; 3 *id.* at 657–58; 4 *id.* at 245, 249 (martial law in time of insurrection). *Cf.* Charge of Mr. Justice Story on the Law of Treason, Delivered to the Grand Jury of the Circuit Court of the United States, Holden at Newport, for the Rhode-Island District, June 15, 1842, 30 Fed. Cas. 1046, No. 18, 275 (C.C.D.R.I. 1842).

28. See note 26 *supra. Cf.* the same problem as posed by Jefferson's use of the terms of the Statute of Edward III in his proposed revision of the Virginia criminal code, in Ch. 3, pp. 87–89 *supra. Cf.* 8 Holdsworth, History of English Law (2d ed. 1937) 318 (hereinafter cited Holdsworth).

29. *Cf.* McKinney, *Treason under the Constitution of the United States* (1918) 12 Ill. L. Rev. 381; Warren, *What is Giving Aid and Comfort to the Enemy?* (1918) 27 Yale L. J. 331.

30. The concern shown in the Convention discussion that the phrase regarding "aid and comfort" be added to "adhering" in order to limit the latter, shows that a theory of a wholesale liberal construction of this offense is not supportable. See pp. 132–133 *supra.*

31. 2 Farrand 348.

32. 2 Elliott 469.

33. See notes 15, 16 *supra; Lectures on Law,* 3 Works of Hon. James Wilson (Bird Wilson ed. 1804) 96, 98, 99. It should be remembered, however, that as counsel for the defense in the *Carlisle* case in 1778, Wilson had argued for a strict construction of the Pennsylvania statute defining adherence to the enemy. See Ch. 3, pp. 85, 90 *supra,* and note 23 *supra.*

34. (Lodge ed. 1908) No. 43, at 269, 463. *Cf. id.* No. 74 (Hamilton); 4 Tucker, *op. cit. infra* note 42, at App., Note B, 11, 40–41.

35. The quotations are from Iredell (note 18 *supra*); "Cassius" (note 18 *supra*); and Hartley (note 21 *supra*). *Cf.* grand jury charges of Iredell, J., in 2 McRee, *op. cit. supra* note 18, at 391 (1793), 468 (1796).

36. 5 King, Life and Correspondence of Rufus King (1898) 73–75. *Cf.* Hamilton's opinion against the radical treason act proposed by Lloyd in 1798, in a letter of June 29, 1798, to Wolcott: "Let us not establish a tyranny. Energy is a very different thing from violence." 6 Hamilton, Works (1851) 307. 3 Adams, History of the United States (1890) 468, after noting that laymen might think Marshall could have reached another result in some of his rulings in the *Burr* trial, if he had so chosen, comments: "On the other hand, the intent of the Constitution was clear. The men who framed that

instrument remembered the crimes that had been perpetrated under the pretence of justice; for the most part they had been traitors themselves, and having risked their necks under the law they feared despotism and arbitrary power more than they feared treason. No one could doubt that their sympathies, at least in 1788, when the Constitution was framed, would have been on the side of Marshall's decision. If Jefferson, since 1788, had changed his point of view, the chief-justice was not under obligations to imitate him."

37. Richard Dobbs Spaight, a member of the Philadelphia convention, expressed astonishment at the extreme fears about the treason clause voiced by some opponents of the Constitution: "But the gentleman . . . says, that any man who will complain of their oppressions, or write against their usurpation, may be deemed a traitor. . . . What an astonishing misrepresentation! Why did not the gentleman look at the Constitution, and see their powers? Treason is there defined. . . . Complaining, therefore, or writing, cannot be treason." 4 Elliott 205, 209.

38. See note 27 *supra*.

39. See pp. 133–134 *supra*.

40. 1 Stat. 112 (1790) c. IX, § 1, 18 U. S. C. § 1 (1940). The penalty provision was subsequently modified by the addition of alternative penalties of fine and imprisonment. The Journal of Senator Maclay (Harris, ed. 1880) 128, 129, 158, 163, 164, 165, records stages in the passage of the bill containing the treason section through the Senate. He notes that there was little debate on any aspect of the bill and records no mention of the treason section.

41. By the Act of Sept. 6, 1788, c. VI, the governor and judges of the Northwest Territory adopted a "Law respecting Crimes and Punishments" which declared the offense of treason against the United States and against the territory, in terms reminiscent of the Revolutionary period, and in several respects probably in excess of the constitutional provision (conspiracy included; no evidentiary provision). See The Laws of the Northwest Territory, 1788–1800 (Pease ed. 1925), 17 Collections of Illinois State Historical Library, 1 Law Series 13; *cf. id.* at 322. The territorial laws were so obviously inartistic, however, that this act cannot be taken seriously as a contemporary exposition of what crimes might be defined under the constitutional provision.

42. See Rawle, A View of the Constitution of the United States (2d ed. 1829) 139 ff.; Sergeant, Constitutional Law (1822) 367; 2 Story, Commentaries on the Constitution of the United States (2d ed. 1851) 539–40; 4 Tucker's Blackstone's Commentaries with Notes of Reference, to the Constitution and Laws of the Federal Government of the United States and of the Commonwealth of Virginia (1803) 74, n.1; 75, n.2; 76, n.3; App., Note B, ii, 16–17, 39, 40–41.

Rawle, however, does analyze the overt act element of the crime in a fashion which implies that the scope of the offense should be sufficiently broad to give preventitive protection to the state, when he says: "It is one of those crimes which may not be accomplished by a single act; but, on the contrary, is in its very nature progressive yet continuous. Robbery, murder, and many other crimes, are or may be effectuated in a short space of time; and when the body is deprived of life or the goods are taken from the spot, the perpetration of the guilt is full and entire: but the attempt to subvert a government is not a momentary act; combinations are formed, unlawful schemes devised and pursued; opposition is commenced and carried on, and the crime is ever the same; the protraction of time may increase the terror and the injury, but in a legal view they do not enhance the guilt: in its outset it is deemed the highest crime that can be committed, and of course, no subsequent circumstances can raise it higher." Rawle, *op. cit.* 141.

43. In the Philadelphia Convention, see Madison, 2 Farrand 345, 346; King, *id.* at 347, 348. In the ratifying debates, see pp. 136–138 *supra.* See also *Ex parte* Bollman, 4 Cranch 75, 125 (U. S. 1807); Stephan v. United States, 133 F.(2d) 87, 90 (C. C. A. 6th, 1943), *cert. denied,* 318 U. S. 781 (1943); United States v. Haupt, 47 F. Supp. 832, 834, 836 (N. D. Ill. 9142) (on demurrer to indictment), *rev'd on other grounds,* 136 F.(2d) 661 (C. C. A. 7th, 1943); Wimmer v. United States, 264 Fed. 11, 13, (C. C. A. 6th 1920), *cert. denied,* 253 U. S. 494 (1920); United States v. Greathouse, 26 Fed. Cas. No. 15, 254, at 21 (C. C. N. D. Cal. 1863); charge to grand jury, by Nelson, J., 30 Fed Cas. No. 18,271, at 1035 (C. C. S. D. N. Y. 1861); United States v. Hanway, 26 Fed. Cas. No. 15,299, at 126 (C. C. E. D. Pa. 1851); United States v. Hoxie, 26 Fed. Cas. No. 15,407, at 398 (C. C, D. Vt. 1808); United States v. Burr, 25 Fed. Cas. No. 14,692a, at 13 (C. C. D. Va. 1807) (on motion to commit); Iredell, J., and Peters, J., in charge to the jury, in Case of Fries, 9 Fed. Cas. No. 5126, at 909, 910 (C. C. D. Pa. 1799). Executive constructions to the same effect may be seen in Adams' pardon of those convicted in "Fries' Rebellion," and in Van Buren's caution to President Jackson concerning the application of the law of treason to the South Carolina nullification controversy of 1832.

44. See United States v. Burr, 25 Fed. Cas. 55, No. 14,693 (C. C. D. Va. 1807).

45. See note 24 *supra.* Following the acquittal of Burr on what amounted to a directed verdict, Senator Giles introduced a bill to spell out certain conduct which should constitute treason. See 17 Annals of Cong. (1852) 108–109; Anderson, William Branch Giles (1914) 115–21. Though inartistically drawn and vague in scope, this bill would certainly have extended the concept of principals in treason as laid down by Marshall, J., under the constitutional definition, in the *Burr* case; and it may also have been designed in effect to include conspiracy to levy war within the offense. The eventual dropping of the bill was probably due to considerations of politics, but in the debates, Senators Mitchell and Pope objected that it was unconstitutional for Congress to undertake further to specify the constitutionally fixed definition of treason. They criticized the bill for extending the crime, but also took the fundamental position that Congress lacked power to pass even declaratory legislation. See 17 Annals of Cong. (1852) 109, 110–11, 138, 139, 141, 143, 145. Giles replied, in part, that, "The word 'only' . . . in this clause relates

only to the species of treasons embraced by it, and not to any particular acts which may amount to treason under either of these species." *Id.* at 117–19. As has been noted, the framers apparently intended to take the words of the Statute of Edward III, to some ill-defined extent, with the judicial gloss which had been put on them, and this lends color to Giles' argument. In substance, however, the contention fits poorly into the dominant restrictive emphasis of the treason clause. Giles' further reliance on the "necessary and proper" clause begs the question; there may be power to create lesser crimes of a subversive character (see pp. 151–152 *infra*), but on its face Art. III, § 3 deprives Congress of any authority over the scope of treason to which a power under the "necessary and proper" clause could be ancillary. See Senator Pope, *id.* at 141–45.

46. Congress seems to have intended to do this in the Act of July 17, 1862, 12 Stat. 589 (1862), 18 U. S. C. § 2 (1940) which, so interpreted, Field, J., treated as valid in United States v. Greathouse, 26 Fed. Cas. No. 15,254, at 23–24 (C. C. N. D. Cal. 1863). *Cf.* the Sedition Act of 1798, which was treated not as setting penalties for different grades of treason, but as creating distinct, if lesser, offenses. See Iredell, J., and Peters, J., in Case of Fries, 9 Fed. Cas. No. 5126, at 909, 910 ff. (C. C. D. Pa. 1799); answer of Chase, J., to impeachment charges, (Note) 9 Fed. Cas. 934, 939 (1800).

47. *Cf.* Stephan v. United States, 133 F.(2d) 87, 90 (C. C. A. 6th, 1943), *cert. denied,* 318 U. S. 781 (1943); United States v. Werner, 247 Fed. 708, 709 (E. D. Pa. 1918); charge to grand jury by Nelson, J., 30 Fed. Cas. No. 18,271, at 1035 (C. C. S. D. N. Y. 1861); United States v. Greathouse, 26 Fed. Cas. No. 15,254, at 21 (C. C. N. D. Cal. 1863); United States v. Hanway, 26 Fed. Cas. No. 15,299, at 126 (C. C. E. D. Pa. 1851); United States v. Hoxie, 26 Fed. Cas. No. 15,407, at 397, 400 (C. C. D. Vt. 1808); see Case of Fries, 9 Fed. Cas. No. 5126, at 909, 910 (C. C. D. Pa. 1799).

48. *Cf.* United States v. Greathouse, 26 Fed. Cas. No. 15,254, at 24 (C. C. N. D. Cal. 1863); charge to grand jury by Smalley, J., 30 Fed. Cas. No. 18,270, at 1033 (C. C. S. D. N. Y. 1861); United States v. Greiner, 26 Fed. Cas. No. 15,262, at 39–40 (E. D. Pa. 1861); see Case of Fries, 9 Fed. Cas. No. 5126, at 909 (C. C. D. Pa. 1799).

49. Congress has of course exercised its power to reduce the penalty; since the Civil War the death penalty—the only punishment under the first treason act—has been balanced by an alternative of fine and imprisonment. The apparently unlimited power of Congress over the jurisdiction of federal courts would also contribute to the illusory character of a ban on "diminishing" the scope of the crime. *Cf. Ex parte* McCardle, 6 Wall. 318 (U. S. 1867). A state may not authorize its courts to prosecute federal statutory crimes, without congressional approval. It might be argued that this is not true of a crime defined by the United States Constitution, which the state judges are sworn to uphold. But state courts have declared themselves to lack jurisdiction of charges of treason against the United States. People v. Lynch, 11 Johns. 549 (N. Y. 1814); *Ex parte* Quarrier, 2 W. Va. 569 (1866). Moreover, in view of the legislative construction evidenced by the promptness with which the first

Congress declared the crime of treason, substantially in the terms of the Constitution, it might be argued that Art, III, § 3 is not self-executing.

50. See note 27 *supra*.

51. See pp. 133–144 *supra*.

52. See United States v. Haupt, 136 F.(2d) 661, 671, 674, 675 (C. C. A. 7th, 1943); United States v. Robinson, 259 Fed. 685, 694 (S. D. N. Y. 1919); charge to grand jury by Sprague, J., 30 Fed. Cas. No. 18,273, at 1040 (D. Mass. 1861); charge to grand jury by Nelson, J., 30 Fed. Cas. No. 18,271, at 1035 (C. C. S. D. N. Y. 1861); United States v. Greiner, 26 Fed. Cas. No. 15,262, at 40 (E. D. Pa. 1861); Iredell, J., in charge to grand jury, Case of Fries, 9 Fed. Cas. No. 5126, at 840–41 (C. C. D. Pa. 1799) (*cf.* charge to trial jury, *id.* at 909, 914); United States v. Magtibay, 2 Philipp. 703, 705 (1903). *But cf.* Stephan v. United States, 133 F(2d) 87, 94 (C. C. A. 6th, 1943), *cert. denied*, 318 U. S. 781 (1943); United States v. Fricke, 259 Fed. 673, 677, (S. D. N. Y. 1919); Kane, J., in charge to grand jury, 30 Fed. Cas. No. 18,276, at 1049 (E. D. Pa. 1851); Paterson, J., in United States v. Mitchell, 26 Fed. Cas. No. 15,788, at 1280 (C. C. D. Pa. 1795).

53. 317 U. S. 1 (1942).

54. *Id.* at 38. *Cf.* Smith v. Shaw, 12 Johns. 257 (N. Y. 1815); In the Matter of Robert Martin, 45 Barb. 142 (N. Y. 1865).

55. Though such rulings may have the effect of giving trial judges a desirably greater latitude in adjusting the severity of penalty to the viciousness of the criminal, they seem objectionably formalistic from a constitutional point of view, and difficult to reconcile with the substantive policy of the double jeopardy clause. *Cf.* 2 Selected Essays on Constitutional Law (Ass'n of American Law Schools ed. 1938) 1368; Note (1932) 45 Harv. L. Rev. 535.

56. As in Frohwerk v. United States, 249 U. S. 204 (1919), (see p. 160 *infra*), so in Ex parte *Quirin*, the possible bearing of the treason clause on the validity of the prosecution was not satisfactorily explored in the briefs. The defense did not rely on Art. III, § 3. The prosecution argued in part that defendant Haupt had renounced his American citizenship (a contention on which the Court found it unnecessary to pass); and in part, apparently, that Art. III, § 3 defines a civil crime, which must be deemed to be modified in application by the historic scope of the military jurisdiction, imported by the war powers grant to Congress. The Court has, it is true, recognized the two-witness requirement of Art. III, § 3, as one of the procedural guaranties of the Constitution, like that of trial by jury and similar safeguards which a majority of the court defended from the encroachment of military jurisdiction in *Ex parte* Milligan, 4 Wall. 2 (U. S. 1866). See Chambers v. Florida, 309 U. S. 227, 236 (1940). Thus, insofar as the Court satisfied itself in the *Quirin* case that Ex parte *Milligan* did not bar the military jurisdiction, it might be thought to answer any question raised under the procedural guaranty of the treason clause. But the fact that the Court went out of its way to employ the questionable analogy of the double jeopardy decisions to show that treason

was not the gravamen of the charge against Haupt suggests that the particular historic policy represented by Art. III, § 3 might present an uncomfortable issue to the proponents of military jurisdiction, even where the more general doctrine of Ex parte *Milligan* is satisfied. See Robinson, Justice in Grey (1941) 380–81.

It should be noted, also, that even if the procedural (two-witness) aspect of the treason clause is ruled to be superseded by military jurisdiction, the question remains, whether the constitutional definition of treason may set some limits to the substantive scope of crimes of betrayal of allegiance under the laws of war. This issue was implicit in the trial of Vallandigham, before a military commission, for disloyal utterances; but it is not clear whether he relied in part on the restrictive policy of the treason clause when he contended there that "the alleged 'offense' is not known to the Constitution of the United States, nor to any law thereof." See *The Trial of Clement L. vallandigham,* 1 American State Trials (Lawson ed. 1914) 699, 713. The argument from the treason clause was relied on in petitioner's contention in Ex *parte* Vallandigham, 28 Fed. Cas. No. 16,816, at 886–88, 889 (C. C. S. D. Ohio, 1863), but was not passed on by the courts, which ruled that they lacked jurisdiction. See *Ex parte* Vallandigham, 1 Wall. 243 (U. S. 1863). The military prosecutions out of which came Ex parte *Milligan* in substance presented only the issue of military versus civil jurisdiction, and not that of the possible effect of the treason clause in limiting the substantive scope of subversive crimes under the laws of war, for the conduct charged seems clearly to have involved treason. See Pitman, The Trials for Treason at Indianapolis (1865); The Milligan Case (Klaus ed. 1929) 24; Milton, Abraham Lincoln and the Fifth Column 170, c.8.

57. This seems to have been a significant factor in the provision of fine and imprisonment as an alternative to the death penalty, by the Act of July 17, 1862. See Cong. Globe, 37th Cong., 2d Sess. (1862) 2165, 2166, 2167–68, 2169, 2173; cf. id. at 2199. See Cummings and McFarland, Federal Justice (1937) 192, 193; Robinson, Justice in Grey (1941) 202 n., 296; Kenny, Outlines of Criminal Law (15th ed. 1936) 315–16.

58. A penalty may be "cruel and unusual" because unreasonably disproportionate to the offense. Weems v. United States, 217 U. S. 349 (1910); see Chambers v. Florida, 309 U. S. 227, 236 (1940). The contention that severe penalties possible under sedition acts are so disproportionate as to violate the Eighth Amendment has not met with success, and it seems that no legislative excess short of including capital punishment would run afoul of this provision. Cf. Dunne v. United States, 138 F.(2d) 137, 140 (C. C. A. 8th, 1943), cert. denied, 320 U. S. 790 (1943); Chafee, Free Speech in the United States (1941) 480. But cf. Herndon v. Lowry, 301 U. S. 242 (1937); Chafee, op. cit. 396. See 1 Schofield, Essays on Constitutional Law and Equity (1921) 421.

59. See Baldwin, Whiskey Rebels (1939) 266, 269–70; Burgoyne, Homestead (1893) c. XV; Cummings and McFarland, Federal Justice (1937) 68; 2

Morison, Life and Letters of Harrison Gray Otis (1913) 80, 126; Stowell, "Fort Frick" or the Siege of Homestead (1893) c. XXIX; 2 Warren, The Supreme Court in United States History (rev. ed. 1935) 299–30.

60. *Cf.* Foster, A Report of Some Proceedings on the Commission for the Trial of the Rebels in the Year 1746 in the County of Surry; and of other Crown Cases (3d ed. 1792) 196–97.

61. See the examples given on pp. 212–217 of conduct held sufficient as an overt act of treason, though innocent on its face.

62. In the Philadelphia Convention, Rufus King seems to have regarded the effort to limit the application of the death penalty for subversive crimes as the central motive of the restrictive definition of treason, though he was skeptical of the practical results to be achieved. See 2 Farrand 347, 348. *Cf.* the implications of the remarks of Wilson and Iredell, notes 15, 18 *supra.* In the debate over the Act of July 17, 1862, Senator Clark (N. H.) indicated his belief that a crime was not treason, and hence the two-witness requirement did not apply, if the death penalty was not provided. Cong. Globe, 37th Cong., 2d Sess. (1862) 2169; *cf.* note 56 *supra.* This seems clearly an erroneous interpretation of Art. III, § 3, if only because the broad power there allowed to Congress to fix the penalty negates the idea that the penalty defines the crime.

63. See p. 143 *supra; cf.* note 59 *supra.*

64. *Cf.* Anderson, J., dissenting in Taylor v. State, 194 Miss. 1, 54–57, 11 So. (2d) 663, 681–82 (1943) (*rev'd sub nom.* Taylor v. Mississippi, 319 U. S. 583 (1943), on basis of the First Amendment). See 3 Holdsworth 289–90, 292.

65. See 10 Oxford English Dictionary (Murray ed. 1926) 304; 2 Holdsworth 450; 3 *id.* at 289–93; 4 *id.* (1925) at 492–500; 8 *id.* at 307–322.

66. Coke, Third Part of the Institutes of the Laws of England (5th ed. 1671) includes in his catalog of crimes the separate offenses of misprision of treason (p. 36), felony by 3 H. 7 for a member of the King's household to compass the King's death or that of a Privy Counsellor (p. 37), heresy (p. 39), receiving Jesuits (p. 101), praemunire (p. 119). See, likewise, 4 Blackstone, Commentaries on the Laws of England (1770) c. IV, VII, VIII, IX; 1 Hale, History of the Pleas of the Crown (Emlyn ed. 1736) 371, 383, 662, 681, 687–90; 1 Hawkins, Treatise of the Pleas of the Crown (7th, Leach, ed. 1795) 6, 22–83, 127, 128, 130, 149, 151. *Cf.* 2 Holdsworth 451, 452; 4 *id* (1925) at 506; 8 *id.* at 322, 327, 328, 403.

67. See chapter 3, *supra, passim.*

68. The only comment in point is the brief observation by Rufus King "that the controversy relating to Treason might be of less magnitude than was supposed; as the legislature might punish capitally under other names than Treason." 2 Farrand 347. There is no direct indication of what his colleagues thought of this interpretation; but King's remark did not stop the detailed discussion of restrictive phrasing for the definition. Moreover, his comment was made in the context of a discussion of whether, because of the same conduct, an individual might be guilty of treason against both the nation and a state, and hence its relevance is questionable when the issue is

not one of the distribution of powers within the federal system, but the scope of the treason clause as a part of the Bill of Rights. *Cf.* 2 Farrand 348. Though his view was undoubtedly colored by partisanship, King later took a stronger stand on the treason clause as a guaranty of individual liberty. See note 36 *supra.*

69. 1 Stat. 112 (1790), 18 U. S. C. §§ 1, 2, 3, (1940). *Cf.* Report of a select committee to consider petitions for repeal of the Alien and Sedition Laws, 9 Annals of Cong. (1851) 2985, 2988. § 14 of the Act of April 30, 1790 punished counterfeiting public securities of the United States. State v. M'Donald, 4 Port. 449, 462–63 (Ala. 1837), relies on this to show that the treason clause has not been deemed to prevent the Congress from denouncing as criminal conduct which was once treason in England. But counterfeiting seems to have a peculiar history which robs it of any such broad significance in this connection. It was included in the Statute of Edward III apparently because of borrowing of the Roman concept that the offense was a sacrilege against the emperor, whose image appeared on the coin, or perhaps also as a protection of what was regarded as a personal prerogative of the king, and not because it was regarded as a political offense. See 2 Pollock and Maitland, History of English Law (2d ed. 1923) 505; 3 Holdsworth 289. Thus, no more weight should be given to its inclusion in "treason" than to the fact that at times that crime was extended to cover murder, assault, or extortion. See 2 *id.* at 450; 3 *id.* at 289; 4 *id.* (1925) at 498.

70. See § 1 of the Act of July 14, 1798, 1 Stat. 596 (1798); *cf.* 1 Stat. 613 (1799), See also the remarks of Albert Gallatin and John Nicholas, 8 Annals of Cong. (1851) 2111; 9 *id.* at 3003; *cf.* Report of a select committee to consider petitions for repeal of the Alien and Sedition Laws, *id.* at 2987.

71. 4 Cranch 75, 126 (U. S. 1807). *Cf.* Iredell, J., and Peters, J., in charge to jury in Case of Fries, 9 Fed. Cas. No. 5126, at 909, 910 (C. C. D. Pa. 1799); answer of Chase, J., to impeachment charges, (Note) 9 Fed. Cas. 934, 939 (1800) In 1807, following the acquittal of Burr, Attorney General Rodney gave his opinion that the Congress could constitutionally make conspiracy to levy war a separate offense of "conspiracy to commit treason against the United States," punishable by fine: "The Constitution has wisely defined the crime of treason; but it must be obvious that, before this crime is consummated by an overt act of levying war, the public peace may be disturbed and the public safety endangered, by the previous preparations for such an event." Caesar A. Rodney to Hon. John Randolph, Dec. 2, 1807, 1 American State Papers (1834) 717; 18 Annals of Cong. (1852) 1718–19. The provision considered by Rodney was contained in substantially similar form both in the bill introduced in the Senate by Giles and that sponsored in the House by Randolph, as rebukes to Marshall's rulings in the *Burr* trial. See 17 Annals of Cong. (1852) 105; 18 *id.* at 1717. See Senator Pope's attack on the constitutionality of this conspiracy legislation. 17 *id.* at 147, 148.

The historic coexistence of other subversive crimes with that of treason certainly presents a more convincing argument against a sweeping interpretation of the treason clause restrictions than either of two other contentions which might be advanced. (1) It might be argued that since the betrayal of either a "natural" or a "local" allegiance is an historic element of treason, a crime against the security of the state which did not involve any such element of allegiance could not in any event fall within any ban set by the treason clause. *But cf.* People v. Lloyd, 304 Ill. 23, 42–43, 136 N. E. 505, 515 (1922). Of course a prosecution against a person in fact owing no kind of allegiance could not be limited by Art. III, § 3. *Cf. Ex parte* Quirin, 317 U. S. 1, 38 (1942). But plainly the treason clause was intended as one of the protective benefits accruing to those who did owe allegiance to this government, and it would seem a clear evasion of the constitutional policy if one might convict a person owing allegiance for that for which he could not be convicted if the allegation of allegiance were an element of the offense. (2) It might be argued that it is historically characteristic of the genus "treason" that it is a capital offense, and that, therefore, if the legislature sets a lower maximum penalty, "treason" is no longer involved in any sense. *Cf.* Peters, J., in Case of Fries, *loc. cit. supra.* But the fact that the Constitution couples its careful restrictions on "treason" with a broad grant of power to Congress to fix the penalty seems sufficient to show that the degree of punishment was not regarded as the essential criterion of the offense.

72. See p. 87 *supra.* Inspired by the assassination of Garfield and McKinley, an amendment was proposed to include in the treason definition attempts to murder the President. See Musmanno, Proposed Amendments to the Constitution (1889); H. R. Doc. No. 551, 70th Cong., 2nd Sess. (1929) 148.

73. See 8 Holdsworth (1925) 314–15; Chapter 2, *supra.* Of course the growth of constructive levying of war was in its way an equally expansive use of "treason" to suppress such competition of interests in the community as was objectionable to those holding power. But these cases do, nevertheless, involve breaches of the peace; and hence do not present as clear-cut a basis for a guaranty against abusive prosecutions as where peaceful political processes are involved.

74. 8 Holdsworth (1925) 309.

75. 8 Holdsworth (1925) 311, 312–13, 315, 316–18.

76. See Chapter 2.

77. See Coke, *op. cit. supra* note 66, at 174 (see 8 Holdsworth (1925) 339 on cases in *Coke's Reports*); 4 Blackstone, *op. cit. supra* note 66, at 123, 150–53; 1 Hawkins, *op. cit. supra* note 66, c. 23, p. 151.

78. See Chafee, *op. cit. supra* note 58, at 18; *cf. id.* at 16–17, 20–22.

79. See notes 34–36 *supra.* As will be seen in chapter 5, this policy factor has bulked large in the first judicial explanations of the policy represented by the treason clause.

80. See pp. 188–189, 200–201, 206.

81. See United States v. Werner, 247 Fed. 708 (E. D. Pa. 1918), *aff'd,* 251 U. S. 466 (1920), and cases cited in note 118 *infra;* Michael and Wechsler, Criminal Law and Its Administration (1940) 1144 n.; Robinson, Justice in Grey (1941) 288; Black, *Debs v. The United States — A Judicial Milepost on the*

Road to Absolutism (1932) 81 U. of Pa. L. Rev. 160, 161–62, 170; Hall, *Criminal Attempt* (1940) 49 Yale L. J. 789, 818; Sears, *Civil Liberties in Wartime*, in War and the Law (Puttkammer ed. 1944) 17. *Cf.* Herndon v. Lowry, 301 U. S. 242 (1937), and Chafee, *op. cit. supra* note 58, at 391, 396.

82. See note 18 *supra; cf.* Chafee, *op. cit. supra* note 58, at 19–20. Schofield observes: "Many of the publications on politics in the Colonies before the Revolution were seditious and even treasonable under the English common law and its administration. One of the objects of the Revolution was to get rid of the English common law on liberty of speech and of the press." He cites the declaration of principle of the Continental Congress of 1774, and the Virginia religious liberties act of 1777. 2 Essays on Constitutional Law and Equity (1921) 510, 521–22. Madison's original coolness to the insertion of a restrictive definition of treason in the Constitution (see p. 130 *supra*) is hard to understand, and is at variance with his general philosophy.

83. See Chafee, *op. cit. supra* note 58, at 16–18.

84. See 2 Elliott 78, 339, 436, 449, 453 ff., 488 ff., 540; 3 *id.* at 191, 202–204, 246; 4 *id.* at 139–41, 148–49, 259–60, 315.

85. 3 *id.* at 46, 51, 103; *cf.* note 99 *infra*. And when Henry incautiously argued that Congress "may legislate, in criminal cases, from treason to the lowest offense," Nicholas and Randolph both pounced on him, to assert that, the new government being one of delegated powers only, the effect of the few precisely defined powers granted Congress in this field was to exclude the creation of any additional offenses. 3 Elliott 451, 466.

86. 4 Elliott 209, 219. Subsequently, James Iredell underlined and expounded at greater length the point made by Spaight: "A gentleman who spoke some time ago (Mr. Lenoir) observed, that the government might make it treason to write against the most arbitrary proceedings. He corrected himself afterwards, by saying he meant *misprision of treason*. . . . Where is the power given to them to do this? They have power to define and punish piracies and felonies committed on the high seas, and offences against the law of nations. They have no power to define any other crime whatever."

The persistent Lenoir rose to declare that he meant such punishments might be inflicted within the federal district, where the new government would have exclusive powers of legislation. Iredell's final answer to this was to recur to the character of the government as one of delegated powers: "The powers of the government are particularly enumerated and defined; they can claim no others such as are so enumerated. In my opinion, they are excluded as much from the exercise of any other authority as they could be by the strongest negative clause that could be framed." *Id.* at 219, 220.

So also in the Pennsylvania convention, Hartley, after making the familiar argument that a bill of rights was unnecessary because the new government possessed only those powers granted to it, which did not include authority to commit the abuses feared by its opponents, linked this contention with the significance of the treason clause: "Some articles, indeed from their pre-eminence in the scale of political security, deserve to be particularly specified, and these have not been omitted in the system before us. The definition of treason, the writ of habeas corpus, and the trial by jury in criminal cases, are here expressly provided for; and in going thus far, solid foundation has been laid." McMaster and Stone, *op. cit. supra* note 15, at 291, 375.

87. See note 71 *supra;* Legal Tender Cases, 12 Wall. 457, 535 (U. S. 1872).

88. See note 86 *supra.* Significant in this respect is the absence of any substantial criticism of abuses of treason trials in the pre-Constitutional period. See p. 126 *supra; cf.* pp. 91–92 *supra.*

89. Thus note the bold sweep with which the policy of the First Amendment is painted, in Madison's report of the committee of the Virginia House of Delegates, to which was referred the communications of various states regarding the Virginia Resolutions on the Alien and Sedition Laws. 4 Elliott 596–98; Sen. Doc. No. 873, 62d Cong., 2d Sess. (1912) 148 ff.

90. Alleged violations of the guaranty of a republican form of government have been held, of course, to present only political, nonjusticiable issues. But, as the discussion in the Convention hereafter noted shows, any effort by violence to deprive a state of a republican form of government would undoubtedly involve conduct amounting to a levying of war against the United States. This link between Art. III, § 3, and Art. IV, § 4, was made explicit by Tench Coxe: "The United States guarantee to every state in the union a separate republican form of government. From thence it follows, that any man or body of men, however rich or powerful, who shall make an alteration in the form of government of any state, whereby the powers thereof shall be attempted to be taken out of the hands of the people at large will stand guilty of high treason; or should a foreign power seduce or over-awe the people of any state, so as to cause them to vest in the families of any ambitious citizens or foreigners the powers of hereditary governors, whether as Kings or Nobles, that such investment of powers would be void in itself, and every person attempting to execute them would also be guilty of treason." *An Examination of the Constitution for the United States of America,* No. IV, reprinted in Ford, *op. cit. supra* note 18, at 145–46. Coxe, it will be noted, does not seem to limit his doctrine to cases of violence; but it may be doubted that, practically, the situation of a peaceful change of the frame of government would arise.

91. 2 Farrand 47.

92. *Id.* at 47–49. Mason summed up the position by pointing out that "if the Genl. Govt. should have no right to suppress rebellions agst. particular States, it will be in a bad situation indeed. As Rebellions agst. itself originate in & agst. individual States, it must remain a passive Spectator of its own subversion." *Id.* at 47. And Gorham further pointed up the underlying policy, when he commented: "With regard to different parties in a State; as long as they confine their disputes to words they will be harmless to the Genl. Govt. & to each other. If they appeal to the sword it will then be necessary for the Genl. Govt., however difficult it may be to decide on the merits of their contest, to interpose & put an end to it." *Id.* at 48.

93. See *id.* at 47–49; *cf.* note 27 *supra.*

94. See, in the Philadelphia Convention, Randolph, 2 Farrand 48; Iredell, in the North Carolina ratifying convention, 4 Elliott 195; Tench Coxe, note 90 *supra*. *Cf.* President Jackson's view that the enactment by a state legislature of militia legislation to implement a decision to secede from the Union would be an overt act of treason. 2 Messages and Papers of the Presidents (Richardson ed. 1927) 1173, 1184–86, 1203, 1217; see the exchange between Jackson and Van Buren, 4 Correspondence of Andrew Jackson (Bassett ed. 1929) 500, 506, 507; 5 *id.* at 3.

95. See p. 151 *supra*.

96. Act of July 14, 1798, § 1, 1 Stat. 506 (1798), 18 U. S. C. § 6 (1940).

97. See note 9 *supra*.

98. 8 Annals of Cong. (1851) 2158; *cf. id.* at 2159; Adams, Life of Albert Gallatin (1879) 204.

99. See Sen. Doc. No. 873, 62d Cong., 2d Sess. (1912) *passim*. Likewise, George Nicholas, who had advanced the treason clause in praise of the Constitution in the Virginia ratifying debate (note 19 *supra*) did not rely on that guaranty in his attack on the Sedition Act. See A Letter from George Nicholas, of Kentucky, to His Friend, in Virginia (reprint, 1799) 12–13, making the familiar arguments from the lack of any affirmative grant of power to Congress to pass such legislation, and from the First Amendment. *Cf.* Carroll, *Freedom of Speech and of the Press in the Federalist Period; The Sedition Act* (1920) 18 Mich. L. Rev. 615, 618.

100. See 2 Parrington, Main Currents in American Thought (1927) 14–19.

101. Sen Doc. No. 873 62d Cong., 2d Sess. (1912) 85.

102. *Id.* at 99–100. Earlier, mingling the arguments from the treason clause and the First Amendment, Taylor had said: "a power to restrain treason was more necessary in a Government than to regulate sedition; that our Constitution had yet limited the power over treason to a few cases. . . . However, Congress might still regulate punishment in case of treason, and it was possible that they might establish in such case a punishment short of death, a punishment even inferior to that of sedition. What then would result? Treason was the genus, sedition a species. If the first were limited and the second not, what security had we? He then read the 3d article of the amendments to the Constitution [sic] concerning freedom of speech, etc., and asked in what sense this clause was understood at the time of adoption. Could it then have been contemplated by anyone, that such a law as this would ever have been passed? . . . " Sen. Doc. No. 873, 62d Cong., 2d Sess. (1912) 7.

See also *id.* at 29, 36; *cf.* speech of Daniel, *id.* at 71 ff. *Cf.* the less satisfactory distinction of the Virginia Ordinance of 1776, attempted by John Nicholas (Va.) in the House, 9 Annals of Cong. (1851) 3010–3011.

103. Taylor, An Inquiry into the Principles and Policy of the Government of the United States (1814) 473–74; *cf.* his New Views of the Constitution of the United States (1823) 198, to similar effect.

104. See, however, State v. M'Donald, 4 Port. 449 (Ala. 1837), sustaining

against a claim under the treason clauses of the federal and state constitutions a statute punishing with death the aiding or being concerned with any slaves in an actual or plotted rebellion.

105. 249 U. S. 204 (1919).

106. *Id.* at 210.

107. *Cf.* pp. 147–148 *supra.*

108. The defense raised the treason clause in terms essentially as summarized by Holmes, J., but without citation of authority of any kind. (Note comments on the totally inadequate presentation of the defense in this case, in Chafee, *op. cit. supra* note 58, at 83). Without citation of any evidence from history or any direct precedent, the Government briefly argued that "If the treason clause of the Constitution were to be construed as depriving Congress of the power to protect the raising and supporting of armies against wilful obstruction thereof, in cases where the crime of treason as defined in the Constitution may not have been committed, then this power to raise and equip armies and, consequently, the power of national self-defense might be rendered nugatory." Government brief, p. 21. The argument is pertinent, but equally pertinent is the historical evidence that the treason clause was the product of sober and deliberate action, taken by men fully aware that states might be subjected to grave peril of their existence. *Cf.* Brandeis, J., concurring, in Whitney v. California, 274 U. S. 357, 372 (1927). The Government argued further that most violations of the important economic regulations essential to waging modern war arise from commercial, rather than treasonable motives, and that defendant's argument would deny all power to punish such offenses. But, in its historic context, the treason clause may limit the power to punish utterances, without preventing the punishment of economic crimes. See note 71 *supra.*

109. 251 U. S. 466 (1920).

110. *Id.* at 493.

111. People v. Steelik, 187 Cal. 361, 375–76, 203 Pac. 78, 84 (1921); *cf.* notes 24–26 *supra.*

112. 264 Fed. 11 (C. C. A. 6th, 1920), *cert. denied,* 253 U. S. 494 (1920).

113. 264 Fed. at 12–13.

114. See pp. 153–154 *supra.*

115. See Chapter 2.

116. See pp. 151–152 *supra.*

117. See pp. 154–157 *supra.*

118. See Berg v. State, 29 Okla. Cr. Rep. 112, 233 Pac. 497 (Okla. Cr. Ct. App. 1925), and separate opinion of Doyle, J., in *Ex Parte* Wood, 71 Okla. Cr. Rep. 200, 204 110 P. (2d) 304, 309 (Okla. Cr. Ct. App. 1941). No rationalization of significance is developed in the other cases. Some are satisfied simply to invoke the authority of the *Frohwerk* and *Wimmer* cases. Lockhart v. United States, 264 Fed. 14, 17 (C. C. A. 6th, 1920), *cert. denied,* 254 U. S. 645 (1920); Schoborg v. United States, 264 Fed. 1, 7 (C. C. A. 6th, 1920); Equi v. United States, 261 Fed. 53 (C. C. A. 9th, 1919), *cert. denied,* 251 U. S. 560 (1920);

People v. Lloyd, 304 Ill. 23, 136 N. E. 505 (1922); Taylor v. State, 194 Miss. 1, 11 So. (2d) 663 (1943), *rev'd on other grounds,* 319 U.S. 583 (1943). Marshall's dictum in Ex parte *Bollman* (p. 152 *supra*) is the principal reliance of State v. M'Donald, 4 Port. 449 (Ala. 1837), and State v. Laundy, 103 Ore. 443, 460, 204 Pac. 958, 964 (1922); *cf.* People v. Mintz, 106 Cal. App. 725, 290 Pac. 93 (Cal. D. C. App. 1930), *rev'd sub nom.* Stromberg v. California, 283 U. S. 359 (1931) (on grounds which would not affect the *Bollman* dictum). State v. Hennessy, 114 Wash. 351, 195 Pac. 211 (1921), seems to treat the issue as one of federalism, failing to see, or ignoring, the issue of individual liberty.

119. See Minturn, J., dissenting, in Colgan v. Sullivan, 94 N. J. L. 201, 206, 109 Atl. 568, 570 (1920) (malicious prosecution: charge of seditious utterances); Anderson, J., dissenting in Taylor v. State, 194 Miss. 1, 54–57, 11 So. (2d) 663, 681–82 (1943).

120. See Million, *Political Crimes* (1940) 5 Mo. L. Rev. 164, 167.

121. See State v. M'Donald, 4 Port. 449 (Ala. 1837), and State v. Hennessy, 114 Wash. 351, 195 Pac. 211 (1921); *cf. Ex Parte* Quarrier, 2 W. Va. 569 (1866); People v. Lynch, 11 Johns. 549 (N. Y. 1814).

122. Schenck v. United States, 249 U. S. 47, 52 (1919).

123. Coke, *op. cit. supra* note 66, at 14.

5

Treason Under the Constitution

(a) General Policy

The doctrinal development of the law of "treason" after the adoption of the Constitution is contributed primarily by the judges; treatise discussions are scissors and paste-pot affairs, or horn-book recitations of question-begging generalities. The judges, however, shine mainly by comparison. In view of the potentialities for good and evil in the instrument of treason prosecutions, it is surprising how little judicial imagination has been stirred to clarifying analysis in such cases as have presented themselves. Indeed the American cases have on the whole served little more than to annotate the doctrine which was, explicitly or implicitly, in the seventeenth and eighteenth-century English treatises. When the Supreme Court at the present Term reviewed for the first time a conviction of treason in *Cramer v. United States*,[1] it divided five to four on the law of the case. The majority opinion, moreover, in its efforts to develop the implications of the constitutional definition of the crime, either invented some bad law or added confusion to an already muddled subject.

Perhaps this continuing lack of helpful judicial exploration in the field may be explained by the fact that after the nineteenth century the executive and legislative branches no longer considered the treason charge as the principal bulwark of state security. There have been less than two score treason prosecutions pressed to trial by the Federal government; there has been no execution on a federal treason conviction; and the Executive has commonly intervened to pardon, or at least mitigate the sentence of those convicted. In the states this trend is even more marked. The trials of Thomas Dorr, and of John Brown, for treason by levying war against the states of Rhode Island and Virginia, respectively, are the only completed treason prosecutions by state authorities. As the Supreme Court observed in the *Cramer* case, "We have managed to do without treason prosecutions to a degree that probably would be impossible except while a people was singularly confident of external security and internal stability."[2]

The policy most frequently expressed in judicial opinions, and one consistent with the history of treason prosecutions, has been, pursuant to the wisdom of the framers, one of careful restriction of the scope of the crime. It is now made clear, in *Cramer v. United States,* that this historic policy should be viewed as taking two forms: it both bans the addition of new categories of subversive conduct to the two branches of "treason" stated in the Constitution, and limits the kinds of conduct which may be charged under either of those two branches.[3]

Some opinions have simply praised the constitutional provision for giving "definite" meaning to the offense.[4] Other opinions, by undertaking to explain the reasons behind the restrictive policy, furnish a little more light, even if they remain vague as to the tangible forms of the application of that policy. Three explanations are advanced. The one near-

est to the familiar English doctrine justifies a restrictive policy
by the inherent danger, if the contours of the crime are vague
and ill-defined, of abuse of treason prosecutions by the
authorities and the resulting intimidation of citizens. This is a
broader ground of policy than the more specific fear that
"treason" prosecutions may be used in the rough and tumble
of domestic faction; and suggests a general public interest in a
reasonable certainty as to the extent of political crimes, so that
men may speak and act their political roles with proper
freedom and live with a decent sense of security. Speaking for
the Court in Ex parte *Bollman,* Mr. Chief Justice Marshall
declared that

> to prevent the possibility of those calamities which result from the
> extension of treason to offences of minor importance, that great
> fundamental law which defines and limits the various departments
> of our government, has given a rule on the subject both to the
> legislature and the courts of America, which neither can be
> permitted to transcend.[5]

Other, and more specific explanations consider two other
"kinds of dangers against which the framers were concerned
to guard the treason offense," which the Court in the *Cramer*
case describes as "(1) perversion by established authority to
repress peaceful political opposition; and (2) conviction of the
innocent as a result of perjury, passion, or inadequate evidence."[6]

A calculating use of the convenient vagueness of "treason"
charges against foes in domestic factionalism seems the
characteristic abuse of the charge of levying war. In this
aspect, a restrictive definition serves the policy of preserving
the free, nonviolent competition of interests in political,
social, and economic life. With his usual capacity for casting
out varied, suggestive lines for doctrinal development, Mr.

Chief Justice Marshall, in ruling on the motion for commitment of Burr, indicated that the dangers of political factions underlay the constitutional limits set to the crime of treason:

> As this is the most atrocious offence which can be committed against the political body, so is it the charge which is most capable of being employed as the instrument of those malignant and vindictive passions which may rage in the bosoms of contending parties struggling for power. It is that of which the people of America have been most jealous, and therefore, while other crimes are unnoticed, they have refused to trust the national legislature with the definition of this. . . .[7]

And in Ex parte *Bollman,* the Chief Justice gave a warning of the dangers of perjury and passion, repetition of which, Mr. Justice Jackson declares in the *Cramer* case, "can never be untimely":

> As there is no crime which can more excite and agitate the passions of men than treason, no charge demands more from the tribunal before which it is made, a deliberate and temperate inquiry. Whether this inquiry be directed to the fact or to the law, none can be more solemn, none more important to the citizen or to the government; none can more affect the safety of both.[8]

In the light of the experience of World War I, the greatest danger of unjust accusations born and prosecuted out of the heat of public passion would seem to be that of an expansion of "treason" to cover unpopular opinions or attitudes.[9] For, in the nature of the case, there will normally be very few occasions on which public prejudice can satisfy itself by accusing the wrong man of an undoubted act of treason. There may be some reason to fear that public prejudice will particularly influence prosecutions for adherence to the

190 The Law of Treason in the United States

enemy, since the elements of that offense ensure that such
prosecutions will spring out of wartime events, when general
feeling is high.[10]

Of the three policies advanced in various American opinions to explain the restrictive character of the constitutional
treason clause, only the second has a clearcut counterpart in
the English authorities. The general policy against vagueness
in so important a crime, and in favor of free speech and free
pursuit of interests generally in the community, was not
articulated in the English materials. And the policy of protection of the accused individual against the waves of public
passion is an aspect of the treason clause policy which seems
to have been brought to the fore by the special rigor of the
two-witness requirement in the United States Constitution.
Of these three policies, moreover, only the second, which is
designed to curb the abuses of political faction, finds clear
expression in the discussions attendant upon the framing and
ratification of the Constitution. Even the brief comments in
the Convention regarding insertion of the two-witness requirement, notably Dr. Franklin's warning of the peculiar
"virulence" of treason prosecutions, imply more the peril of
political abuse of the offense than the danger of public
prejudice.

As was indicated in dealing with the materials pertinent to
the framing and ratification of the Constitution, the question
of the relevance of English authorities to the construction of
the terms borrowed from the Statute of Edward III blurs the
lines of the constitutional provision's restrictive policy.[11] The
words of the treason clause are obviously broad, and the need
for interpretation inescapable in the face of the refusal of
facts to fit into neat moulds.[12] But the constitutional prohibition on creation of new "treasons" limits the courts as well as
the Congress.[13] And, as the *Burr* and *Cramer* cases demonstrate, this requires restraint not only in the adoption of

offenses outside the constitutional definition, but also in the determination of what evidence will suffice to make out the elements of the offenses of adherence to enemies or levying of war.[14] In both situations the limits set by the Constitution might be evaded if the courts imported the full scope of English decisions interpreting and applying the Statute of Edward III.

Counsel have sometimes argued, and judges have sometimes spoken, as if the policy of the Constitution required a wholesale refusal of any guidance from English authorities.[15] This extreme position is not, however, the law of the American opinions, which overwhelmingly assert the relevance of English constructions of the Statute of Edward III.[16] But it is significant that in early opinions, close to the times and ideas of the framers, two limitations were suggested on the use of English materials. In the first place, it was suggested that English doctrine developed under charges of compassing the death of the king had no proper relation to cases arising under the constitutional provision which pointedly omitted any analogue of that branch of the Statute of Edward III. Thus, in charging the jury in the first trial of Fries, Judge Peters found the greater part of the objection to the doctrine of "constructive treason" to be "totally irrelevant here.—The subject of them is unknown, and may it ever remain so, in this country. I mean the compassing the death of the king."[17] Secondly, it was declared that a broad discretion was properly to be exercised in rejecting English precedents, from the days of great political turmoil or arbitrary power in that country, which expanded the scope of "treason." So, in the first Fries trial, Mr. Justice Iredell distinguished the products of "the bad times of English history" from "the better and more modern decisions," and added that he did not believe "that any judge since the revolution in England has ever considered that he was bound to follow every arbitrary example of the English courts, or the crown laws which had taken place in dark ages."[18] Later courts have not had occasion to develop or deny these suggested doctrinal limitations on the adoption of English treason authorities. The limitations, however, seem consistent with the restrictive policy evidence in the terms and history of the constitutional provision, and with the generally conservative approach taken in expounding the law by almost all of the American opinions. Nor does the impeachment of one of their chief exponents, Mr. Justice Chase, cast doubt on their validity, for the impeachment charge was not that Chase's distinction of the early English cases was inherently arbitrary or unreasonable, but that he denied counsel opportunity to make their own statement of that law to the jury. The impeachment of Chase was, moreover, too clearly partisan to carry weight on a professional matter.[19]

This persistence of the general, stated policy of strict construction of the scope of "treason" is an element of continuity between the materials seen in the period of the framing and adoption of the Constitution and the subsequent decisions. And, though it appears less in opinions and charges of more recent years, it has been strongly reaffirmed by the Supreme Court in *Cramer v. United States.*[20] Moreover, though the reported decisions in treason trials are not numerous, when they are examined with a view to checking the practical reality of the restrictive policy the preponderance of acquittals and of specific rules laid down with careful regard to the protection of the accused indicates that the restrictive policy has expressed an operative attitude and not merely a pious hope.[21] Nor does there seem to be any basis, either in the doctrine or in the results of the cases, for applying the restrictive policy in a different degree to the two branches of treason under the constitutional definition, although experience suggests that each bears its peculiar dangers.[22]

(b) The Intent: Limitation of "Levying War"

Perhaps because it is at the heart of the definition of the crime, the intent element in the concept of treason is apt to be discussed, as the most obvious ingredient of the positive case for the prosecution, in rather summary fashion. In fact, however, the expression of the restrictive policy governing the scope of the offense has turned as much on a carefully restrictive definition of the intent as upon the overt act element.

"To make treason the defendant not only must intend the act, but he must intend to betray his country by means of the act."[23] Thus, the Supreme Court, in *Cramer v. United States,* stressed the critical importance of a defined purpose in the defendant's mind one step beyond the immediate intention to do the overt act, and seems to indicate that "treason" is a crime of specific intent. However, doubt is cast on this interpretation by the further, unqualified assertion of the *Cramer* opinion that

> the law of treason, like the law of lesser crimes, assumes every man to intend the natural consequences which one standing in his circumstances and possessing his knowledge would reasonably expect to result from his acts.[24]

This latter statement may be taken to lend support to those texts which have declared that a specific intent is not necessary to make out "treason."[25]

The definition of intent in the court's latter statement would seem to run counter to the logic of the offense and the history behind the restrictive policy which has controlled the evolution of that policy in English and American law. The idea of betrayal of allegiance connotes a specific intent. And, historically, most of the excesses of the English law of treason, prior to the eighteenth century, can be described in terms of a treasonable intent found by inference under the head of compassing the death of the king; men were convicted not on evidence fairly showing that they had planned the king's death and the overthrow of the government, but on the basis of the expression or advocacy of ideas or measures whose "natural" consequences, as deduced by their political foes, might involve harm to the king or the state.[26] The evidence is overwhelming that the treason clause of the United States Constitution was intended to limit the scope to be given to the offense of treason; and it is upon that admonition of policy that the courts' opinions have since centered. Moreover, as the treason clause is the product not of theory, but of history, the practical meaning of its restrictive policy should be drawn from history. The most obvious manner in which the Constitution narrows the scope of treason is by omitting any analogue to the crime of compassing the king's death. Since most of the reprobated doctrines of the English law had developed under that head, it makes historical sense to look there for the kinds of doctrine which the framers wished to bar from the American law of treason. There is of course some truth in the observation that the crime of compassing the king's death has no ready analogy in a republic; but, unless a bloodless logic is substituted for living policy, it is clear that the framers rejected the doctrine for other reasons of substance.[27] In this light, one historic target of the framers' restrictive policy was the raising of a treasonable intent from inferences drawn at second or third hand under the convenient vagueness of a test of responsibility for the "natural consequences" of actions.

There is loose language in the opinions, it is true, to the effect that one accused of treason may not disavow the "natural consequences" of his act by pleading that he sought merely a commercial profit by selling supplies to an enemy or rebel, or that he helped an enemy or rebel agent merely out of friendship or compassion.[28] The crucial fact in the court's mind in these situations seems always to be, however, the defendant's knowledge that he is dealing with the enemy or rebel. If, having such knowledge, the defendant then sells supplies or gives money or concealment, he in fact specifically intends the ultimate, prohibited effect, to aid the enemy, or to contribute to the levy of war. In this state of proof, the plea of profit or friendship seeks to raise not the issue of his intention, but the more remote question of his motive; and it is merely applying elementary doctrine to hold that if defendant had the specific intention to bring about a result which the law seeks to prevent, his motive is irrelevant.[29] Of course the mercy of juries is always an incalculable factor here, and one deliberately preserved in our system.[30]

The prosecution is not limited to the accused's direct statements of intention to prove specific intent, however; and obviously a practical compromise must be struck in dealing with a crime which threatens the life of the community. Thus the man who is apprehended as he rows out to sell his foodstuffs to a known hostile frigate is held to have had a treasonable intent, though he pleads that his purpose was merely to make a dollar.[31] But the man who joins a "wildcat" strike in a munitions plant in time of war, and then pleads that his purpose was merely to get a raise, will not be held to possess a treasonable intent, though the "natural consequence" of the strike is the interruption of production needed to save the country.[32] It is hard to reconcile these positions by any more precise test than one of the proximity of defendant's immediate intention to the forbidden ultimate result of aid and comfort to the enemy.

The way in which the scope of treason by levying war was narrowed demonstrates the manner in which the historic policy restrictive of "treason" may be effectuated through a strict definition of the intent element. The problem first arose where forcible opposition to the execution of a single statute

or other act of authority was charged to be a levying of war.
The English decisions prior to the middle of the eighteenth
century went far in finding that riotous assemblies for any
non-private ("public") purpose amounted to constructive
levying of war; and it was so held *a fortiori* if the object of the
mob could be said to be to prevent by force the execution or
procure the repeal of some official act. [33] It was established, in
the cases arising out of the Whiskey Rebellion in 1794 and the
Pennsylvania resistance to the federal property excise in
1799, that this latter is likewise treason under the Constitution. But even Federalist-minded judges laid down the law
with significant and reiterated emphasis on the need for
finding that the force was exerted for a general and public
purpose and not merely to stop the collection of particular
levies, or collection from particular persons, or by a particular
exciseman. [34]

In 1808, in *United States v. Hoxie,* [35] Livingston, Circuit
Justice, in effect directed a verdict on the basis that the
conveying of a raft of logs to Canada, in violation of the
Embargo and with armed opposition to the troops seeking to
enforce it, was not shown to be more than a particular
violation of law for profit, and hence was, for lack of the
requisite intent, not treason. Emphasizing the agreement of
men learned in the law upon "the exceptions, which have
been so cautiously interwoven into" the doctrines regarding
levying of war, "for the very purpose of preventing their
extension to cases of this kind," he noted that it may sometimes be hard to distinguish between treason and some other
offenses involving opposition to authority.

> But, difficult as this may be, every one will at once perceive a very
> wide separation, between regular and numerous assemblages of
> men, scattered over a large portion of country, under known
> officers, and in every respect armed and marshalled in military
> and hostile array, for the avowed purpose, not only of disturbing

and arresting the course of public law, in a whole district, by forcibly compelling the officers of government to resign, but by intimidation and violence, of coercing its repeal, and a sudden, transient, weak, unmilitary, and unsystematized resistance, and that in a solitary instance, and for the single object of personal emolument.[36]

Livingston concentrated here entirely on the intent element as the safeguard against extension of the crime by inference:

In what can we discover the treasonable mind, which common sense, as well as all the authorities tell us, is of the very essence of this offence? . . . These learned judges also consider the intention as the only true guide in ascertaining whether certain acts amount to treason, or a less offence, and regard the universality, or generality of the design, as forming an essential ingredient in the composition of this crime.[37]

Mr. Justice Livingston thus carefully insisted on the specific intent, to ensure that mere resistance to lawful authority, or ordinary crime, would not be treated as a levying of war. In *United States v. Hanway,*[38] Mr. Justice Grier, on circuit, by emphasizing that treason was inherently a crime of deliberate, preconceived intention, developed another facet of a cautiously defined specific intent: mere presence in a riotous assembly or sudden, impulsive joining in damage wrought, would not raise an adequate inference of participation in a design to levy war. Under what amounted to a direction by the court, the jury acquitted of "treason" a defendant, who had participated in a forcible effort to prevent the taking of escaped slaves under the Fugitive Slave Law. Mr. Justice Grier raised a doubt whether, under the English authorities of the generation preceding adoption of the Constitution, a rising against the execution of a particular law was enough to show treasonable intent, or whether the design must not be entirely to subvert the government.[39] But, at any rate, a calculated and general intention, directed to a public and not merely a particular or private object, must be shown, and not a mere "sudden 'conclamatio' or running together."[40] Since Grier noted that the defendant was "confessedly present" at the disturbance, and that being present and aiding overtly or by approval makes one a principal in treason (as, indeed, in other felonies), it seems clear that he does not question the sufficiency of presence as an overt act, but focuses instead on the intent.[41] Grier also charged, as had Livingston, that mere breach of the law, as, for example, by smugglers resisting the revenue officers, though necessarily involving forcible opposition to authority, is not treason. His evident distaste for the doctrine of constructive levying of war led him practically to read it out of the scope of treason, as that offense had been defined in the early English cases:

> A whole neighbourhood of debtors may conspire together to resist the sheriff and his officers, in executing process on their property—they may perpetrate their resistance by force of arms—may kill the officer and his assistants—and yet they will be liable only as felons, and not as traitors. Their insurrection is of a private, not of a public nature; their object is to hinder or remedy a private, not a public grievance.[42]

The new climate of policy reflected in the *Hoxie* and *Hanway* cases is the more striking because both prosecutions were brought as test cases by administrations eager to obtain the support of favorable decisions for hotly controverted public policies. In this light, it is significant that the grounds on which President Adams decided to pardon those convicted in the earlier "state trial" of Fries and his companions, arising out of the excise riots of 1799, amount to an insistence that a levying of war can be established only on a showing of specific intent to overthrow the government.[43]

Reported decisions indicate but one attempt since the Civil War to use the charge of treason by levying war. This has not been for lack of occasions on which, at least under the seventeenth and eighteenth-century English authorities, sufficient overt acts might have been shown. Consider the railroad strike riots of 1877, the Haymarket affair of 1886, Coxey's Army, and the Pullman strike in 1894. [44] But, as a matter of practical construction, the crime of treason by levying war has been restricted here, and perhaps in England, to the offense described by the literal meaning of the words: a direct effort to overthrow the government, or wholly to supplant its authority in some part or all of its territory. [45] In terms of doctrine, this amounts to limiting the scope of the crime by insistence upon the showing of a carefully defined intention.

That it is the intent and not the act element which limits the scope of the crime is plain from the notable instances where the most flagrant overt acts in defiance of law were not charged as treason. The same emphasis upon intention is also seen on the one occasion in which a broader use of the charge of levying war was attempted. Following the Homestead Riot of 1892, several of the strike leaders were indicted for levying war against the state of Pennsylvania, after the grand jury had been charged by the Chief Justice of the state, that

> a mere mob, collected upon the impulse of the moment, without any definite object beyond the gratification of its sudden passions, does not commit treason, although it destroys property and takes human life.
>
> But when a large number of men arm and organize themselves by divisions and companies, appoint officers and engage in a common purpose to defy the law, to resist its officers, and to deprive any portion of the fellow-citizens of the rights to which they are entitled under the Constitution and laws, it is a levying of war against the state, and the offense is treason. [46]

These, as well as other charges, were quietly dropped after the acquittal of three of the men, in prosecutions for murder growing out of the encounter with the Pinkerton men.[47] Significantly, the resort to the treason charge met with prompt and unanimous criticism from conservative professional sources. Criticism ranged from the polite doubts of the *Albany Law Journal* to the biting commentary of the *American Law Review,* which found the indictment "a mass of stale, medieval verbiage, drawn seemingly from some old precedent, not dating later than the reign of William and Mary," and which declared that the charge of Mr. Justice Grier, in the *Hanway* case,

> disposes of any attempt to raise to the grade of treason the act of a lot of half-starved mechanics or their governing committee, where they are organized into a society, in taking unlawful measures to coerce their employer into compliance with their demands. The object is not to bring about any *political change* whatever, but to subject a party to an intended contract to a species of *duress,* such as will compel him to enter into a contract determined upon by the members of the unlawful combination. It is undoubtedly an unlawful conspiracy, provided it has in contemplation the attainment of its object by unlawful means. . . . But it is the wildest dream to dignify such a conspiracy with the name of treason.[48]

The character of the intention, therefore, rather than any difference in the overt acts, marks the line between riot and treason by levying war.[49] Even in the lesser of these offenses, moreover, hardly a score of the approximately 250 cases on riot or unlawful assembly listed in the American Digest System since 1787 involve prosecutions for disturbances arising out of issues of a public, rather than a private character. This distribution may be a concrete manifestation of a legal theory favoring the free competition of interests in the forum of public opinion. However, it is more directly significant for our central inquiry that most of these "public issue" riots could probably have been fitted within the crime of levying war, as that crime had been developed by construction before 1787.[50] The relation between the history of the riot cases and the treason cases is implicit in the recent ruling of the Supreme Court of Utah in *State v. Solomon*.[51] That case reversed the conviction of participants in a riot over "relief" administration on the ground that the district attorney's address to the jury had introduced an irrelevant and highly prejudicial element by implying, without support in the evidence, that the rioters had a subversive intent directed against our form of government. There are some indications in other cases of a similar resort to a careful definition of specific intent in order to limit the dangerous potentialities inherent in the charge of conspiracy to obstruct the execution of the laws.[52]

Decisions concerning adherence to the enemy are as few as those regarding the levying of war, but there also an effort has been made to define the requisite intention in such a way as to protect the innocent. The most illuminating treatment is in *United States v. Pryor*.[53] There Washington, Circuit Justice, at least in part because the evidence did not show specific treasonable intent, in effect directed a verdict. The defendant, who had been taken prisoner by the British squadron blockading the Delaware in 1814, sought to ransom himself and his fellows by going ashore with a British party under a flag of truce to help them purchase provisions. The court instructed the jury that the act of going ashore under a flag of truce was not a sufficient overt act, because, though it evidenced intent, it was not sufficiently far advanced in the execution of that intent. But Mr. Justice Washington also indicated that the existence of a specific intent to betray would affect the determination of what was a sufficiently advanced act to be an "overt act," for some intents are more dangerous than others and hence the law should take earlier preventive steps against those holding the former type of intent. Here, however, there was a flag of truce and "no act of hostility was attempted, nor is there the slightest reason to believe that any was meditated by the prisoner, or by any of the party." In these circumstances,

> All rests in intention merely, which our law of treason in no instance professes to punish. Carrying provisions towards the enemy, with intent to supply them, though this intention should be defeated on the way, would be very different from the act of going in search of provisions for such a purpose, and stopping short before any thing was effected, and whilst all rested in intention. . . . But, if the intention of the prisoner was to procure provisions for the enemy, by uniting with him in acts of hostility against the United States or its citizens, which is chiefly pressed against him by the district attorney; then, indeed, it must be admitted, that his progressing towards the shore, was an overt act of adhering to the enemy, although no act of hostility was in fact committed. . . .[54]

Charges to the jury in cases of adhering, as well as in those of levying war, have carefully instructed that, though the mere fact of mixed motives will not negative guilt, the defendant must have in mind more than the purpose of aiding the individual with whom he deals, as an individual; he must know, or have reason to know, that he is dealing with an agent of the enemy.[55] Though the Supreme Court in the *Cramer* case declared that treasonable intent may be established by the familiar formula of assuming that the "natural consequences" of action were intended,[56] the Court's failure to link this vague test with the implications of the historic policy restrictive of the scope of "treason," elsewhere so strongly recognized in its opinion, creates some ambiguity. However, the "natural consequences" from which intent is inferred are those foreseeable by "one standing in his circumstances and possessing his knowledge,"[57] and this qualification is flexible enough to permit reconciliation of the "natural consequences" formula with the requirement, implicit in previous cases, that a specific intent must be shown.

(c) The Act: Limitation of "Adhering to the Enemy"

Anthony Cramer, German by birth, became a resident of the United States in 1925, and was naturalized in 1936. Since 1929 he had been an intimate friend of Werner Thiel, whom he knew to be a frankly avowed adherent of the German Nazi movement. Cramer, like Thiel, was a member, and for a time an officer, of the organization which preceded the Bund. Before Pearl Harbor, Cramer openly opposed the entry of this country into the war and expressed strong sympathy with Germany in its fight with other European powers. After Pearl Harbor he refused to work on war materials and expressed concern about being drafted into the Army of the United States and "misused" for purposes of "world conquest."

Thiel had returned to Germany in 1941, as Cramer knew, to help that country. In June, 1942, Thiel and seven other German soldiers, armed with explosives with which to destroy the American aluminum industry, were landed on the eastern coast of the United States by submarine. Cramer had not anticipated Thiel's return as a saboteur; but in response to a cryptic message, he met Thiel. The two had a meal in a public restaurant, and on the following evening met again at the same place, together with Kerling, leader of Thiel's saboteur unit. Both meetings were observed by two or more agents of the FBI, who were trailing the saboteurs; but the agents overheard none of the conversations, nor did they observe any actions except Cramer's dining and talking earnestly with the others. From statements later made by Cramer to Thiel's fiancee, his admissions to FBI agents after his arrest, and especially from his admissions on the witness stand, it appeared that as a result of the first meeting, Cramer had reason to, and did, believe that Thiel was in the United States on a mission for the German government. Cramer, however, denied any belief that Thiel's mission was sabotage, but admitted to a belief that Thiel was here to spread rumors and incite unrest. Cramer also had agreed to, and did, write Thiel's fiancee to come to New York for the purpose of meeting Thiel. At the first meeting there had been talk that Cramer should take Thiel's money belt, containing, according to Cramer, about $3600. Cramer was to put the bulk of this money in his safe deposit box, keeping some handy for Thiel's convenience and taking $200 of the money in payment of an old debt owed him by Thiel. By Cramer's own admission the money belt was transferred at the second meeting, and Cramer put in his safe deposit box all the money, except some which he kept in his room to meet Thiel's requests.

Cramer, after indictment for treason by adhering to the enemy and giving him aid and comfort, was tried, found guilty, and sentenced to 45 years imprisonment and a $10,-000 fine. The overt acts submitted to the jury, and considered subsequently by the Supreme Court, were that Cramer "did meet with" Thiel, and with Thiel and Kerling, "enemies of the United States," and "did confer, treat, and counsel with" Thiel and Kerling "for a period of time for the purpose of giving and with intent to give aid and comfort to said enemies. . . ."[58] The conviction was affirmed by the Circuit Court of Appeals for the Second Circuit. Certiorari was granted, and after argument at the October Term, 1943, the Supreme Court invited reargument addressed both to the meaning of "treason" under the Constitutional definition, and the sufficiency thereunder of the proof in Cramer's case. The case was reargued November 6, 1944, and on April 23,

1945, the conviction was reversed in a five to four decision. Mr. Justice Jackson spoke for a majority including Justices Roberts, Frankfurter, Murphy, and Rutledge. The dissenting opinion of Mr. Justice Douglas was concurred in by the Chief Justice, and Justices Black and Reed.

The majority apparently found the Government's case deficient both as to the nature of the overt act laid, and as to the proof thereof. The heart, as well as some of the ambiguities, of the ruling are contained in the following passage:

> The Government contends that outside of the overt acts, and by lesser degree of proof, it has shown a treasonable intent on Cramer's part in meeting and talking with Thiel and Kerling. But if it showed him disposed to betray, and showed that he had opportunity to do so, it still has not proved in the manner required that he did any acts submitted to the jury as a basis for conviction which had the effect of betraying by giving aid and comfort. To take the intent for the deed would carry us back to constructive treasons. [59]

The *Cramer* case thus reaffirms the doctrine, familiar in English law, and established both by the history of the Convention of 1787 and in the almost unbroken line of prior American decisions, that an overt act is a separate and distinct element of the crime of treason. [60] In other words, the prosecutor must produce adequate evidence to establish two propositions: one concerning a state of mind; the other concerning conduct. [61] And the distinct character of the intent and act elements of the crime is further reflected in rulings that, since each must equally be established, the order of proof is in the discretion of the prosecutor. [62]

The function of the intent element of the crime, as indicated by those authorities which would require a showing of specific intent, is to identify the special gravity of the offense, and to define permissible objects of private action in the field of public policy. [63] The function of the overt act element, "the concern uppermost in the framers' minds," says the *Cramer* opinion, is to ensure "that mere mental attitudes or expressions should not be treason." [64] Here, the opinion accords with previous American authority, in which with remarkable unanimity the judges have stated that the function of the overt act element of the crime consists in the demonstration that the defendant has moved from the realm of thought, plan, ideas, or opinions into the world of action. The overt act is to show that the defendant has done something about what was in his mind, something, as is typically said, "in furtherance" of his intention. [65] This function of the act element in treason seems in part to express a policy familiar in the general law of crimes, which commonly insists on the showing of an act as well as an intent, as a curb on arbitrary wielding of official power. [66] The *Cramer* opinion, however, apparently regards the act element as designed more particularly to curb the two dangers which it notes as peculiar to the offense: the use of the treason charge to suppress peaceful political opposition; and conviction of the innocent on perjured evidence or under the spur of passion. [67] In some previous opinions there is like emphasis upon the significance of the overt act requirement as a curb on abusive use of treason prosecutions in political faction. [68]

However, in implementing the function of the overt act, *Cramer v. United States* goes far beyond the current of previous American authority by apparently insisting that the act of adherence to the enemy must be one which successfully confers tangible benefit upon the enemy; an act which is merely a step in furtherance of a design to confer such benefit is not enough, however substantially it may advance that purpose. "The very minimum function that an overt act must perform in a treason prosecution is that it show sufficient action by the accused, in its setting, to sustain a finding that the accused actually gave aid and comfort to the enemy."[69] The literal meaning of the court's words is underlined by the comment footnoted to the word "gave," that "We are not concerned here with any question as to whether there may be an offense of attempted treason."[70] Evidently the majority felt that its concept of "treason" contained nothing which might smack of an attempt.[71] In the instant case,

> There is no showing that Cramer gave [Thiel and Kerling] . . . any information whatever of value to their mission or indeed that he had any to give. . . . Cramer furnished them no shelter, nothing that can be called sustenance or supplies, and there is no evidence that he gave them encouragement or counsel, or even paid for their drinks. . . . without the use of some imagination it is difficult to perceive any advantage which this meeting afforded to Thiel and Kerling as enemies. . . .[72]

The case would have been "quite different," however, if the transfer of the saboteur's money had been proved as the overt act:

> That Thiel would be aided by having the security of a safe-deposit box for his funds, plus availability of smaller amounts, and by being relieved of the risks of carrying large sums on his person—without disclosing his presence or identity to a bank—seems obvious.[73]

But the Court rejected, as a sufficient overt act, the prearranged meeting with a known enemy agent for the purpose of arranging this transfer of funds.[74] The further implication that a *fait accompli* is also the requisite overt act in the other branch of treason is conveyed by the opinion's emphasis that the latter consists in the "actual" levying of war.[75]

Even assuming that a benefit must be shown to have been actually conferred on the enemy, the Court's application of its rule seems unreasonably narrow. Cramer's second meeting with Thiel afforded the essential opportunity to transfer Thiel's money. In the "setting" of Thiel's mission and circumstances this was obviously in itself an aid to him, if, as the Court found, the safekeeping of his money was an aid.[76] If this is insufficient, why should the mere act of receipt of the money by Cramer be enough? Why should it not be necessary to present as the overt act Cramer's deposit of the funds in his safe-deposit box, or his first subsequent disbursement to Thiel? To make sense in its own terms the majority opinion requires some further rationalization in terms of proximate cause, which, however, it does not offer.

The requirement that the overt act constitute "actual" aid is within the scope of the words of the constitutional definition, and might be deemed supported by the early English legislation and judicial constructions which were felt necessary in turbulent times to strike preventively at conspiracies not covered by the Statute of Edward III.[77] But "giving" aid and comfort might also mean simply that the accused have done something in tender of aid, whether or not benefit accrued to the enemy. The Statute of Edward III, from whose terms the definition in the United States Constitution is borrowed, has, like a constitutional provision, had the scope of its meaning unfolded only by experience. By 1787 English doctrine had long treated the overt act element in treason so as to make the crime itself of the nature of an attempt.[78] Thus it was settled that, even if the defendant's "aid" were intercepted before reaching the enemy, treason was made out.[79] There is nothing in the discussions surrounding the framing and ratification of the Constitution, moreover, to suggest that in this respect the familiar terms of the English definition were intended to be taken in their unglossed rigor. The American decisions under the Constitution, with one exception, were in accord before the *Cramer* case.[80] Cases involving adherence to the enemy were markedly liberal in applying what seems the familiar technique of the law of attempts. Such ordinary commercial transactions as purchasing goods, holding money on deposit, provisioning a ship, and borrowing from a bank have been held sufficient overt acts, where they were linked with an intention thereby to give aid and comfort to the enemy.[81] And there seems no logical reason why a meeting might not be a sufficient overt act, without regard to whether its purpose was simply to plan future activity, or to serve as a means to effectuate plans. On the authorities it is clear, however, that a meeting to plan to subvert the government is not an overt act of treason; it is rather "conspiracy to levy war," and ever since Lord Coke pronounced it such, his dictum, given without satisfactory explanation save such as may be inherent in the phrase "levying war," has been religiously followed.[82] But there is no comparable line of historical authority against holding a meeting to plan the giving of aid and comfort to an enemy a sufficient overt act. And it seems taken for granted that harboring an enemy agent is a sufficient overt act of adherence, though the line between this and a meeting to plan the giving of aid might become quite shadowy.[83] If, as in the *Cramer* case, the meeting is not to plan, but instead to effectuate a plan; or even if the meeting is both to plan and to gather in a state of readiness to execute such plans as may be made at the meeting, there is a sufficient overt act under previous authorities even for the charge of levying war.[84]

In *United States v. Greathouse,* the assembling of a ship's company aboard a vessel intended as a privateer, but not yet so equipped, seems to be treated as a sufficient overt act.[85] The intent, of course, will always determine the criminality of a meeting, and thus if the sole evidence of intent is a meeting with a known rebel or enemy, with no evidence of an intention that the meeting serve any purpose of the rebel or enemy, the most that could be made out would be misprision of treason. Moreover, "war" is in its nature a collective activity, and this serves to explain in part at least Marshall's well-known remarks on the necessity of an assemblage to constitute a levying of war: individual action may amount to levying war when men are already waging war, but in no fair sense of the term could the isolated acts of an individual be said to constitute war against a state.[86] But Marshall was also unwilling to overrule ancient authority rejecting conspiracy to levy war as a sufficient overt act, and so he insisted that the assemblage be present in force. In their total context his remarks, despite some ambiguous references to this force as evidencing the intention behind the assembly, simply insist, as would the law of attempts, that defendants be shown to have had some minimum capacity-in-fact, sufficient at least to make them dangerous, to do harm.[87]

The majority opinion in *Cramer v. United States* advances no justification in history or authority for its apparent insistence that, to make out an overt act, "actual" aid be given. As a matter of policy such a ruling does not necessarily follow, as the Court seems to believe, from the announced function of the overt act: to ensure "that mere mental attitudes or expressions should not be treason."[88] The law of attempts is nothing more or less than a standard to achieve this same objective in the general criminal law, and it has there proved a workable device.[89] As soon as one requires the showing of some act reasonably advanced in execution of the criminal intention the danger of prosecuting men for their thoughts alone has been met. It might, of course, be a defensible position to decide that "treason" is a crime so intrinsically open to abuse that it should be abolished. But, if the crime of treason is to be retained, it should be recognized that its value is at least as much in prevention as in punishment. To wait for aid to be "actually" given the enemy risks stultification: the treason may be successful to the point at which there will no longer be a sovereign to punish it.

(d) The Evidence of the Overt Act

It is constitutionally required that at least part of the evidence to establish the crime of treason be of a defined type: "the Testimony of two Witnesses to the same overt Act."[90] The elementary meaning of this is plainly stated by the *Cramer* opinion:

> While to prove giving of aid and comfort would require the prosecution to show actions and deeds, if the Constitution stopped there, such acts could be inferred from circumstantial evidence. This the framers thought would not do. So they added what in effect is a command that the overt acts must be established by direct evidence, and the direct testimony must be that of two witnesses instead of one. In this sense the overt act procedural provision adds something and something important, to the definition.[91]

Cramer v. United States, however, raises the further question, whether the overt act testified to by the two witnesses must, in itself, either (1) provide at least some evidence (if not evidence beyond a reasonable doubt) of treasonable intention, or (2) demonstrate that aid and comfort were given to the enemy. Neither proposition follows necessarily from the elementary meaning of the two witness provision. An act which merely serves to show that the defendant has moved from the realm of thought into that of execution can as well be shown, and required to be shown, by direct evidence as an act having either of the other suggested evidentiary values. Nothing in the *Cramer* opinion seems to claim the contrary.[92]

It was clear on previous authority that the treasonable intention need not be proved by inference from an overt act testified to by two witnesses, and, therefore, it was not necessary to prove by two witnesses conduct offered as evidence of intention which could suffice as an overt act.[93]

The majority opinion in Cramer's case seems to agree with this, and is expressly so construed by the dissent. According to the majority,

> What is designed in the mind of an accused never is susceptible of proof by direct testimony. If we were to hold that the disloyal and treacherous intention must be proved by the direct testimony of two witnesses, it would be to hold that it is never provable. It seems obvious that adherence to the enemy, in the sense of a disloyal state of mind, cannot be, and is not required to be, proved by deposition of two witnesses.[94]

However, it is, of course, "permissible" to draw inferences as to intent from the overt acts as well as from other conduct of the defendant.[95]

Actually, the majority opinion has only conceded a truism. Consistent with all this it might still be held that, insofar as acts of the defendant are relied on as the basis for inferring intent, any and all such acts must be proved by the testimony of two witnesses. This would not be to require proof of intent by "direct" testimony of two witnesses.

The majority, it is true, purported to reject the more extreme argument of the defendant, that the overt act must in itself "manifest" the treasonable intention. This contention is contrary to the long settled doctrine that the intent and the act are distinct elements of the crime, and "would place on the overt act the whole burden of establishing a complete treason."[96] Moreover, the demand that an act, in itself and apart from extrinsic evidence, evidence the intention with which it is done, or the effect which it may or does produce, rests on an unsound conception of the meaning, for these purposes, of the term "act." The law treats a physical movement as an act only if it is willed. Thus behind every jural act there is, *ex hypothesi,* some purpose, for it would seem psychologically impossible to will a movement without some purpose. Some acts, as, for example, the tying of a shoelace, may conceivably have a purpose (as distinguished, perhaps, from the more remote question of motive), which in all normal cases may be inferred from observation of the acts alone. This is not a theoretical matter, but is true simply because some acts are capable of serving a narrower range of human satisfactions or designs than others. But, when one is dealing with ends as broad as the subverting of a government by domestic disturbance or by aid to its enemies, the range of acts which may fit such purposes is as broad as the possible economic, political, social, racial, sectional, or class factors which affect the health or existence of a community. The acts which can serve to advance purposes of such range may, conversely, be acts which might in another context serve innocent purposes in economic, political, social, racial, sectional, or class dealings. Indeed, so varied is the character of the conduct which may serve the broad purposes penalized by the treason clause, that even the man whose purpose seems to be merely the obvious and undivided one of tying a shoelace may be conveying military intelligence to an observer according to a prearranged code. If thus in theory no act has a meaning in itself, in the sense of a significance which can be grasped by observation of the act alone, so in practice one understands the meaning of acts only insofar as he knows other facts in context with the acts.[97] This is particularly likely to be true in dealing with the kind of purposes penalized by the treason clause, since they may be served by manifold acts which can also serve many other purposes. Thus, in prior cases, acts have been found treasonable which on their face were "innocent"[98] and acts appearing on their face to be treasonable have been found innocent[99] Indeed, if acts could have meaning in themselves, it is difficult to see why, after the centuries of experience represented by the criminal law, it was found necessary or desirable to develop the concept of intent as a separate element of crimes.

This seems partially recognized by the majority opinion in the *Cramer* case, which notes that

> it is only overt acts by the accused which the Constitution explicitly requires to be proved by the testimony of two witnesses. It does not make other common-law evidence inadmissible nor deny its inherent powers of persuasion. It does not forbid judging by the usual process by which the significance of conduct often will be determined by facts which are not acts. Actions of the accused are set in time and place in many relationships. Environment illuminates the meaning of acts, as context does that of words. What a man is up to may be clear from considering his bare acts by themselves; often it is made clear when we know the reciprocity and sequence of his acts with those of others, the interchange between him and another, the give and take of the situation.[100]

But, if the majority thus rejects the extreme argument of the defense, it also observes disapprovingly that

> on the other hand, the Government's contention that it may prove by two witnesses an apparently commonplace and insignificant act and from other circumstances create an inference that the act was a step in treason and was done with treasonable intent really is a contention that the function of the overt act in a treason prosecution is almost zero.[101]

The majority described the "minimum function" of the overt act as being to show the giving of aid and comfort, and purported to decide the case on the insufficiency of the act to show this, rather than on its insufficiency to show intention.[102] But the last-quoted statement ambiguously condemns reliance on an "apparently commonplace and insignificant act" both because it fails to evidence intent and because it does not show that aid was given. And, when the Court concedes that it may be that in some cases the overt acts, sufficient to prove giving of aid and comfort, will fall short of showing intent to betray and that questions will then be raised as to permissible methods of proof that we do not reach in this case. . . , [103]

it raises at least a doubt whether intent can be established at all, outside the scope of the two-witness testimony. Cramer's act of taking the saboteur's funds for safekeeping, which the majority indicates would be a sufficient overt act if properly proved, is apparently given no weight by the Court on the issue of intent, though the transaction was admitted by Cramer, because it was not submitted as an overt act proved by two witnesses. [104]

The Court's remarks on the admissibility of evidence extrinsic to that of the overt act testified to by two witnesses, but tending to prove the "environment" of the act, seem equally applicable to the proof that aid was given as to the issue of intent, though made with particular reference to the latter issue. [105] But the Court introduced doubt by its declaration that

> . . . the protection of the two-witness rule extends *at least* to all acts of the defendant which are used to draw incriminating inferences that aid and comfort have been given. [106]

Analyzing the evidence of Cramer's meetings with the saboteur, the Court further observed that

> the Government recognizes the weakness of its proof of aid and comfort, but on this score it urges: "Little imagination is required to perceive the advantage such meeting would afford to enemy spies not yet detected. . . ." The difficulty with this argument is that the whole purpose of the constitutional provision is to make sure that treason conviction shall rest on direct proof of two witnesses and not on even a little imagination. And without the use

of some imagination, it is difficult to perceive any advantage which this meeting afforded to Thiel or Kerling as enemies . . . there is no proof either by two witnesses or by even one witness or by any circumstance that Cramer gave them information or established any "contact" for them with any person other than an attempt to bring about a rendezvous between Thiel and a girl, or that being "seen in public with a citizen above suspicion" was of any assistance to the enemy. . . .[107]

Thus, though the Court made passing comment on the insufficiency of the extrinsic evidence offered, the stress is on the weakness of the overt act. The Court kept this same emphasis when, though conceding that Cramer's receipt of the saboteur's money for safekeeping would be a sufficient overt act if submitted as such, it refused to consider this transaction, though admitted by Cramer, as evidence that the meeting afforded aid to the saboteur, because, "We cannot sustain a conviction for the acts submitted on the theory that, even if insufficient, some unsubmitted ones may be resorted to as proof of treason."[108] It is difficult to see why the second meeting between Cramer and the saboteur does not satisfy the two-witness requirement, unless, despite its theoretical concession of the admissibility of extrinsic evidence of the "setting" of the act, the majority opinion practically ruled, as indeed the dissent understood it to do, "that the related acts and events which show the true character of the overt act charged must be proved by two witnesses."[109] On no other theory does it seem possible to describe as an "apparently commonplace and insignificant act" a prearranged meeting with a known enemy agent for the probable purpose of undertaking the safekeeping of his funds.[110]

The only historic evidence we have of the intended function of the two-witness requirement is Madison's note that "Docr Franklin wished this amendment to take place— prosecutions for treason were generally virulent; and perjury too easily made use of against innocence."[111] Judge Learned Hand has argued that it is necessary to insist that the overt act be such an act as evidences the treasonable intent because the safeguard against perjury would be easily evaded if it were only necessary to obtain a corroborating witness for some innocent detail of a single witness's story.[112] Apparently, Judge Hand's reasoning on this point was wholly *a priori*. Dean Wigmore, however, did not see the special virtue of the two-witness requirement in any implication that the overt act must evidence the intent or anything else, but in a consideration which might apply to any conduct sufficient to constitute an attempt according to familiar criminal law standards; namely, that "the opportunity of detecting the falsity of the testimony, by sequestering the two witnesses . . . and exposing their variance in details, is wholly destroyed by permitting them to speak to different acts.[113]

Whatever the rule which the majority intended by its vacillating language in the *Cramer* case, its opinion developed neither arguments of policy nor evidence from history to support any of the functions which it may be construed to have assigned to the two-witness requirement. Certainly there is no sound basis in English or American history to require that the overt act be such as to evidence the intent.[114] And, since it was apparent in the English authorities even before *Lord Preston's Case*[115] that actual conferring of aid upon the enemy was not necessary to make out a case of treason, no support can be found in that quarter, even by analogy, for a requirement that the overt act demonstrate the giving of aid. Moreover, even if the current of previous American doctrine is departed from, and it is assumed that accomplished aid and comfort must be shown, the Court advances no evidence that the framers intended the two-witness requirement to apply here. The Constitution in its terms requires only the testimony of two witnesses to an "act," not to the effect of that act.

Therefore, except for some references to the proof of the

required intent which, curiously, suggest a broadening of the scope of the offense, the majority opinion in *Cramer v. United States* has cast such a net of ambiguous limitations about the crime of "treason" that it is doubtful whether a careful prosecutor will ever again chance an indictment under that head. The uncertain meaning of the decision will alone be as strong a deterrent as any doctrine elicited from it. Perhaps this is what the majority desire. The opinion concludes with what amounts to an invitation to Congress "to enact prohibitions of specified acts thought detrimental to our wartime safety," if the limits set to "treason" are deemed too stringent:

> The loyal and the disloyal alike may be forbidden to do acts which place our security in peril, and the trial thereof may be focussed upon defendant's specific intent to do these particular acts thus eliminating the accusation of treachery and of general intent to betray which have such passion-rousing potentialities.[116]

As the law of "treason" is founded directly upon the Constitution, the majority's self-denying policy amounts to a shift of power from the executive and judicial branches to the legislative branch of the Federal government. The consequences of this are obviously unpredictable; but the destruction of a protective instrument which the Constitution placed in the hands of the Executive, and thus beyond the authority of the Congress to expand or impair, may come to have significance if crisis ever brings sharp division between the branches of the government.[117]

NOTES

1. 325 U.S. 1.
2. *Id.* at 26; *cf.* 2 Stephen, A History of the Criminal Law of England (1883) 251, 283.

3. 325 U. S. 1, 27 (1945). No previous opinion had spelled out precisely what form the general restrictive policy should take.

4. See Chase, C. J., in Case of Fries, 9 Fed. Cas. No. 5127, at 930 (C. C. D. Pa. 1800) (second trial); Nelson, C. J., Charge to Grand Jury, 30 Fed. Cas. No. 18,271, at 1035 (C. C. S. D. N. Y. 1861); Stephan v. United States, 133 F. (2d) 87, 90 (C. C. A. 6th, 1943), *cert. denied,* 318 U. S. 781 (1943).

See also the argument of Sitgreaves, for the prosecution, and Ewing and Lewis for the defense, in the first trial of Fries, 9 Fed. Cas. No. 5126, at 847–48, 887, 895–96 (C. C. D. Pa. 1799); argument of William Pinkney, for the defense, in United States v. Hodges, 26 Fed. Cas. 332, No. 15,374 (C. C. D. Md. 1815).

5. 4 Cranch 75, 125–26 (U. S. 1807). *Cf.* Livingston, C. J., in charge to the jury in United States v. Hoxie, 26 Fed. Cas. No. 15,407, at 398, 402, 403 (C. C. D. Vt. 1808). See also Cramer v. United States, 325 U. S. 1, 27 (1945).

Mr. Justice Curtis, in charging the grand jury, found the Statute of Edward III to have been "enacted . . . mainly for the purpose of restraining the power of the crown to oppress the subject by arbitrary constructions of the law of treason." 30 Fed. Cas. No. 18,269, at 1025 (C. C. D. Mass. 1851). *Cf.* Field, C. J., in charge to jury in United States v. Greathouse, 26 Fed. Cas. No. 15,254, at 21 (C. C. N. D. Cal. 1863); Nelson, C. J., Charge to Grand Jury, 30 Fed. Cas. No. 18,271, at 1035 (C. C. S. D. N. Y. 1861); Leavitt, D. J., Charge to Grand Jury, 30 Fed. Cas. No. 18,272, at 1036 (C. C. S. D. Ohio, 1861).

The line between desirable freedom of discussion and political action and "treason" is put at the point where men "pass from words to . . . criminal acts of resistance to law" by Sprague, D. J., Charge to Grand Jury Regarding Mob Resistance to Execution of the Fugitive Slave Law, 30 Fed. Cas. No. 18,263, at 1016 (D. Mass. 1851); *cf.* Leavitt, D. J., Charge to the Grand Jury, *loc. cit. supra* at 1037. Compare also the decision of the Attorney General not to prosecute the leaders of the Pittsburgh meeting of September 7, 1791, though the resolutions there adopted criticizing government policy and petitioning Congress and the state legislature were a significant step in the unrest which culminated in the "Whiskey Rebellion." (Note) 26 Fed. Cas. 499, 501, 503 (1795). See also Brandeis, J., dissenting in Schaefer v. United States, 251 U. S. 466, 482, at 493 (1920); Mayer, D. J., in charge to jury in United States v. Fricke, 259 Fed. 673, 677 (S. D. N. Y. 1919); *cf.* Haywood v. United States, 268 Fed. 795, 799–800 (C. C. A. 7th, 1920), *cert. denied,* 256 U. S. 689 (1921) (conspiracy).

The thread of insistence on a policy, in the interest of individual security and free give-and-take in community life, against vagueness in the definition of the crime, comes up to the present in the charge to the jury in United States v. Stephan, 50 F. Supp. 738, 740, n.1 (E. D. Mich. 1943). See Stephan v. United States, 133 F. (2d) 87, 99 (C. C.A. 6th, 1943), *cert. denied,* 318 U. S. 781 (1943).

6. 325 U. S. 1, 27 (1945).

7. United States v. Burr, 25 Fed. Cas. No. 14,692a, at 13 (C. C. D. Va. 1807). See also Livingston, C. J., in charge to the jury in the United States v.

Hoxie, 26 Fed. Cas. No. 15,407, at 397–98 (C. C. D. Vt. 1808). This comment takes on particular emphasis because the charge as a whole so clearly reflects Livingston's sensitivity to the impeachment proceedings against Chase, J., for his "strong" expositions of the law of levying of war in the trial of Fries and his ardent expositions of the Alien and Sedition Laws to juries. Indeed, after discounting the fervor of advocacy, it is still significant of a prevailing attitude toward the policy of the treason clause that, in his answer to the impeachment charges brought against him, Mr. Justice Chase reasoned from the historic danger of abuse of treason prosecutions in political faction to justify his refusal to permit defense counsel in the trial of Fries to parade before the jury the excesses of the earlier English treason cases. See answer of Chase, J., to impeachment charges, (Note) 9 Fed. Cas. 934, at 938 (1800); *cf.* argument of defense counsel in United States v. Hanway, 26 Fed. Cas. No. 15,299, at 117 (C. C. E. D. Pa. 1851). In his charge to the jury in the Fries case, 9 Fed. Cas. No. 5,127, at 930 (C. C. D. Pa. 1800), Chase had, however, confined himself to brief, opening praise for the constitutional definition and proof requirements. The argument based on the excesses of English treason trials, which he prevented Lewis and Dallas from making to the jury, seems to have been directed essentially to enlisting the jury's sympathies for the policy of curbing factional use of "treason" prosecutions. See, *e.g.,* argument of Dallas on the first trial of Fries, 9 Fed. Cas. No. 5,126, at 878, 883, 879–81 (C. C. D. Pa. 1800); and the argument of Lewis, *id.* at 897–99.

8. 4 Cranch 75, 125 (U. S. 1807); *cf.* Leavitt, D. J., Charge to Grand Jury, 30 Fed. Cas. No. 18,272, at 1038 (C. C. S. D. Ohio 1861). See Cramer v. United States, 325 U. S. 1, 47 (1945).

The suggestion made in Ex Parte *Bollman* has been adopted in several cases which, however, create some ambiguity by linking the protection against public passion primarily to the two-witness provision. See Sprague, D. J., Charges to Grand Jury, 30 Fed. Cas. Nos. 18,273, at 1039; 18,274, at 1042 (D. Mass. 1861, 1863). Mingling, as it does, a substantive (overt act) and an evidentiary (two witnesses) safeguard, the objects of this provision are themselves somewhat ambiguous; but the cases stress more the danger of convicting the "wrong man" than of expanding unduly the concept of "treason." Thus in United States v. Haupt, 136 F. (2d) 661, 671 (C. C. A. 7th, 1943), *rev'g,* 47 F. Supp. 832 (N. D. Ill. 1942); 47 F. Supp. 836 (N. D. Ill. 1942), the court declared that the charge of treason presents special dangers of unfair trials in a time of national crisis; and it linked this warning with a ruling that the trial court had abused its discretion in denying motionsfor severance of the trials of the several defendants after the admission of much highly prejudicial evidence which did not relate to all of the defendants. Significantly, the Circuit Court of Appeals cited the *Bollman* case in connection with its warning. See also Chambers v. Florida, 309 U. S. 227, 236–37 (1940), where the Court lists the two-witness requirement of the treason clause among the constitutional provisions inserted "as assurance against ancient evils." On the other hand, the charge to the jury in United States v. Fricke, 259 Fed. 673, 677 (S. D. N. Y. 1919), relates the danger of injustice through public passion both to the hazards of undue expansion of the scope of "treason" and of conviction of the wrong man.

9. *Cf.* Chafee, Free Speech in the United States (1942) 51–60.

10. See United States v. Fricke, 259 Fed. 673, 677 (S. D. N. Y. 1919); United States v. Haupt, 136 F. (2d) 661, 671 (C. C. A. 7th, 1943).

11. See p. 140 *supra*.

12. See Peters, D. J., in charge to jury in Case of Fries, 9 Fed. Cas. No. 5,126, at 909 (C. C. D. Pa. 1799) (first trial); Livingston, C. J., in charge to jury in United States v. Hoxie, 26 Fed. Cas. No. 15,407, at 398 (C. C. D. Vt. 1808).

13. See Cramer v. United States, 325 U. S. 1, 24 (1945); *Ex parte* Bollman, 4 Cranch 75, 127 (U. S. 1807); United States v. Burr, 25 Fed. Cas. No. 14,692a, at 13 (C. C. D. Va. 1807).

14. See Cramer v. United States 325 U. S. 1, 35 (1945) (majority opinion), 59 (dissenting opinion); United States v. Burr, 25 Fed. Cas. Nos. 14,692a, at 13; 14,693, at 159 (C. C. D. Va. 1807).

15. See Nelson, D. J., Charge to Grand Jury, 30 Fed. Cas. No. 18,271, at 1035 (C. C. S. D. N. Y. 1861); argument of Lewis, for the defense, in Case of Fries, 9 Fed. Cas. No. 5,126, at 897 (C. C. D. Pa. 1799) (first trial). Chase, C. J., refused, in the second trial of Fries, to permit defense counsel to present to the jury a picture of the extreme constructions given to the Statute of Edward III by English judges. Defense counsel then withdrew from the case. Subsequently, in response to a request by President Adams, Dallas and Lewis sent to the President a memorandum of the argument which they had proposed to make at the second trial. This included the statement that "as the spirit of the constitution is opposed to implied powers, and constructive expositions, we are bound to take the plain manifest meaning of the words of the definition, independent of any glossary which the English courts, or writers, may have affixed to the words of the English statute." *Id.* at 948.

Probably mindful of the fact that the impeachment of Chase rested in part on his refusal to let counsel argue this point, Livingston, C. J., noted the issue, in United States v. Hoxie, 26 Fed. Cas. No. 15,407, at 398 (C. C. D. Vt. 1808), but cautiously avoided it. Because he found that no treason had been committed in that case, even within the definitions of the English authorities, he found it unnecessary to decide whether they had any binding effect, or to "discuss a question which has been much agitated — whether, by the use of these terms, it was intended to adopt the technical meaning which they had already received in England, or whether, considering treason as a new offence against a newly created government, the constitution on this point was to be interpreted by itself, without reference to, or with the aid of any common law decisions whatever?"

16. See *e.g.,* Cramer v. United States, 325 U. S. 1, 18 (1945); Iredell, C. J., and Peters, D. J., in charges to the jury in Case of Fries, 9 Fed. Cas. No. 5,126, at 909, 912 (C. C. D. Pa. 1799); Marshall, C. J., in direction to the jury in United States v. Burr, 25 Fed. Cas. No. 14,693, at 159–60 (C. C. D. Va. 1807); Kane, D. J., Charge to Grand Jury, 30 Fed. Cas. No. 18,276, at 1048 (C. C. E. D. Pa. 1851); Curtis, C. J., Charge to Grand Jury, 30 Fed. Cas. No. 18,269, at

1025 (C. C. D. Mass. 1851); Cadwalader, D. J., in United States v. Greiner, 26 Fed. Cas. No. 15,262 at 38 (E. D. Pa. 1861); Field, C. J., in charge to jury in United States v. Greathouse, 26 Fed. Cas. No. 15,254, at 21 (C. C. N. D. Cal. 1863); Sprague, D. J., Charge to Grand Jury, 30 Fed. Cas. No. 18,273, at 1039 (D. Mass. 1861); United States v. Cramer, 137 F. (2d) 888, 894 (C. C. A. 2d, 1943); *cf.* Druecker v. Salomon, 21 Wis. 621, 626 (1867).

17. 9 Fed. Cas. No. 5,126, at 909 (C. C. D. Pa. 1799); *cf.* the exchange between the prosecutor and Chase, J., in the second trial of Fries, 9 Fed. Cas. No. 5,127, at 927 (C. C. D. Pa. 1800). See also the answer filed by Chase, J., to his impeachment, (Note) 9 Fed. Cas. 934, at 938 (1800).

18. 9 Fed. Cas. No. 5,126, at 912 (C. C. D. Pa. 1799); see, also, Peters, D. J., *id.* at 909; Grier, J., in United States v. Hanway, 26 Fed. Cas. No. 15,299, at 127 (C. C. E. D. Pa. 1851). Though he does not make clear how far he would carry his strong condemnation of the incorporation of English judicial constructions of the words of Edward III's Statute into the constitutional definition, Tucker would probably agree substantially with the soundness of thus distinguishing the earlier and later English decisions as guides to policy. See 5 Blackstone's Commentaries with Notes of Reference, to the Constitution and Laws of the Federal Government of the United States and of the Commonwealth of Virginia (Ed. Tucker 1803) 85, n.18, App. Note "B," pp. 13, 40–41, 46.

19. See notes 7, 15, 17 *supra.* The views of Chase, J., on the exclusion of English precedents antedating 1688 are set forth in great detail in his answer to the impeachment charges filed against him. The impeachment did not rest on objections to these doctrines, but on the Justice's action in preventing counsel from arguing them to the jury. See 11 American State Trials (Lawson ed. 1919) 197, 241, 242, 316, 345, 351.

20. 325 U. S. 1, 47 (1945).

21. See Appendix, I, pp. 260–265 *infra.*

22. However, the materials surrounding the framing and ratification of the Constitution tend to center the emphasis on the dangers of abuse of treason prosecutions in political strife. See p. 141 *supra.*

23. 325 U. S. 1, 31 (1945).

24. *Ibid.* This statement comes after, but does not necessarily follow from, the obvious point made by the opinion that intention can generally be proved only by inference from conduct. This is true, but does not rule out the proof of specific intent by such inference; the standard of proof is simply more precise and exacting. Note also, as bearing out the implication of the quotation above, the assertion in the majority opinion that statutory crimes forbidding specific acts are safer than reliance on "treason," because "the trial thereof may be focused upon defendant's specific intent to do those particular acts thus eliminating the accusation of treachery and of general intent to betray which have such passion-rousing potentialities." *Id.* at 45.

25. See, *e.g.,* Miller, Criminal Law (1934) 502. Even apart from its inconsistency with the history of the American law of treason, this proposition seems contrary to the familiar doctrine that a specific intent is necessary in crimes of the nature of an attempt. See Keedy, *Ignorance and Mistake in the*

Criminal Law (1908) 22 Harv. L. Rev. 75, 89; Sayre, *Criminal Attempts* (1928) 41 Harv. L. Rev. 821, 822, 841; Skilton, *The Mental Element in A Criminal Attempt* (1937) 3 Univ. of Pitt. L. Rev. 181, 182; Turner, *Attempts to Commit Crimes* (1934) 5 Camb. L. J. 230, 235; *cf.* Harno, *Intent in Criminal Conspiracy* (1941) 89 U. of Pa. L. Rev. 624, 636, 637.

26. See 8 Holdsworth, History of English Law (1937) 327 *ff.*

27. *But see* Cramer v. United States, 325 U. S. 1, 20(1945). *Cf.* p. 87 *supra.*

28. See, *e.g.*, United States v. Hoxie, 26 Fed. Cas. No. 15,407, at 398 (C. C. D. Vt. 1808); United States v. Stephan, 50 F. Supp. 738, 744 (E. D. Mich. 1943) (trial court charge). John Brown's defense to the charge of treason by levying war against the state of Virginia was, in part, that he had no intent further than "to free slaves." See *The Trial of John Brown,* 6 American State Trials (Lawson ed. 1916) 700, 801, 802. There was evidence, however, that Brown had envisioned his effort to help the slaves as possibly involving the creation of a separate commonwealth, and, although he seems to have raided Harper's Ferry with no well thought-out plan for the steps to follow, his intent seems plainly to have embraced such overturning of existing institutions as might be necessary "to free slaves." See Warren, John Brown (1929) 350, 384; Villard, John Brown (Rev. ed. 1943) 427.

29. Thus the profit motive does not excuse the selling of provisions to the enemy. Hanauer v. Doane, 12 Wall. 342 (U. S. 1871); Carlisle v. United States, 16 Wall. 147 (U. S. 1873); Sprott v. United States, 20 Wall. 459 (U. S. 1874); United States v. Lee, 26 Fed. Cas. 907, No. 15,584 (C. C. D. C. 1814). And the mingling of friendship or sympathy for the known enemy with the intent to aid him, knowing him an enemy, does not negative the treasonable intent. United States v. Stephan, 50 F. Supp. 738, 740, n. 1, at 744 (E. D. Mich. 1943), 133 F. (2d) 87, 99 (C. C. A. 6th, 1943); United States v. Cramer, 137 F. (2d) 888, 893 (C. C. A. 2d, 1943). Nor does hostile duress acting on persons other than the defendant, or directed at property, justify giving aid. United States v. Hodges, 26 Fed. Cas. 332, No. 15,374 (C. C. D. Md. 1815); United States v. Pryor, 27 Fed. Cas. 628, No. 16,096 (C. C. D. Pa 1814). *Cf.* United States v. Hughes, 26 Fed. Cas. 420, No. 15,418 (S. D. Ohio, 1864), Thompson, *A Treason Trial in Ohio* (1883) 4 Ohio Bar Assn. Appendix II, 54.

A contrary doctrine concerning sale of supplies to the enemy might seem to have evolved in the Confederate States of America. Though originally regarded as clearly involving treason, there trade with the enemy "came to be more generally regarded as an offense against the revenue laws than as an act of treason." Robinson, Justice in Grey (1941) 177. The circumstances strongly suggest, however, that this course of opinion reflected a practical compromise with facts; such trade as was going on seemed probably of greater benefit to the South than to the North.

30. Thus, despite the confused argument of Pinckney for the defense, and the unsatisfactory charge of Duval, C. J., the issue of motive seems the real defense attempted in United States v. Hodges, cited in note 29 *supra;* and the jury's verdict of acquittal may amount to interposition of mercy.

31. *Cf.* United States v. Lee, 26 Fed. Cas. 907, No. 15,584 (C. C. D. C. 1814).

32. *Cf.* Cramer v. United States, 325 U. S. 1, 29 (1945): "On the other hand, a citizen may take actions which do aid and comfort the enemy — making a speech critical of the government or opposing its measures, profiteering, striking in defense plants or essential work, and the hundred other things which impair our cohesion and diminish our strength — but if there is no adherence to the enemy in this, if there is no intent to betray, there is no treason." Note that the implication of the Court's observation rejects the broad possibilities seen for the treason clause in McKinney, *Treason under the Constitution of the United States* (1918) 12 Ill. L. Rev. 381 and Warren, *What is Giving Aid and Comfort to the Enemy?* (1918) 27 Yale L. J. 331.

33. See 8 Holdsworth, History of English Law (1937) 335 *ff.*

34. See Paterson, C. J., in United States v. Vigol, 28 Fed. Cas. 376, No. 16,621 (C. C. D. Pa. 1795); Iredell, C. J., and Peters, D. J., in Case of Fries, 9 Fed. Cas. No. 5,126, at 840, 909, 912; Chase, C. J., in the second trial of Fries, 9 Fed. Cas. No. 5,127, at 930. Needless to say, the Jeffersonian Congress' impeachment of Mr. Justice Chase was not based on any objection to such parts of his charge to the jury in the Fries trial as confined the definition of treasonable intention; and, significantly, Chase's answer to his impeachment boldly makes capital out of the fact that his refusal to allow defense counsel to describe early English treason law to the jury was based on its excessive scope, both in intent and in act. See (Note) 9 Fed. Cas. 934, 938 *ff.*

35. 26 Fed. Cas. 397, No. 15,407 (C. C. D. Vt. 1808).

36. *Id.* at 400, 402. Livingston's ruling is the more striking because, though the particular enterprise was only a somewhat unusually open and brash smuggling attempt, it probably represented a type of conduct which then met with the approval of that substantial part of the community which was violently opposed to the Embargo. A different temper of mind towards the scope of "treason" might have led the court to find that a case existed. *Cf.* Moulton, *A Vermont Treason Trial* (1935) 29 Vt. Bar Assn. 121, 128–32.

37. 26 Fed. Cas. No. 15,407, at 399, 401–402 (C. C. D. Vt. 1808).

38. 26 Fed. Cas. 105, No. 15,299 (C. C. E. D. Pa. 1851).

39. See note 18 *supra.*

40. See 26 Fed. Cas. No. 15,299, at 128 (C. C. E. D. Pa. 1851): "Not because the numbers of [or?] force was insufficient. But (1) for want of any proof of previous conspiracy to make a general and public resistance to any law of the United States; (2) because there is no evidence that any person concerned in the transaction knew there were such acts of congress, as those with which they are charged with conspiring to resist by force and arms, or had any other intention than to protect one another from what they termed 'kidnappers' (by which slang term they probably included not only actual kidnappers, but all masters and owners seeking to recapture their slaves, and the officers and agents assisting therein).

"The testimony of the prosecution shows that notice had been given that certain fugitives were pursued; the riot, insurrection, tumult, or whatever you may call it, was but a sudden conclamatio or running together, to prevent the capture of certain of their friends or companions, or to rescue them if arrested. Previous to this transaction, so far as we are informed, no attempt had been made to arrest fugitives in the neighbourhood under the new act of congress by a public officer."

Insistence on specific intent underlies Grier's admission of defense evidence that in the previous nine months there had been rough seizure of Negroes in the neighbourhood by men of dubious character, who acted without show of official authority. This was recognized as a critical point, and was hard fought, on both sides. See Hensel, The Christiana Riot and the Treason Trials of 1851 (1911) 78. The prosecution objected that the evidence was irrelevant. Grier answered: "The objection of the prosecution would be irresistible if Hanway was indicted simply for resisting an officer of government. But in treason there must be some previous agreement." *Id.* at 112.

So also Grier and Kane, D. J., agreed that the prosecution, not having previously supplied the defense with a list of the witnesses on the point as the statute required, could not now introduce "rebuttal" evidence that for the year previous armed bands of Negroes had ranged the neighbourhood seeking out whites trying to reclaim slaves. Judge Kane declared that "the two elements of the crime are the act and the preconcert. . . . The evidence which is now offered is merely to prove that preconcert. It was an indispensable element of the original case." *Id.* at 114.

41. See *id.* at 126.

42. *Id.* at 128. Grier's observations are the more striking in view of the clarity with which District Judge Kane, who sat with Grier in the *Hanway* trial, had charged the grand jury on the theory that an attempt by force generally to prevent the enforcement of a single law was treason by levying war. See Charge to Grand Jury, 30 Fed. Cas. No. 18,276, at 1048 (C. C. E. D. Pa. 1851). Judge Kane, a former district attorney and Attorney-General of Pennsylvania, was herein merely reflecting his "well known views" on the need for strict enforcement of the constitutional right of slave owners to the return of their property. See Hensel, *op. cit. supra* note 40, at 57–58. Justice Grier's evident distaste for the doctrine of constructive levying of war is further pointed by the contrast of his remarks with the clear presentation of the broader doctrine by the district attorney in his address to the jury. See Robbins, Report of the Trial of Castner Hanway (1852) 45, 53.

Mr. Justice Grier's sweeping exclusion of the mortgage debtor's case can also be contrasted with the resort to force to stop the general operation of the mortgage foreclosure system in farm states at the depth of the depression of the 1930's. See Skilton, Government and the Mortgage Debtor (1944) 74. So far as appears, no effort was ever made to charge these disturbances as constructive levying of war, though they seem within the scope of the older English authority.

43. See Appendix, III, pp. 268–269 *infra*.

44. There seems to be no evidence that any stronger measures than the use of Federal troops were considered in connection with the 1877 riots. In view of the broad construction of "conspiracy" used to convict the leaders in the Haymarket meeting, it is notable that no charge of treason was attempted. *Cf.*Spies v. People, 122 Ill. 1, 12 N. E. 865 (1887); *The Trial of the Chicago Anarchists,* 12 American State Trials (Lawson ed. 1919) 1; David, History of the Haymarket Affair (1936) c. XIV.

The *Spies* decision was declared by (1887) 18 Weekly L. Bull. 326, 327 to be "the most portentous and dangerous . . . ever pronounced by a court of justice in the United States," because "the theories laid down in the Chicago case are essentially the exploded idea of constructive treason revived and applied to the crime of murder."

Whatever the pacific protestations of its organizers, Coxey's "petition in boots" was the sort of mass movement on the legislature which earlier English doctrine would almost certainly have regarded as within the scope of constructive levying of war; but, despite real official concern for the dangerous potentialities of the movement, the only prosecutions which eventuated were for the misdemeanors of unlawful parading on the Capitol grounds and trampling the grass. See McMurry, Coxey's Army (1929) 104–106, 116, 123.

The value of fastening a serious criminal charge on the leadership of the Pullman strike both as a matter of influencing public opinion and breaking the morale of the strikers was fully appreciated by the government, which, yet, relied on a conspiracy charge rather than the more intimidating accusation of treason; and there seems to be no evidence that the possibility of the latter was considered. See Lindsey, The Pullman Strike (1942) c. XII, 276, 278, 279, 280; *cf.* Consolidated Coal & Coke Co. v. Beale, 282 Fed. 934, 936 (S. D. Ohio 1922). Any theory of constructive levying of war was conspicuously absent in strong charges delivered to grand juries in connection with the strike. See *In re* Charge to Grand Jury, 62 Fed. 828 (N. D. Ill. 1894); *In re* Grand Jury, *id.,* at 834 (S. D. Cal. 1894); *In re* Grand Jury, *id.,* at 840 (N. D. Cal. 1894).

There are numerous dicta through the Civil War period to the effect that effort by force to prevent the general execution of a single law is a levying of war. See Story, C. J., Charge to Grand Jury, 30 Fed. Cas. No. 18,275, at 1,047 (C. C. D. R. I. 1842); Sprague, D. J., Charge to Grand Jury, 30 Fed. Cas. No. 18,263 at 1,015 (D. Mass. 1851); Nelson, C. J., Charge to Grand Jury, 30 Fed. Cas. No. 18,261, at 1,012 (C. C. S. D. N. Y. 1851); Kane, D. J., Charge to Grand Jury, 30 Fed. Cas. No. 18,276, at 1,048 (C. C. E. D. Pa. 1851); Curtis C. J., Charge to Grand Jury, 30 Fed. Cas. No. 18,269, at 1,025 (C. C. D. Mass. 1851); United States v. Greiner, 26 Fed. Cas. No. 15,262, at 39 (E. D. Pa. 1861); Field, C. J., in charge to jury in United States v. Greathouse, 26 Fed. Cas. No. 15,254, at 22 (C. C. N. D. Cal. 1863); Charge to Grand Jury, *In re* Riots of 1844, 4 Pa. Law Jour. Rep. 29, 35 (Phila. Quar. Sess. 1844), also quoted at 26 Fed. Cas. 116; Druecker v. Salomon, 21 Wis. 621, 626 (1867).

45. *Cf.* 8 Holdsworth, (2d ed. 1937) 320, 328–29; Kenny, Outlines of Criminal Law (15th ed. 1936) 315.

46. Paxson, C. J., in Commonwealth v. O'Donnel, 12 Pa. Co. 97, 104–105 (Oyer & Tr., Allegheny Cty. 1892).

47. See Burgoyne, Homestead (1893) 294; Stowell, "Fort Frick" or the Siege of Homestead (1893) 291.

48. (1892) 26 Am. L. Rev. 912, 914; *cf.* (1892) 46 Alb. L. Jour. 345; (1892) 31 Am. L. Reg. (N.S.) 691, 699; (1893) 15 Crim. L. Mag. 191, 197. Former Chief Justice Agnew, of Pennsylvania, is quoted as stating in a letter to the press that "it is easy to distinguish treason from riot. It lies in the purpose or intent of the traitor to overthrow the government or subvert the law or destroy an institution of the state. Riot is a breach or violation of law, but without a purpose against the state." See Burgoyne, Homestead (1893) 202.

49. See Seagle, *Riot* in 13 Enc. Soc. Sci. (1934) 388.

50. See Appendix, IV, pp. 270–273 *infra.*

51. 96 Utah 500, 503, 504–505, 87 P. (2d) 807, 808–809 (1939); *cf.* 93 Utah 70, 71 P. (2d) 104 (1937).

52. See Harno, *Intent in Criminal Conspiracy* (1941) 89 U. of Pa. L. Rev. 624, 646. The practical protection against a finding of "guilt by association" afforded by insistence upon a showing that any given defendant shared the specific intent to commit the plotted crime is shown in United States v. Bryant, 245 Fed. 682 (N. D. Tex. 1917), *aff'd,* 257 Fed. 378 (C. C. A. 5th, 1919). See, especially, 257 Fed. at 384.

A strict construction of the intent element in the general federal conspiracy statute was the instrument employed to prevent a dangerously vague extension of the crime in Haywood v. United States, 268 Fed. 795, 799–800 (C. C. A. 7th, 1920), *cert. denied,* 256 U. S. 689 (1921). *Cf.* Baldwin v. Franks, 120 U. S. 678 (1887), for the same rationale of interpretation, though erroneously applied. See Field, J., dissenting in 256 U. S. at 703, 705; Deady, D. J., in *In re* Impaneling and Instructing the Grand Jury, 26 Fed. 749, 754 (D. Ore. 1886).

53. United States v. Pryor, 27 Fed. Cas. 628, No. 16,096 (C. C. D. Pa. 1814). And compare the acquittal of Joshua Hett Smith, for lack of convincing proof of intent to join in Arnold's treason. See note 97 *infra.*

54. *Id.* at 630, 631.

55. See, *e.g.,* United States v. Stephan, 50 F. Supp. 738, 740, n.1, at 744, *charge approved,* 133 F. (2d) 87, 99 (C. C. A. 6th, 1943); United States v. Fricke, 259 Fed. 673, 676, 682 (S. D. N. Y. 1919); Douglas, J., dissenting in Cramer v. United States, 325 U. S. 1, 49, n.2 (1945).

56. See p. 193 *supra.*

57. *Ibid.*

58. The remaining overt act submitted to the jury was based on falsehoods told by Cramer after his arrest to FBI agents, admittedly for the purpose of shielding the saboteur. The Supreme Court does not pass on the "complicated" problem presented by this phase of the case, since it reverses

on the error found in submitting as overt acts Cramer's meetings with Thiel. See 325 U.S. 1, 36,n.45 (1945). The falsehoods would seem clearly to constitute a giving of aid, although Thiel was already under arrest when Cramer falsified; and the latter fact would seem irrelevant if prior doctrine were followed, and successful conferring of a benefit on the enemy did not have to be shown. Since the lies were told to two or more of the Federal agents, they would seem to be established satisfactorily under the two-witness provision.

59. Cramer v. United States, 325 U.S. 1, 39–40 (1945).

60. See Appendix, V, pp. 273–276 *infra.*

61. See, *e.g.,* Paterson, C. J., in United States v. Vigol, 28 Fed. Cas. 376, No. 16,621 (C. C. D. Pa. 1795). Thus, though it be assumed that there is incontrovertible evidence of treasonable plotting to subvert the government, a conspiracy to levy war is not treason within the constitutional definition, says Mr. Chief Justice Marshall, because plotting does not amount to a sufficient overt act. *Ex parte* Bollman, 4 Cranch 75,126 (U. S. 1807). See Peters, D. J., in charge to jury in first trial of Fries, 9 Fed. Cas. No. 5,126, at 909 (C. C. D. Pa. 1799), and charge to Chase, C. J., on second trial, 9 Fed Cas. No. 5,127, at 931 (C. C. D. Pa. 1800); Livingston, C. J., in charge to jury in United States v. Hoxie, 26 Fed. Cas. No. 15,407, at 398 (C. C. D. Vt. 1808); Story, C. J., Charge to Grand Jury, 30 Fed. Cas. No. 18,275, at 1,047 (C. C. D. r. i. 1842); Sprague, D. J., Charge to Grand Jury, 30 Fed. Cas. No. 18,263, at 1,015 (D. Mass. 1851); Grier, C. J., in charge to jury in United States v. Hanway, 26 Fed. Cas. No. 15,299, at 127 (C. C. E. D. Pa. 1851); Nelson, C. J., Charge to Grand Jury, 30 Fed. Cas. No. 18,271, at 1,035 (C. C. S. D. N. Y. 1861); Leavitt, D. J., Charge to Grand Jury, 30 Fed. Cas. No. 18,272, at 1,037 (S. D. Ohio 1861); *cf.* Wimmer v. United States, 264 Fed. 11, 13 (C. C. A. 6th, 1920), *cert. denied,* 253 U. S. 494 (1920).

On the other hand, where there was a clear overt act of armed resistance to constituted authority—as by an armed clash with troops seeking to enforce the Jeffersonian Embargo, or a forcible resistance to execution of the Fugitive Slave Law—verdicts were nevertheless directed when evidence of treasonable intent was lacking, or the evidence was ambiguous as to whether force was not applied for particular or private purposes and hence would not sustain the prosecution's burden of proof. See, *e.g.,* United States v. Hoxie, 26 Fed. Cas. 397, No. 15,407 (C. C. D. Vt. 1808); United States v. Hanway, 26 Fed. Cas. 105, No. 15,299 (C. C. E. D. Pa. 1851); *cf.* United States v. Leiner, S. D. N. Y. 1943 (unreported) (reprinted in Brief for Petitioner, p. 47, in United States v. Cramer, 325 U.S. 1 (1945)).

62. See, *e.g.,* United States v. Burr, 25 Fed Cas. No. 14,692a, at 54 (C. C. D. Va. 1807); United States v. Lee, 26 Fed. Cas. 907, No. 15,584 (C. C. D. C. 1814); *The Trial of Thomas Wilson Dorr,* 2 American State Trials (Lawson ed. 1914) 5, 22 (R. I. Sup. Ct. 1844); Pitman, Report of the Trial of Thomas Wilson Dorr (1844) 10; *cf.* United States v. Fricke, 259 Fed. 673, 675 (S. D. N. Y. 1919). See also Douglas, J., dissenting in Cramer v. United States, 325 U.S. 1, 54, n.1 (1945). Marshall pointed out in effect that, if one of the two

elements were merely corroborative of the other, it would plainly be improper and capable of prejudicial effect on defendant's rights to permit the prosecutor to prove the corroborative fact before establishing the fact corroborated. See United States v. Burr, 25 Fed. Cas. No. 14,692a, at 54 (C. C. D. Va. 1807), and 7 Wigmore, Evidence (3d ed. 1940) § 2038 (praising the "lucid opinion by Marshall, C. J.").

63. See Harno, *op. cit. supra* note 52, at 646.

64. 325 U.S. 1, 28 (1945).

65. See *Ex parte* Bollman, 4 Cranch 75, 126 (U.S. 1807); United States v. Mitchell, 26 Fed. Cas. No. 15,788, at 1,280 (C. C. D. Pa. 1795); Case of Fries, 9 Fed. Cas. No. 5,126, at 840 (charge to grand jury), 909 (first trial) (C. C. D. Pa. 1799); Case of Fries, 9 Fed. Cas. No. 5,127, at 924, 931 (C. C. D. Pa. 1800) (second trial); United States v. Burr, 25 Fed. Cas. No. 14,692a, at 13–14 (C. C. D. Va. 1807), United States v. Burr, 25 Fed. Cas. No. 14,693, at 168 (C. C. D. Va. 1807); United States v. Pryor, 27 Fed. Cas. No. 16,096, at 630 (C. C. D. Pa. 1814); United States v. Fricke, 259 Fed. 673, 677 (S. D. N. Y. 1919); United States v. Robinson, 259 Fed. 685, 690 (S. D. N. Y. 1919); United States v. Haupt, 47 F. Supp. 836, 839 (N. D. Ill. 1942), *rev'd on other grounds,* 136 F.(2d) 661 (C. C. A. 7th, 1943); United States v. Stephan, 50 F. Supp. 738, 742–43 (E. D. Mich. 1943), *approved,* 133 F.(2d) 87, 99 (C. C. A. 6th, 1943).

All of the rulings and dicta refusing to recognize a conspiracy as a sufficient overt act of levying war contain similar language or implications. See cases cited, note 61 *supra.* The familiar analysis is in the background of those contemporary decisions refusing to concede that "mere words," as punished under sedition acts, could constitute treason, because they do not amount to sufficient execution of such treasonable intent as they evidence. See cases cited in notes 106, 111, 112, and 118, all in chapter 4 *supra.* To the same effect are numerous charges to grand and petit juries regarding disturbances against the Fugitive Slave Law and the outbreak of the Civil War. See Charge to Grand Jury, 30 Fed. Cas. 1,015, No. 18,263 (D. Mass. 1851); Charge to Grand Jury, 30 Fed. Cas. 1,047, No. 18,276 (C. C. E. D. Pa. 1851); United States v. Hanway, 26 Fed. Cas. 105, No. 15,299 (C. C. E. D. Pa. 1851); Charge to Grand Jury, 30 Fed. Cas. 1,024, No. 18,269 (D. Mass. 1851); United States v. Greiner, 26 Fed. Cas. 36, No. 15, 262 (E. D. Pa. 1861);United States v. Greathouse, 26 Fed. 18, No. 15,254 (C. C. N. D. Cal. 1863); Charge to Grand Jury, 30 Fed. Cas. 1,034, No. 18,271 (C. C. S. D. N. Y. 1861); Charge to Grand Jury, 30 Fed. Cas. 1,036, No. 18,272 (C. C. S. D. Ohio 1861); *cf.* 10 Ops. Att'y Gen. 513 (1863).

66. The function of the overt act in treason is identified with this general policy of the criminal law in the charge to the jury in United States v. Stephan, 50 F. Supp. 738, 740, n.1, at 742–43 (E. D. Mich. 1943), *approved,* 133 F.(2d) 87, 99 (C. C. A. 6th, 1943). See Hall, *Criminal Attempt—A Study of Foundations of Criminal Liability* (1940) 49 Yale L. J. 789, 818.

67. 325 U.S. 1, 28 (1945).

68. See United States v. Fricke, 259 Fed. 673, 677 (S. D. N. Y. 1919); Charge to Grand Jury, 30 Fed. Cas. No. 18,272, at 1,037 (C. C. S. D. Ohio

1861). This rationale is implicit in the decisions which sustain criminal syndicalism legislation against the claim that it trenches on the treason clause, by pointing out that legislation penalizing "mere words" does not *ipso facto* purport to punish treason. See cases cited in notes 106, 111, 112, and 118, all in chapter 4 *supra*.

69. *Ibid.* 325 U.S. 1, 34 (1945).

70. *Ibid.*

71. *Id.*, 38. Compare also the comment that "where the sufficiency of the overt acts has been challenged because they were colorless as to intent, we are persuaded the reason intent was left in question was that the acts were really indecisive as a giving of aid and comfort." Acts "that are trivial and commonplace," it continues, "hence are doubtful as to whether they gave aid and comfort to the enemy." *Id.*, 35. Likewise, in the court's summation, cited in note 59 *supra*, its insistence that the act of meeting with the saboteur is insufficient, because this would be "to take the intent for the deed," points to a requirement that aid actually be conferred on the enemy. The majority's approving quotation of Lord Reading's formula that "aid" is "an act which strengthens or tends to strengthen the enemy" (325 U.S. 1, 28) is somewhat ambiguous and in isolation might suggest that something less than accomplished aid and comfort would suffice. But the formula may also mean simply that a net accretion to the enemy's strength need not be shown, if it appears that some effect of defendant's efforts has at least reached the enemy. More ambiguous are the majority's examples (*id.*, 29) of "actions which do aid and comfort the enemy," such as "making a speech critical of the government . . . profiteering, striking in defense plants. . . ," for such acts would probably require the conjunction of other events to constitute them effective aid to the enemy.

72. *Id.*, 37.

73. *Ibid.*

74. See Note 59 *supra*.

75. 325 U.S. 1, 28 (1945).

76. See United States v. Fricke, 259 Fed. 673 (S. D. N. Y. 1919); *cf.* Douglas, J., dissenting in Cramer v. United States, 325 U.S. 1, 55, n.2 (1945).

77. See 2 Stephen, History of the Criminal Law of England (1893) 263; 4 Holdsworth, History of English Law (1924) 496–97; *Cf.* Learned Hand, J., in United States v. Robinson, 259 Fed. 685, 689–90 (S. D. N. Y. 1919).

78. See Appendix, VI, pp. 276–279 *infra*.

79. See cases discussed by Douglas, J., dissenting in Cramer v. United States, 325 U.S. 1, 64 (App. 73–74).

80. *Cf. Ex parte* Bollman, 4 Cranch 75, 126 (U. S. 1807); United States v. Lee, 26 Fed. Cas. 907, No. 15,584 (C. C. D. C. 1814); United States v. Pryor, 27 Fed. Cas. No. 16,096, at 631 (C. C. D. Pa. 1814); Story, C. J., Charge to Grand Jury, 30 Fed. Cas. No. 18,275, at 1,047 (C. C. D. R. I. 1842); United States v. Greathouse, 26 Fed. Cas. No. 15,254, at 24 (C. C. N. D. Cal. 1863); United States v. Fricke, 259 Fed. 673, 678, 679 (S. D. N. Y. 1919); see United States v. Stephan, 50 F. Supp. 445, 448 (E. D. Mich. 1943). That the law of

treason is probably, in fact, the origin of the general law of attempt, see Hall, *Criminal Attempt* (1940) 49 Yale L. J. 789, 794–97, 815. That treason is of the nature of a "direct attempt," see Strahorn, *Effect of Impossibility of Criminal Attempts* (1930) 78 U. of Pa. L. Rev. 962, 964. This is also the executive construction of the scope of "treason" in the President's proclamation of April 16, 1917, warning of the nature and penalties of treasonable activities. See 18 U. S. C. A. § 1, annotation, at 4 (1940). *Contra:* United States v. Robinson, 259 Fed. 685 (S. D. N. Y. 1919); Respublica v. Malin, 1 Dall. 33 (U. S. 1778). See Strahorn, *op. cit. supra* at 994–95.

81. See, *e.g.,* Hanauer v. Doane, 12 Wall. 342 (U. S. 1870) (sale of goods, intended for enemy use); United States v. Lee, 26 Fed. Cas. 907, No. 15,584 (C. C. D. C. 1814) (purchase of provisions, intended for enemy); United States v. Greathouse, 26 Fed. Cas. 18, No. 15,254 (C. C. N. D. Cal. 1863) (fitting out a sailing vessel, intended to act as a privateer); United States v. Werner, 247 Fed. 708 (E. D. Pa. 1918) (words); United States v. Fricke, 259 Fed. 673 (S. D. N. Y. 1919) (holding of funds on deposit, or borrowing money, when for convenience of enemy agent); United States v. Haupt, 136 F.(2d) 661 (C. C. A. 7th, 1943) (holding funds, securing lodgings, furnishing mailing address, when for convenience of enemy agent).

82. See Marshall, C. J., in *Ex parte* Bollman, 4 Cranch 75, 126 (U. S. 1807), and cases cited in note 61 *supra.*

83. This was one of the overt acts charged in *United States v. Haupt,* in an indictment the substantive validity of which was not involved in the reversal of the convictions. 47 F. Supp. 836, 839 (N. D. Ill. 1942), *rev'd,* 136 F. (2d) 661 (C. C. A. 7th, 1943).

84. See United States v. Mitchell, 26 Fed. Cas. No. 15,788, at 1,278 (C. C. D. Pa. 1795); Case of Fries, 9 Fed. Cas. No. 5,126, at 914 (C. C. D. Pa. 1799) (first trial); Case of Fries, 9 Fed. Cas. No. 5,127, at 931 (C. C. D. Pa. 1800) (second trial); *Ex parte* Bollman, 4 Cranch 75, 134, (U. S. 1807); United States v. Burr, 25 Fed. Cas. No. 14,692a, at 14 (C. C. D. Va. 1807), United States v. Burr, 25 Fed. Cas. No. 14,693, at 165, 168 (C. C. D. Va. 1807); Charge to Grand Jury, 30 Fed. Cas. 1,015, No. 18,263 (D. Mass. 1851); United States v. Haupt, 47 F. Supp. 836, 839 (N. D. Ill. 1942), *rev'd on grounds not affecting the substance of indictment,* 136 F.(2d) 661 (C. C. A. 7th, 1943). *Cf.* Stephan v. United States, 133 F.(2d) 87, 93, 94 (C. C. A. 6th, 1943). *But cf.* Story, C. J., Charge to Grand Jury, 30 Fed. Cas. No. 18,275, at 1,047 (C. C. D. R. I. 1842); Grier, C. J., in charge to jury in United States v. Hanway, 26 Fed. Cas. No. 15,299, at 126 (C. C. E. D. Pa. 1851).

85. See 26 Fed. Cas. No. 15,254, at 24 (C. C. N. D. Cal. 1863).

86. See United States v. Burr, 25 Fed. Cas. No. 14,693, at 165, 168 (C. C. D. Va. 1807).

87. *Id.* at 169.

88. See note 71 *supra.*

89. See note 80 *supra.*

90. U. S. Const. Art. III, § 3. The clause, of course, also recognizes confession in open court as a basis for conviction.

91. 325 U. S. 1, 30 (1945); see Marshall, C. J., in United States v. Burr, 25 Fed. Cas. No. 14,693, at 176 (C. C. D. Va. 1807); Baldwin, C. J., in United States v. Doebler, 25 Fed. Cas. No. 14,977, at 886 (C. C. E. D. Pa. 1832). The suggestion of Judge Hand in United States v. Robinson, 259 Fed. 685, 691 (S. D. N. Y. 1919), that the requirement of direct evidence represents a continuance of an archaic philosophy of proof by oath bearers seems without conviction in logic, and is certainly without evidence in history. It seems clear that a rational theory of probative values, whether mistaken or not, underlies the two-witness requirement. Indeed, it would be difficult to find two members of the Federal Convention less likely to have been moved by considerations drawn from a "system of trial not rational in its processes" (*Id.* at 691), than Benjamin Franklin and James Wilson, whose remarks alone are recorded on the point. See p. 133 *supra;* 7 Wigmore, Evidence (3d ed. 1940) § 2039; 259 Fed. at 692–93. The cases cited in this note discuss the basis of the two-witness requirement wholly in terms of probative values, and the same approach has been taken toward the requirements for proof of overt acts in English law. See 7 Wigmore, Evidence (3d ed. 1940) §§ 2036, 2037.

92. When the Court says (325 U. S. 1, 35) that "The two-witness principle is to interdict imputation of *incriminating acts* to the accused by circumstantial evidence or by the testimony of a single witness," it seems merely to state its conclusion, not an argument therefor, since the meaning of the assertion depends on the content of the "incriminating" act. This is true also of the statement that "The words of the Constitution were chosen, not to make it hard to prove merely routine and everyday acts, but to make the proof of acts that convict of treason as sure as trial processes may be." *Ibid.* The germ of an argument why aid or intent must be evidenced by the act seems at first glance implied in the remark that the framers, "having thus by definition made treason consist of something . . . capable of direct proof," wrote the two-witness requirement to safeguard the trial procedure. *Id.,* 29. But, again, the significance of the statement turns on the meaning of the act, for obviously an act which merely furthers defendant's plan of aiding the enemy is, *qua* act, as much "capable of direct proof" as an act which completes the aid.

93. *Cf.* Case of Fries, 9 Fed. Cas. No. 5,126, at 909, 914 (C. C. D. Pa. 1799) (first trial); see United States v. Doebler, 25 Fed. Cas., No. 14,977, at 885–86 (C. C. E. D. Pa. 1832); 7 Wigmore, Evidence (3d ed. 1940) § 2037.

94. 325 U. S. 1, 31 (1945); *cf.* Douglas, J., dissenting, at 59.

95. 325 U. S. 1, 31 (1945).

96. *Id.,* 34, *cf.* Douglas, J., dissenting, *id.,* 58. The fact that the intent and the act elements have always been recognized as distinct, so that the prosecution must equally establish each, and that distinct functions have been ascribed to them, in itself suggests that the evidence sufficient to establish one element may not necessarily be required to be of a character relevant to establishing the other. As an *a priori* matter, it may of course be argued also that both elements are designed, ultimately, to prove the intent, which is the basic factor which may make the accused a dangerous man; and that it would not be irrational, in promotion of the obvious concern of the framers to

safeguard the rights of the accused, if the "overt act" were intended to be such as would offer corroborative evidence of the intent. It may fairly be urged that men in all ages would be perfectly willing to punish one whom they were sure was adhering to the state's enemies by treacherous thoughts; that the practical problem is one of securing adequate proof to assure against abusive prosecutions of the innocent; and that, hence, if the overt act element is construed to require proof which will provide cumulative evidence of intent, this is not to say that the overt act requirement is rendered meaningless. Whatever the persuasiveness of this latter analysis, certainly it must carry the burden of proof, for, by familiar principles of construction, distinct elements in a constitutional, legislative, or judge-made rule of law are to be taken *prima facie* as intended to serve distinct purposes. See Marshall, C. J., in Marbury v. Madison, 1 Cranch 137, 174 (U. S. 1803). Further, if the evidence to establish the overt act is required to be such as will corroborate the existence of the intent, it is difficult to understand the decisions which so rigorously insist on full proof of each element, acquitting those whose intent is assumed treasonable, but who have not been shown guilty of an "overt act." Likewise, it is hard to see how it can be said to be immaterial which element of the crime is proved first (see note 62 *supra*), if one is corroborative of the other. True, in the cases of ruling on the order of proof, the issues arose because the prosecution sought first to introduce its evidence on intent, and it might be argued that it is hence wholly consistent with a corroborative function of the act element to introduce the principal evidence on intent first. But the rulings make no such distinction, and Marshall, C. J., plainly says that there is none, an answer which is the more to the present point because it was in response to the contention that the *act* must be proved first.

97. *Cf.* United States v. Schulze, 253 Fed. 377, 379 (S. D. Cal. 1918), *aff'd without reference to the point here relevant,* 259 Fed. 189 (C. C. A. 9th, 1919); Hall, *op. cit. supra* note 80, at 794–97, 824–25.

98. See cases cited in note 81 *supra*.

99. See, *e.g.*, United States v. Hodges, 26 Fed. Cas. 332, No. 15,374 (C. C. D. Md. 1815) (delivery of prisoners to enemy); United States v. Hoxie, 26 Fed. Cas. 397, No. 15,407 (C. C. D. Vt. 1808) (armed clash with troops seeking to enforce national embargo); United States v. Hanway, 26 Fed. Cas. 105, No. 15,299, (C. C. E. D. Pa. 1851) (forcible resistance to execution of Fugitive Slave Law); United States v. Magtibay, 2 Philipp. 703 (1903) (duress); United States v. Leiner, Cr. No. 113–120 (S. D. N. Y. 1943) (unreported, see note 61 *supra*) (misstatements to authorities regarding identity of spy). Distinguish cases where the prosecution fails because the acts shown are not deemed sufficiently advanced in execution of the intent. See, *e.g.*, United States v. Pryor, 27 Fed. Cas. 628, No. 16,096 (C. C. D. Pa. 1814); United States v. De Los Reyes, 3 Philipp. 349 (1904).

There is no more striking example of conduct on its face clearly treasonable, but in fact found innocent, than the case of Joshua Hett Smith. Smith, a resident of the West Point area, arranged to have two of his tenants row him on the night of September 21, 1780, to the British sloop Vulture, lying in the

Hudson. He hailed the vessel as a friend, boarded her and was aboard for fifteen to twenty minutes, after which he returned to the rowboat accompanied by Major Andre, whom he then brought ashore for the meeting with Arnold. Smith took Andre to his house and furnished him with the civilian coat which Andre wore at the time of his capture. Smith was tried before a court-martial, convened under a resolution of the Congress authorizing the commander in chief thus to try any citizen who should harbor or secrete any of the subjects or soldiers of Great Britain, knowing them to be such, or should be instrumental in conveying intelligence to the enemy. His defense, apart from a challenge to the jurisdiction of the court martial, was that Arnold had enlisted his aid on the pretext that this was a means of obtaining information helpful to the American cause. The most careful student of the Arnold conspiracy apparently believes that Smith was telling the truth. Van Doren, Secret History of the American Revolution (1941) 330, 331, 337. The court-martial acquitted the defendant, finding that although he had aided Arnold, "yet they are of opinion, that the evidence is not sufficient to convict the said Joshua H. Smith of his being privy to, or having a knowledge of the said Benedict Arnold's criminal, traitorous and base designs." See *The Trial of Joshua H. Smith for Assisting the Enemy,* 6 American State Trials (Lawson ed. 1916) 486; 2 Chandler, American Criminal Trials (1844) 255; Smith, An Authentic Narrative of the Causes which Lead to the Death of Major Andre (1809) 118.

    100. 325 U. S. 1, 32–33 (1945).

    101. *Id.,* 34.

    102. See notes 59 and 71 *supra.*

    103. 325 U. S. 1, 35 (1945).

    104. *Id.,* 38–39.

    105. See note 100 *supra.*

    106. 325 U. S. 1, 33 (1945). Emphasis added.

    107. *Id.,* 37–38.

    108. *Id.,* 39.

    109. Douglas, J., dissenting in 325 U. S. 1, 59 (1945).

    110. See *id.,* 34.

    111. See pp. 133–134 *supra.*

    112. See United States v. Robinson, 259 Fed. 685, 691–91 (S. D. N. Y. 1919).

    113. 7 Wigmore, Evidence (3d ed. 1940) § 2037.

    114. The only effort to defend this position seems to be that of Judge Hand in United States v. Robinson, 259 Fed. 685, 689–90 (S. D. N. Y. 1919), and the scant historical evidence which he adduces does not present a convincing case. His interpretation of the significance of the repeal of 21 Rich. II, c. 3 (1397–98), by 1 Hen. IV, c. 10 (1399), is not unreasonable on the face of the statutes, considered in isolation. But see 1 Hale, History of the Pleas of the Crown. (Emlyn ed. 1736–1739) 85, 111, 266, 267; 2 Stephen, History of the Criminal Law of England (1883) 254. His attempt to derive the

principle of the two-witness rule from the law of "oath bearers" seems to have no plausible relation to the hard-headed men who framed the treason clause. See note 91 *supra*. His argument that a heavy burden of proof must be laid on the prosecution, if the two-witness clause is to mean anything seems wholly *a priori,* and ignores the practical, evidentiary value which may be derived from the simple comparison of the testimony of two separate witnesses to what is allegedly the same transaction. See note 113 *supra*. And see, generally, note 96 *supra*.

115. The King v. Lord Preston, 1 Salk. 278, 91 Eng. Rep. 243 (1691).

116. 325 U. S. 1, 45 (1945).

117. The constitutional authority of Congress, under Art. III, § 3, to mitigate the penalty for treason, of course, limits but cannot be said to destroy the political, as compared to the legal, significance of the constitutional status of the crime. See pp. 146, 149–150 *supra*.

6

Treason Cases
and Doctrine,
1945-1970

AFTER THE Supreme Court decided *Cramer* v. *United States,*
World War II produced ten more reported treason prosecutions pressed to conviction. In seven of these cases court
opinions dealt with substantive and procedural doctrine
concerning the elements of treason and the manner of
proving it. Three of the seven cases—*Haupt* v. *United States,*
decided by the Supreme Court in 1947, *Chandler* v. *United
States,* decided by the First Circuit Court of Appeals in 1948,
and *Kawakita* v. *United States,* decided by the Supreme Court
in 1942—have leading importance for the development of
treason doctrine.[1]

Defendant Haupt, a naturalized United States citizen of
German origin, was the father of one of the German saboteurs landed secretly by submarine in this country in June,
1942. When the son came to Chicago, defendant gave him
shelter for several days in the building in which defendant
lived, accompanied him on visits to foremen of a war-
materials plant so that the son might seek employment there

in furtherance of his mission, and accompanied and assisted him in buying an automobile which the son needed for the activities of his sabotage group; defendant's admissions to federal agents after his arrest and his statements to fellow prisoners in jail, established that he knew of and sympathized with his son's sabotage mission.

Defendant Chandler, living in Europe when Germany went to war with the United States, volunteered his services to a German government corporation engaged in a continuing program of wartime radio propaganda, became a salaried member of the corporation's staff, participated in regular planning sessions in which propaganda directives were discussed and programs tailored to their demands, and made recordings designed for use in the enemy's propaganda broadcasts.

Defendant Kawakita was born in the United States, and was hence (under the 14th Amendment) a citizen of this country; since his parents were Japanese nationals, he was by Japanese law also a national of that country. While in Japan as a student, before the outbreak of war, he renewed an oath of allegiance to the United States before a United States consul, incident to renewing a passport. After war broke out, he remained in Japan, caused himself to be registered in an official record of Japanese nationals, and took employment as a civilian interpreter in a Japanese private factory producing war materials. While working in this factory, but acting outside the scope of his assigned duties as civilian interpreter, he inflicted physical brutalities on United States prisoners of war assigned to work in the factory and its related mines. These brutalities, the courts found, were calculated to increase production by the prisoners of war and reduce their readiness to escape or otherwise refuse to perform labor in the service of the enemy. Testimony of prisoner witnesses tended to establish defendant's animus against the United States, and his intent to aid the victory of Japan.

All of these defendants—Haupt, Chandler, and Kawa-kita—were ruled to have been guilty of overt acts which aided an enemy of the United States, with intent to adhere to the enemy's cause. Four of the other treason prosecutions which resulted in court announcements of doctrine directly related to treason doctrine, involved the kind of conduct involved in *Chandler* v. *United States*—participation in enemy wartime radio propaganda programs—and followed the doctrine laid down in that case.[2]

(a) General Policy

Official opinions in treason cases after *Cramer* consistently continue the familiar emphasis on the restrictive policy of the Constitution toward the scope of the crime. In none of the ten reported decisions dealing directly with treason doctrine was there application of this restrictive emphasis to weight choice in favor of a narrower rather than a broader definition of elements of the offense; nine decisions found treason by adhering to the enemy, giving him aid or comfort; in one case tried before a military commission, the conviction was over-turned on appeal within the military justice system for defects in the evidence of overt acts. The pattern of decision casts no doubt on the vitality of the restrictive policy, for all of these World War II cases fell within a conservative concept of the offense.[3] True, *Haupt* defined the crime in terms less difficult for the prosecutor than *Cramer*. But, as I note later, in doing so *Haupt* only corrected what seems error in *Cramer*, without diminishing the proper force of the limiting admonition of the Constitution.

In a number of cases not involving prosecution for treason, judges took note of the restrictive policy of the Constitution toward that crime by the care they took, or the arguments they made, to differentiate it from other offenses against national security. These instances were of two types, one promoting the broad scope of legislative and executive power to define and implement other security offenses, the other drawing on the limiting policy toward treason to narrow certain assertions of official power.

There was acknowledgment that the treason clause of the Constitution set the exclusive definitions of treason; Congress might not vary the elements of treason or escape the substantive constitutional definition or the requirement of two witnesses to the same overt act by attaching a different label to levying war or adhering to an enemy.[4] Somewhat analogous was a policy declared by Congress to limit military trials. The Uniform Code of Military Justice declared that one might be brought to court martial for conduct engaged in before his discharge from military service only if the accused was not subject to trial therefor in a civil court. Hence, it was held that where the individual's acts constituted adhering to and aiding the enemy, the availability of the treason charge precluded trial before a military tribunal.[5]

On the other hand, in two important prosecutions under the Federal Espionage Act, the Second Circuit Court of Appeals fulfilled previous declarations of the law by ruling that the treason clause did not bar Congress from creating an offense against national security with elements materially different from treason. The applicable statute provided penalties for "whoever, with intent or reason to believe that it is to be used to the injury of the United States or to the advantage of a foreign nation" communicates or delivers to any foreign government or its agents information relating to the national defense.[6] *United States* v. *Rosenberg* presented charges of conspiracy to violate this statute by communicating protected information to the USSR between 1944 and 1950. The Court of Appeals held (1952) that the treason clause did not bar creation of this offense, because "in the Rosenbergs' case, an essential element of treason, giving aid to an 'enemy' is irrelevant to the espionage offense."[7] *United States* v. *Drummond* presented a charge of conspiracy to violate the same statute by a serviceman in the United States Navy who between 1957 and 1962 delivered classified military materials to USSR agents. Again the Court of Appeals held that the treason clause did not bar creation of the espionage offense. The court seemed to go out of its way to enlarge the distinctions between the crimes, finding it "unnecessary" to invoke the difference relied on in *Rosenberg,* because it found differences in the required mental element. Now it pointed out (1965) that the espionage act required a showing only (a) that the defendant transmitted information with intent "or reason to believe" that it would be used to a forbidden result, and (b) with intent or reason to believe that it would be used either "to the injury of the United States or to the advantage of a foreign nation." In contrast, the court implied, treason requires a specific intent, and a specific intent both to aid the enemy and to injure the United States.[8] The two decisions are consistent with the historic scope of the constitutional definition of treason, and with doctrine announced in *Cramer.*

The concerns over possible abuse of government power which lay back of the restrictive constitutional policy on treason had analogies—with varying results—in the development of other areas of public policy. No clear over-all pattern emerged, but the balance inclined toward borrowing the cautions on treason to limit application of other legal sanctions against alleged disloyalty.

In two decisions, the Court of Appeals for the District of Columbia ruled that the Administrator of Veterans Affairs had improperly terminated veterans' disability benefits under a federal statute which authorized such action concerning a beneficiary whom the Administrator found "guilty of mutiny, treason, sabotage, or rendering assistance to any enemy of the United States." In *Wellman* v. *Whittier* (1958) the court found that the Administrator grounded his action upon the beneficiary's membership in the Communist Party as established by his conviction under the Smith Act for conspiracy to advocate overthrow of the government by force. The court ruled that an overt act of assistance to an enemy of the United States must be shown, since the statute showed the intention of Congress to analogize that category of its terms to the requirements of proving treason; mere membership in the party was thus not within Congress's intent under the statute.[9] In *Thompson v. Gleason* the Administrator based forfeiture of disability benefits on findings that the beneficiary had published pamphlets and made speeches sharply critical of the United States military involvement in Korea. The majority of a three-judge district court thought that the Administrator acted within the statute, for—citing treason cases— "It is well settled that aid and assistance to the enemy may be extended in the form of verbal utterance alone, as was the case in this instance." Circuit Judge Fahy (who as Solicitor General had presented the government's case in *Cramer* before the Supreme Court) dissented strongly; it was not claimed that the Administrator had found acts of treason here, and in the context of the statute's reference to treason, it should not be interpreted to penalize domestic political opposition.[10] Reversing the district court, the Court of Appeals (1962) ruled that to avoid a serious question under the First Amendment the statute should be construed to require a finding that the beneficiary had committed a crime in aiding the enemy, and since the record did not show a crime, the benefits must be reinstated. The Court of Appeals did not mention treason, but in the whole context of the case its opinion in substance agrees with Fahy's dissent below.[11]

Several cases growing out of World War II presented an issue analogous to that of adherence and aid to an enemy, where petitioners of dual nationality (citizens of the United States by place of birth, and of the enemy nation by birth to nationals of that country) sought declarations that their service in the enemy's army in wartime under conscription was not an act of expatriation. In *Knauer* v. *United States* (1946)—with concern made manifest by its own reexamination of the full record—the Supreme Court sustained revocation of a decree of naturalization because it had been obtained by fraud; the record, the Court found, clearly sustained the finding that when petitioner foreswore allegiance to the German Reich he swore falsely. Rutledge, J., dissented, joined by Murphy, J. A native-born person, Rutledge argued, might lose his citizenship only for conviction of treason or other felony, with all the safeguards surrounding a determination that the requisite offense had been committed (after, for example, a "rigidly safeguarded trial for treason"); nothing in the Constitution or our traditions, he felt, warranted subjecting a naturalized person to any greater range of hazard of losing citizenship.[12] *Knauer* might seem to forecast stiff handling of the later expatriation cases. But to the contrary the decisions gave full benefit of the doubt to those native-born citizens who, having been lawfully present in enemy countries at the outbreak of war, found themselves conscripted into enemy military service on the basis of their dual nationality. In *Nishikawa* v. *Dulles* (1958) the Supreme Court held that—contrary to the ordinary rule that duress is a matter of affirmative defense—the government had the burden of proving by clear, convincing and unequivocal evidence that an apparent act of expatriation was voluntary; unless voluntariness were put in issue, it would be assumed, but when petitioner showed that he was inducted under a conscription law of the country of his dual nationality, and claimed that the induction was against his will, the government must sustain its burden of proof.[13] The strong preponderance of lower federal court decisions before *Nishikawa* had already in effect come to the same result. Most of these decisions did not explicitly invoke the treason clause or cases, though at least one court intimated that the availability of the treason charge was a further reason why an expansive interpretation should not be given to the statutory provisions for expatriation.[14] The prevailing emphasis of the cases was, rather, on the uniquely basic status which citizenship is, and on the doctrine established in statute and apparently of constitutional force, that no conduct may result in expatriation unless it be voluntary.[15] However, where individuals served in enemy armies, the courts' insistence on clear proof of intent inconsistent with loyalty to the United States constituted a value judgment which in effect belongs with the restrictive traditions of the treason clause. In 1961 Congress highlighted the presence of a significant value choice by amending the Nationality Act to reverse the *Nishikawa* allocation of the burden of proof on duress, putting it on the citizenship claimant.[16]

The Supreme Court drew on the restrictive policy toward treason to support the rule that wrongful intent should be presumed intended as an element in federal crimes,[17] and more specifically to support its ruling that under the Smith Act the United States must prove specific intent to advocate overthrowing the government by force.[18] On the other hand, dissenting Justices were conspicuously unsuccessful in persuading the Court that since treason requires proof of an overt act, in order to forestall using the treason charge against unpopular speech or publication in the course of domestic political controversy, so laws directed at subversive activity other than treason should be interpreted to require proof of overt acts other than the communicating of ideas or opinions.[19]

The march of events raised a new point relevant to general limitations on the treason offense. In earlier doctrine there was an assumption, more often implied than stated, that treason by adhering to and aiding an "enemy" could be committed only during a formally declared state of war.[20] By mid-20th century the country found itself in shooting wars which Congress had not formally declared. In two matters connected with the undeclared Korean war, where treason charges were not directly in issue but policy concerning the scope of treason figured in the handling of the matters at issue, some judges apparently assumed that a foreign power which was shooting at United States forces was an "enemy" within the meaning of the treason clause despite absence of a declaration of war.[21] There is realism in this position. But there were also enough possibilities of uncertain definition in it to run counter to the traditional restrictive policy of the Constitution.

(b) The Intent

Post-*Cramer* decisions reaffirmed familiar doctrine on the nature of the wrongful intent which is an element of treason by adhering and giving aid to the enemy. Intent is a distinct element of the crime, in addition to the required showing of an overt act.[22] The requisite intent is one to benefit the enemy's war effort and to harm that of the United States.[23] Duress amounting to immediate threat of death or serious bodily harm is a recognized defense which would negative the required wrongful intent; in the setting of two defendants' detailed, long-continued involvement in conducting enemy wartime radio propaganda programs the courts had no difficulty in supporting jury verdicts which found that the defense was not proved.[24]

The World War II cases added to previous doctrine on intent by responding to three kinds of claims that defendants had been of a divided state of mind—out of dual purposes, loyal motive, or dual allegiance. The Supreme Court in *Haupt* held proper a jury instruction that the defendant lacked treasonable intent if his intention "was not to injure the United States, but merely to aid his son as an individual, as distinguished from assisting him in his purposes, if such existed, of aiding the German Reich, or of injuring the United States." In ruling that the evidence supported the jury's verdict of conviction, in the context of the instruction it approved, the Court apparently holds that if defendant intended to aid the enemy he acted with the requisite wrongful intent, though he may also have acted to implement a father's concern; a mixture of purposes will not negative the crime, if the mixture includes an intent to betray.[25] Defendants Chandler and Best presented a related, but distinct, point when they argued that they lacked treasonable intent because, though they intended their propaganda broadcasts to help Germany win and the United States to lose the war, they acted so out of conviction that defeat would serve the best long-term interests of the United States by halting the march of a Jewish Communist conspiracy for world domination. The argument in effect would excuse purpose (an immediate intended objective result of conduct) by motive (an intended more remote result, or at least a different intended result valued for its service to different interests). In both cases the First Circuit Court of Appeals held that motive was irrelevant, if there were an immediate purpose to aid the enemy.[26] Finally, the World War II cases presented what in effect were issues of intent, created in the first instance by problems of defining the legal nature of allegiance where individuals lawfully were present in the foreign country at war's outbreak, especially when they were of dual nationality—citizens of the United States because they were born here, and citizens of the foreign country of which their parents were then nationals. Any person owes temporary allegiance to the ordinary domestic laws of a foreign sover-

eign whose protection he enjoys in that sovereign's territory.[27] In addition, a United States citizen, lawfully present at
the outbreak of war in a foreign country of which by dual
nationality he is also a citizen, owes that country the ordinary
duties of citizenship apart from direct war service.[28] Given
the need to earn a living, and given the broad scope of
controls characteristic of a modern war economy, individuals
whom the outbreak of war found in the hostile country would
not be held to have treasonable intent merely because they
took employment there, though the employment made some
contribution to the enemy's strength.[29] So, as we have already
seen, conscripted service in the enemy army will be taken to
reflect duress and not a voluntary change of allegiance.[30] But
the radio-broadcast defendants committed themselves to spe-
cial-skills activities not of an ordinary employment nature,
focused upon specialized aid to the enemy. Defendant Kawakita took what might be rated as ordinary employment—as civilian interpreter dealing with prisoners of war
assigned to work in a mine and metals processing factory
producing materials useful to the war effort—but exerted
himself in physical abuse of prisoners beyond his job assign-
ment. All of these defendants were shown to have repeatedly
declared their animus against the United States war effort
and their desire that the enemy prevail. In these contexts the
courts had no difficulty in ruling that claims of allegiance
owed by presence or of allegiance owed also by dual nationality did not negative the existence of intent to betray the
United States.[31] That Congress by statute allowed United
States citizens voluntarily to expatriate themselves—thereby
ending the allegiance which could open them to conviction of
treason—did not set up an unconstitutionally arbitrary classification as against those who kept their United States citizenship; differentiation of legal responsibility according to allegiance was a reasonable classification for a national state to
make.[32]

(c) The Overt Act

The decisions after *Cramer* materially clarified or added to the law concerning the overt act in treason in three respects—the relation between the intent and act elements of the crime, the required causal tendency or likely effect of the act, and the bearing of the act element on values of protected speech and dissent.

Mr. Justice Jackson's opinion for the Court in *Cramer* left badly confused the relation between the intent and act elements of treason. The opinion stated clearly that these were distinct elements, and at one point disclaimed holding that to be a sufficient overt act the act must be of such character as itself to evidence intent to betray. But in ruling insufficient the two-witness testimony there offered, of defendant's two meetings with an enemy saboteur in public restaurants, Jackson's opinion seemed nonetheless to reject the evidence because in itself it implied nothing of evil purpose: If the government's argument was that it might meet its burden of proof by showing "an apparently commonplace and insignificant act and from other circumstances create an inference that the act was a step in treason and was done with treasonable intent. . . . [then] the function of the overt act in a treason prosecution is almost zero."[33] Along with this ambiguous talk, the *Cramer* opinion said that its ground was that the acts proved constituted "no showing that Cramer gave [the saboteurs] . . . any information whatever of value to their mission . . . furnished them no shelter, nothing that can be called sustenance or supplies," so that "without the use of some imagination it is difficult to perceive any advantage which this meeting afforded to [the saboteurs] . . . as enemies."[34] Again speaking for the Court, in *Haupt* Mr. Justice Jackson somewhat clarified the matter. Haupt's acts—sheltering his saboteur son, helping him buy an automobile, and accompanying him in seeking employment in a war-

materials factory—were conduct which a jury could reasonably believe helped the saboteur in his mission, without need
to prove other acts of defendant. Hence the two-witness
testimony to these acts satisfactorily established overt acts of
aiding the enemy. It was immaterial that the conduct did not
on its face evidence wrongful intent.[35] The *Haupt* opinion
does not foreclose that a given act might be a legally sufficient
overt act, though on its face it was not of such likely effect as
to persuade a jury that aid was given by it, provided that
other evidence could put it in a context that would show that
aid was given; however, *Haupt* intimates—as *Cramer* perhaps
held—that this evidence of the act's context must also be
supplied by two witnesses to the same circumstances.[36]

Sufficient acts of aid were shown where defendants participated in staff conferences and made broadcast recordings for
enemy radio propaganda programs,[37] and where a defendant
committed brutalities on prisoners of war calculated to extort
more production from them and intimidate them from
resisting demands made on them as forced labor in a mine
and factory producing material useful to the enemy war
effort.[38] In all these cases the same two-witness evidence
which proved the particular acts also served to prove the
setting in which it was apparent that they were calculated to
give aid. That the aid was not effective, or not substantial, was
no defense.[39] Thus it was immaterial how many in the United
States heard a defendant's broadcasts for the enemy, or even
whether his recordings were used; in making the recordings,
he fulfilled his assigned role for the enemy.[40]

The radio-broadcast defendants inevitably raised that aspect of the restrictive policy toward treason which emphasized protection of rights of speech and political dissent.
The courts had no difficulty in rejecting the defense. True,
sound policy opposed using treason charges to suppress
ordinary domestic political controversy. And mere speech,
however disloyal in intent, would not make out an overt act if

in its setting it would not give aid.[41] But expression was an act, and where it was part of a planned enemy propaganda campaign it amounted to a sufficient overt act. Moreover, the First Circuit Court of Appeals indicated, there could here be no substantial question of protecting the freedom of political dissent, for this behavior was outside the framework of domestic political combat: "Trafficking with the enemy, in whatever form, is wholly outside the shelter of the First Amendment."[42]

(d) Sufficiency of Evidence

The decisions after *Cramer* elaborated the law concerning the sufficiency of evidence of treasonable intent, without major addition. Intent need not be proved by two witnesses, nor by the character of the overt acts proved by two witnesses.[43] On the other hand, intent might be inferred from the overt acts.[44] So, intent to betray might be inferred from the content of recordings made by a United States listening post of defendant's radio broadcasts for the enemy, where the trial court carefully charged the jury that the evidence used for this purpose was not to be taken as a substitute for the required two-witness testimony to overt acts.[45] Defendants fruitlessly challenged use of their out-of-court admissions to prove intent. The most pointed defense argument was that the Constitution should be taken to bar evidence of the defendant's admissions because Article III, Section 3 stipulated that conviction might not be had "unless on the testimony of two witnesses to the same overt act, or on confession in open court." The Supreme Court expressed doubt whether the Constitution's reference to confession applied to any out-of-court admission of a fact other than a complete confession of guilt of the crime.[46] In any event, it ruled such admissions competent where they corroborated other evidence, such as inferences drawn from properly proved overt acts, or testimony of third parties as to defendants' statements to them. The Supreme Court did intimate some doubt whether intent might be sufficiently proved only by the defendant's admissions.[47] Defendant's statements contemporary with properly proved overt acts are proper evidence of intent.[48] Defendant's statements made long before indictment, should be admitted with caution lest their use trench on protected domestic political dissent, but where the statements were "explicit" in showing sympathy for a country later our enemy, and hostility to the United States, they were held admissible.[49]

Problems of proving the overt act all centered on the two-witness requirement. The courts continued to declare a standard of strict adherence to the substance of the requirement. Two witnesses must testify directly to the same overt act; it would not be enough that there was two-witness evidence of a separate act from which it might be inferred that the charged act occurred.[50] Two-witness testimony to defendant's admissions of an act did not meet the requirement of two-witness evidence to the act itself.[51] To charge defendant with conspiring with others to commit the act did not relieve the government of the need to produce two-witness evidence that the defendant did the act.[52]

However, the decisions defined with some flexibility favorable to the prosecution the boundaries of the act to which two witnesses must testify. Their testimony need not be identical or precise as to all aspects of the cited behavior, nor need it minutely cover every element into which an episode of behavior might be analyzed. The evidence was sufficient if it joined in identifying what reasonable jurors could regard as a connected, patterned transaction. So in *Haupt* the Supreme Court held that it was not fatal to the government's case that the two-witness testimony did not show the saboteur entering defendant's apartment, where it did show that he entered the building in which defendant had an apartment, and entered only as defendant's licensee, since by other two-witness testimony it was established that no other tenant in the building sheltered him.[53] So, too, defendant's help to the saboteur in buying an automobile was properly proved by the testimony of the auto salesman and the showroom sales manager, though the two witnesses did not participate together in every incident of the transaction, where the sales manager joined in several steps of it.[54] Again, in decisions sustaining convictions of defendants who participated in enemy radio propaganda efforts, the courts indicated that it met the constitutional standard of proof that two witnesses established a defendant's continuing cooperation in a connected, planned program; in each of these cases there was direct two-witness testimony to particular significant acts, but the courts intimated that they would have accepted testimony of two witnesses to separate phases of a closely woven net of behavior.[55]

NOTES

1. Haupt v. United States, 330 U. S. 631 (1947); Kawakita v. United States, 343 U. S. 717 (1952); Chandler v. United States, 171 F (2d) 921 (C. C. A 1st 1948), cert den., 336 U. S. 918 (1949), See Appendix II for further details.

2. Gillars v. United States, 182 F. (2d) 962 (Ct. App. D. C. 1950); Best v. United States, 184 F. (2d) 131, cert. den., 340 U. S. 939 (1951); Burgman v. United States, 188 F. (2d) 637 (Ct. App. D. C. 1951), cert. den. 342 U. S. 838 (1951); D'Aquino v. United States, 192 F. (2d) 338 (C. C. A. 9th. 1951), cert. den. 343 U. S. 935 (1952).

3. See, especially, Magruder, circ. j., for the court, in Chandler v. United States, 171 F. (2d) 921, 938, 939 (C. C. A. 1st. 1948), cert. den., 336 U. S. 918 (1949).

4. See Rosenberg v. United States, 195 F (2d) 583, 610–611 (C. C. A. 2d. 1952), cert. den., 344 U. S. 838 (1952); United States v. Drummond, 354 F. (2d) 132, 152 (C. C. A. 2d. 1965).

5. Martin v. Young, 134 F. Supp. 204 (N. D. Cal. 1955). For discussion of a number of cases of alleged assistance to the enemy by United States servicemen held as North Korean prisoners of war (in an undeclared war: see

note 21, *infra*), prosecuted or considered for prosecution by military tribunals as violations of Article 104 of the Uniform Code of Military Justice, see Comment, 6 Catholic University of America Law Review 56, 57 (1956), and Steinhaus, "Treason, A Brief History with Some Modern Applications", 22 Brooklyn Law Review 255, 272–273, note 93 (1956). None of these cases seems to have produced a reported judicial decision. In some instances the defense unsuccessfully pressed the argument that in the given contexts the substance of the charge was treason, and that hence proceedings under the Uniform Code violated the exclusive policy of the treason clause of the Constitution.

6. 40 Stat. 218, 219 (1917), 62 Stat. 737 (1948), 68 Stat. 1219 (1954), 18 U. S. C. A. sec. 794.

7. 195 F. (2d) 583, 611 (C. C. A. 2d 1952), cert. den., 344 U. S. 838 (1952).

8. 354 F. (2d) 132, 152 (C. C. A. 2d. 1965). *Cf.* Gorin v. United States, 312 U. S. 19 (1941).

9. Wellman v. Whittier, 259 F. (2d) 163, 167 and 167, n. 15 (Ct. App. D. C. 1958).

10 Thompson v. Whittier, 185 F. Supp. 306, 314, 315 (dissent) (Dist. Ct. D. C. 1960).

11. Same case, sub. nom. Thompson v. Gleason, 317 F. (2d) 901 (Ct. App. D. C. 1962).

12. Knauer v. United States, 328 U. S. 654, 679 (dissent).

13. Nishikawa v. Dulles, 356 U. S. 129, 134 (1958). See Mandoli v. Acheson, 344 U. S. 133, 135 (1952).

14. See Terada v. Dulles, 121 F. Supp. 6, 7 (D. Hawaii, 1954); *cf.* Nationality Act of 1940, 54 Stat. 1137, 1169 (1940), 8 U. S. C. A. sec. 1481, and Perez v. Brownell, 356 U. S. 44, 56 (1958).

15. See, *e.g.,* Perri v. Dulles, 206 F.(2d) 586 (C. C. A. 3rd. 1963); Tomasicchio v. Acheson, 98 F. Supp. 166 (Dist. Ct. D. C. 1951); Kanbara v. Acheson, 103 F. Supp. 565 (S. D. Cal. 1952); Gensheimer v. Dulles, 117 F. Supp. 836 (D. N. J. 1954); *cf.* Perez v. Brownell, 356 U. S. 44 (1958). But *cf.* Kondo v. Acheson, 98 F. Supp. 884 (S. D. Cal. 1951), and Hamamoto v. Acheson, *id.,* 904 (S. D. Cal. 1951).

16. 75 Stat. 656 (1961), 8 U. S. C. A. sec. 1481 (c). The change seems impliedly acknowledged in Woodby v. Immigration Service, 385 U. S. 276, 285, n.17 (1966).

17. See Morisette v. United States, 342, U. S. 246, 262, n.21 (1952).

18. See Dennis v. United States, 341 U. S. 494, 499–500 (1951).

19. See Jackson, J., dissenting in part in American Communications Association v. Douds, 339 U. S. 382, 437 (1950); Black and Douglas, J. J., dissenting in part in Yates v. United States, 354 U. S. 298, 339, 342–343 (1957); Douglas, J., dissenting in Scales v. United States, 367 U. S. 203, 266 (1961); Douglas, J., dissenting from denial of certiorari in Epton v. New York, 390 U. S. 29, 31, 32 (1968). Though the majority opinion in Yates v. United States did not mention the treason cases, in effect it squarely rejected the idea that the kind of overt act required in treason should be interpreted

as required in a statute punishing conspiracy to advocate overthrow of the government by force. See Harlan, J., for the Court, 354 U. S. 298, 334 (1957). Ege v. United States, 242 F.(2d) 879, 883 (C. C. A. 9th. 1957) explicitly rejected the argument from treason doctrine as applicable to conspiracy charges (here a conspiracy to violate the Mann Act): " . . . the overt act of the crime of treason of Article III, section 3 of the Constitution is a substantial part of the crime. Insubstantial overt acts may qualify to move a garden variety of conspiracy agreement into the zone of crime and away from 'talking' and 'thinking'. Yet such overt acts may fall short of the substance required for a treasonable overt act. Thus, in a way, treason is sui generis." Compare, also, State v. Raley, 136 N. E. (2d) 295, 306, 307 (Ct.App. Ohio. 1954) (Federal Constitution's treason clause does not preempt field so as to prevent a state investigation of treason or seditious activity against either the United States or a state).

20. *Cf.* United States v. McWilliams, 54 F. Supp. 791, 793 (Dist. Ct. D. C. 1944): An indictment for conspiracy to impair armed forces' morale is not duplicitous for also charging conspiracy to commit treason, since averments of defendants' conduct between 1933 and 1940 "cannot be deemed a charge of conspiracy to commit treason. . . . since an essential element therein is aid and comfort to 'enemies' and Germany did not become a statutory enemy until December, 1941."

21. Martin v. Young, 134 F. Supp. 204, 207, 208 (N. D. Cal. 1955), discussed in text at note 5, *supra;* majority and dissenting opinions in Thompson v. Whittier, 185 F. Supp. 306, 314, 315 (Dist. Ct. D. C. 1960), and text at notes 10, 11, *supra.* On the absence of a declaration of war in the Korean fighting, see Hearings before the Committee on Armed Services and the Subcommittee on Department of Defense of the Committee on Appropriations, on S. 2950, U. S. Senate Documents, 89th Congress, 2d Session, p. 279 (1966). On the issue of the existence of such a "war" as would make the treason clause applicable, see Loane, "Treason and Aiding the Enemy," 30 Military Law Review 43, 62 (1965), and Ruddy, "Permissible Dissent and Treason", 4 Criminal Law Bulletin 145, 151–153 (1968).

22. Haupt v. United States, 330 U. S. 631, 634–635 (1947), and s. c., 152 F.(2d) 771, 789 (C. C. A. 7th. 1946).

23. Haupt v. United States, 330 U. S. 631, 635, 636, 641–642 (1947); Kawakita v. United States, 343 U. S. 717, 735, 744 (1952); Gillars v. United States, 182 F.(2d) 962, 968 (Ct. App. D. C. 1950); Best v. United States, 184 F.(2d) 131, 137 (C. C. A. 1st. 1950), cert. den., 340 U. S. 939 (1951); see Martin v. Young, 134 F. Supp. 204, 208 (N. D. Cal. 1955). At p. 641 the Supreme Court's opinion in Haupt refers to the intent as that "of aiding the German Reich, or of injuring the United States," but in the whole context of the opinion it is clear that these are not alternatives; intent to benefit the enemy cause is the core, and where this is present there will also be intent (measured by responsibility for the predictable consequences of action) to harm the United States. See Chandler v. United States, 171 F.(2d) 921, 943 (C. C. A. 1st. 1948), cert. den., 336 U. S. 918 (1949).

24. Gillars v. United States, 182 F.(2d) 962, 974, 975, 976–977 (Ct. App. D. C. 1950); D'Aquino v. United States, 192 F.(2d) 338, 358, 359–363 (C. C. A. 9th. 1951), cert. den., 343 U. S. 935 (1952). As the plea of duress was presented in the D'Aquino case, it emphasized the peculiarly unsupported and friendless condition of a United States citizen caught in the enemy country by the outbreak of war. Whatever appeal lay in this aspect of the facts, the court found overcome by the duration, detail, and liberal salaried status of defendant's employment along with the want of evidence of serious incidents of focused threats to her safety.

25. Haupt v. United States, 330 U. S. 631, 641 (1947). Dissenting, Murphy, J., thought that intent had not been proved. He does not, however, seem to say that defendant must be found not guilty if he had mixed purposes, but rather that the father-son relation here gave so ambiguous a cast to the purpose of defendant's actions that, in view of the general restrictive policy on the scope of the treason offense, as a matter of law doubt should here be resolved in favor of the defendant as having intended only to help his son because he was his son. Id., 647.

26. Chandler v. United States, 171 F.(2d) 921, 944 (C. C. A. 1st. 1948), cert. den., 336 U. S. 918 (1949); Best v. United States, 184 F.(2d) 131, 137 (C. C. A. 1st. 1950), cert. den., 340 U. S. 939 (1951).

27. See Gillars v. United States, 182 F.(2d) 962, 980 (Ct. App. D. C. 1950); United States v. Shinohara, C. M. O. 9, 1948, p. 280.

28. See Kawakita v. United States, 343 U. S. 717, 735 (1952); cf. Nishikawa v. Dulles, 356 U. S. 129, 137 (1958).

29. See Kawakita v. United States, 343 U. S. 717, 733–735 (1952); Chandler v. United States, 171 F.(2d) 921, 945 (C. C. A. 1st. 1948), cert. den., 336 U. S. 918 (1949). Cf. D'Aquino v. United States, 192 F.(2d) 338, 366 (C. C. A. 9th. 1951), cert. den., 343 U. S. 935 (1952) (what Geneva Convention may permit enemy country to exact of prisoners of war does not excuse intent to betray U. S.).

30. See notes 13–16, supra.

31. Allegiance by presence: Chandler v. United States, 171 F.(2d) 921, 930, 945 (C. C. A. 1st. 1948), cert. den., 336 U. S. 918 (1949); Best v. United States, 184 F.(2d) 131 (C. C. A. 1st. 1950), cert. den., 340 U. S. 939 (1951); Gillars v. United States, 182 F.(2d) 962, 979 (Ct. App. D. C. 1950); Burgman v. United States, 188 F.(2d) 637 (Ct. App. D. C. 1951), cert. den., 342 U. S. 838 (1951), Allegiance by dual nationality as well as presence: Kawakita v. United States, 343 U. S. 717, 728, 733–735 (1952); cf. D'Aquino v. United States, 192 F.(2d) 338, 349 (C. C. A. 9th. 1951), cert. den., 343 U. S. 935 (1952).

32. D'Aquino v. United States, 192 F.(2d) 338, 349 (C. C. A. 9th. 1951), cert. den., 343 U. S. 935 (1952). The United States also properly held individuals to present clear evidence that they had made the choice to expatriate themselves, as against liability for treason. Kawakita v. United States, 343 U. S. 717, 723–726 (1952) (actions consistent with dual nationality held insufficient to establish choice of expatriation); Gillars v. United States,

182 F.(2d) 962, 983 (Ct. App. D. C. 1950) (signing of vague statement of loyalty to enemy, given to government corporation employer, insufficient); Burgman v. United States, 188 F.(2d) 637, 640 (Ct. App. D. C. 1951) (requested instruction, that defendant could not be guilty of treason if he believed that he was no longer a United States citizen, held properly refused where record showed no evidence for a reasonable basis of such belief).

33. Cramer v. United States, 325 U. S. 1, 34 (1945).

34. *Id.*, 37.

35. Haupt v. United States, 330 U. S. 631, 634, 635 (1947). Jackson's opinion is at pains to assert that it is not altering, but only applying, the formulae of *Cramer*. *Id.*, 635. In total emphasis, however, the *Haupt* opinion more sharply differentiates the matter of likely effect of the act (its capability of conferring help on the enemy) from the matter of its commonplaceness or suspicious character (its relevance as evidence on intent) than did the *Cramer* analysis: Cramer's conviction "was reversed because the Court found that the act which two witnesses saw could not on their testimony be said to have given assistance or comfort to anyone, whether it was done treacherously or not." *Ibid.* Douglas, J., concurring, thought that the *Haupt* opinion repudiated the *Cramer* formulation on the nature of the required overt act. *Id.*, 645, 646. Murphy, J., dissenting in *Haupt*, apparently reads *Cramer* as requiring both that the overt act not be ambiguous as evidence of intent and that it constitute a giving of aid. Hence he would free defendant because defendant's acts of sheltering his son as much evidenced a father's normal concern as father as it evidenced intent to betray his country; in view of the strict policy of our law toward proof of treason, this ambiguity of the act as evidence of intent in Murphy's view made the act an insufficient overt act: "An act of assistance may be of the type which springs from the well of human kindness, from the natural devotion to family and friends, or from a practical application of religious tenets. Such acts are not treasonous, however else they may be described. They are not treasonous even though, in a sense, they help in the effectuation of the unlawful purpose. To rise to the status of an overt act of treason, an act of assistance must be utterly incompatible with any of the foregoing sources of action." *Id.*, 647. Murphy does not ground his dissent on a finding that the total evidence of treasonable intent was insufficient in *Haupt;* thus it appears that he dissents specifically because he finds a fatal defect in proof of the overt act, because in its context in this case the act of sheltering could support different inferences as to defendant's intent in doing it.

36. Though a somewhat clearer rule emerges by comparing the *Cramer* and *Haupt* opinions, Mr. Justice Jackson's second effort still falls short of desirable clarity. What appears to suffice about the overt acts proved in *Haupt* is that they could reasonably be believed to confer aid without proof of any other acts; in contrast, one could not know from the two restaurant meetings proved in *Cramer* that they gave aid without proof of other acts or circumstances involving Cramer's cooperative behavior (that he undertook to arrange a meeting with the saboteur's girl friend, that he agreed to and did

at the second meeting take charge of the saboteur's reserve money supply, that after the first meeting he concealed his knowledge of the saboteur's presence) on which two-witness evidence was not tendered. See Cramer v. United States, 325 U. S. 1, 37–39 (1945). So the *Haupt* opinion explains that "there can be no question that sheltering, or helping to buy a car, or helping to get employment is helpful to an enemy agent. . . . They have the unmistakable quality which was found lacking in the *Cramer* case of forwarding the saboteur in his mission. We pointed out that Cramer furnished no shelter, sustenance or supplies. . . . No matter whether young Haupt's mission was benign or traitorous, known or unknown to defendant, these acts were aid and comfort to him. In the light of his mission and his instructions, they were more than casually useful; they were aid in steps essential to his design for treason." 330 U. S. 631, 635 (1947). Further, the *Haupt* opinion intimates that if other acts or circumstances environing defendant's acts must be shown in order to create a reasonable basis for inferring that he gave aid, these further acts or circumstances must also be proved by two witnesses in a way that meets the constitutional requirement. Such seems the implication of the rationale by which the Court's opinion distinguishes *Cramer:* Cramer's conviction "was reversed because the Court found that the act which two witnesses saw could not on their testimony be said to have given assistance or comfort to anyone, whether it was done treacherously or not. To make a sufficient overt act, the Court thought it would have been necessary to assume that the meeting or talk was of assistance to the enemy, or to rely on other than two-witness proof." *Id.*, 635. But this statement leaves the matter less than clear, for—as the next-to-last quotation shows—the *Haupt* opinion itself assessed the proved acts as acts of aid only in the light of a context ("in the light of [the saboteur's] . . . mission and his instructions") which was itself not directly proved by two-witness evidence. Mr. Justice Douglas's concurring opinion also fails to achieve a clearcut formulation. But Douglas seems properly to make the point that the act of sheltering was "quite innocent on its face" and "without more, was as innocent as Cramer's conversation with the agent," because "nothing would be more natural and normal or more 'commonplace' (325 U. S. p. 34), or less suspicious or less 'incriminating' (325 U. S. p. 35), than the act of a father opening the family door to a son." *Id.*, 644, 645. What Douglas is in effect highlighting is that, though the Court's *Haupt* opinion finds that the likely aid effect of the acts there proved by two witnesses was a reasonable inference from the acts alone, in fact this was not so, but depending upon other facts of context which were no more proved in *Haupt* by two witnesses than they were in *Cramer.* Perhaps the implicit explanation turns on whether the context necessary to show the likely effect of defendant's acts consists in other acts of defendant (in which situation, the inference may be, additional two-witness evidence is required) or in acts of other persons (in which case, apparently, two-witness evidence is not required). Justification for this distinction might arguably lie in the fact that the Constitution's proof requirement focuses on proof of the defendant's own

overt acts. If this is the explanation, it is not made explicit in either the
Jackson or Douglas opinions in *Haupt*.

37. Chandler v. United States, 171 F. (2d) 921, 941 (C. C. A. 1st. 1948),
cert. den., 336 U. S. 918 (1949); Gillars v. United States, 182 F. (2d) 962, 968
(Ct. App. D. C. 1950); Best v. United States, 184 F. (2d) 131, 137 (C. C. A. 1st
1950), cert. den., 340 U. S. 939 (1951); Burgman v. United States, 188 F. (2d)
637 (Ct. App. D. C. 1951), cert. den., 342 U. S. 838 (1951); D'Aquino v.
United States, 192 F. (2d) 338 (C. C. A. 9th. 1951), cert. den., 343 U. S. 935
(1952). See also, United States v. Best, 76 F. Supp. 857, 861 (D. Mass. 1948),
affirmed, *supra*. *Cf*. Ex parte Monti, 79 F. Supp. 651 (E. D. N. Y. 1948), and
s.c. *sub nom*. United States v. Monti, 100 F. Supp. 209 (E. D. N. Y. 1951), and
168 F. Supp. 671 (E. D. N. Y. 1958). The First Circuit Court of Appeals
opinion in Chandler v. United States perhaps, by inference, conceded some
embarrassment from the Cramer opinion when it notes that "Possibly the
overt acts, viewed in rigid isolation and apart from their setting, would not
indicate that they afforded aid and comfort to the enemy. But viewed in their
setting . . . they certainly take on incriminating significance." 171 F. (2d) 921,
941. However, the two-witness evidence in the Chandler case not only proved
particular acts, but also made plain that the acts were not "commonplace" (*cf*.
325 U. S. 1, 34, 40) occurrences, but participation in meetings of an
apparatus of the German war effort.

38. Kawakita v. United States, 343 U. S. 717, 737, 738, 741 (1952). *Cf*.
Provoo v. United States, 215 F. (2d) 531 (C. C. A. 2d. 1954), reversing 124 F.
Supp. 185 (S. D. N. Y. 1954); Martin v. Young, 134 F. Supp. 204 (N. D. Cal.
1955).

39. Kawakita v. United States, 343 U. S. 717, 738 (1952) ("It is the nature
of the act that is important. The act may be unnecessary to a successful
completion of the enemy's project; it may be an abortive attempt; it may in
the sum total of the enemy's effort be a casual and unimportant step. But if it
gives aid and comfort to the enemy at the immediate moment of its
performance, it qualifies as an overt act within the constitutional standard of
treason."); D'Aquino v. United States, 192 F. (2d) 338, 373 (C. C. A. 9th.
1951), cert. den., 343 U. S. 935 (1952). See also, United States v. Kawakita, 96
F. Supp. 824, 837 (S. D. Cal. 1950), and 190 F. (2d) 506, 520 (C. C. A. 9th.
1951), affirmed, *supra*.

40. Chandler v. United States, 171 F. (2d) 921, 941 (C. C. A. 1st. 1948),
cert. den., 336 U. S. 918 (1949). *Cf*. Gillars v. United States, 182 F. (2d) 962,
977 (Ct. App. D. C. 1950) (evidence that effects of broadcasts were such as
would support inference that defendant's true intent was to aid United States
might be admitted on issue of intent).

41. See Chandler v. United States, 171 F. (2d) 921, 938–939 (C. C. A. 1st.
1948), cert. den., 336 U. S. 918 (1949); *cf*. Gillars v. United States, 182 F. (2d)
962, 971 (Ct. App. D. C. 1950). The First Circuit Court of Appeals took pains
to note, however, that, subject to the clear and present danger test, words
might be punished as sedition in a situation where they did not constitute
treason. 171 F. (2d) 921, 939.

42. Chandler v. United States, 171 F. (2d) 921, 939 (C. C. A. 1st. 1948), cert. den., 336 U. S. 918 (1949). Other broadcast cases were in substance in accord with the Chandler ruling, though not with such explicit statement: Gillars v. United States, 182 F. (2d) 962, 968, 971 (Ct. App. D. C. 1950); Best v. United States, 184 F. (2d) 131, 137 (C. C. A. 1st. 1950), cert. den., 340 U. S. 939 (1951); Burgman v. United States, 188 F. (2d) 637, 639 (Ct. App. D. C. 1951), cert. den., 342 U. S. 838 (1951), affirming 87 F. Supp. 568, 571 (Dist. Ct. D. C. 1949).

43. Haupt v. United States, 330 U. S. 631, 635 (1947); Kawakita v. United States, 343 U. S. 717, 742 (1952); Chandler v. United States, 171 F. (2d) 921, 944 (C. C. A. 1st. 1948), cert. den., 336 U. S. 918 (1949). So, too, the existence of defendant's continuing allegiance to the United States (implicitly including the basis for a finding that defendant had not chosen to expatriate himself) need not be proved by two witnesses. Kawakita v. United States, 190 F. (2d) 506, 515, n. 11 (C. C. A. 9th. 1951), affirmed, *supra.*

44. Kawakita v. United States, 343 U. S. 717, 742 (1952).

45. Chandler v. United States, 171 F. (2d) 921, 944 (C. C. A. 1st 1948), cert. den., 336 U. S. 918 (1949).

46. See Haupt v. United States, 330 U. S. 631, 643 (1947).

47. *Id.,* 643. The Court intimated that a complete confession, out of court, might be admissible as an admission, if it were offered merely to corroborate other evidence. *Ibid.*

48. Kawakita v. United States, 343 U. S. 717, 743 (1952).

49. Haupt v. United States, 330 U. S. 631, 642 (1947); *cf.* Chandler v. United States, 171 F. (2d) 921, 925, 943 (C. C. A. 1st 1948), cert. den., 336 U. S. 918 (1949); Gillars v. United States, 182 F. (2d) 962, 967 (Ct. App. D. C. 1950); Best v. United States, 184 F. (2d) 131, 133–134, 137–138 (C. C. A. 1st. 1950), cert. den., 340 U. S. 939 (1951).

50. See Haupt v. United States, 330 U. S. 631, 640 (1947). In the judgment of the Seventh Circuit Court of Appeals the requirement that the two witnesses present "direct" evidence of the act was a gloss of the Supreme Court upon the Constitution. See 152 F. (2d) 771, 787 (C. C. A. 7th. 1946), affirmed without note of this point, *supra.*

51. Haupt v. United States, 136 F. (2d) 661, 674 (C. C. A. 7th. 1943), reversing first conviction, in part because instructions did not make this point clear to the jury.

52. *Id.,* 675, taking as another ground of reversing the first conviction, that the trial court violated the constitutional two-witness requirement by charging that if the jury found that the defendants agreed among themselves to commit any of the charged overt acts, the act of any one of them in furthering this design became in law the act of all; the Circuit Court of Appeals ruled that "a defendant charged with treason cannot, under a conspiracy theory, be convicted of an overt act committed by some other person." *Id.,* 676.

53. Haupt v. United States, 330 U. S. 631, 638–639 (1947).

54. *Ibid.* Comparison with the Seventh Circuit Court of Appeals observa-

tions in its opinion reversing the first conviction, and of the remarks of the judge dissenting from that court's affirmance of the second conviction, show that the Supreme Court adopted a more flexible definition of the "act", to the government's benefit. See 136 F. (2d) 661, 675 (C. C. A. 7th. 1943), and Minor, circ. j., dissenting, 152 F. (2d) 771, 802, 803 (C. C. A. 7th. 1946).

55. See Chandler v. United States, 171 F. (2d) 921, 940 941 (C. C. A. 1st. 1948), cert. den., 336 U. S. 918 (1949). Implicitly accord: Gillars v. United States, 182 F. (2d) 962, 968, 971 (Ct. App. D. C. 1950); Best v. United States, 184 F. (2d) 131, 137 (C. C. A. 1st. 1950), cert. den., 340 U. S. 939 (1951); Burgman v. United States, 188 F. (2d) 637, 639 (Ct. App. D. C. 1951), cert. den., 342 U. S. 838 (1951); D'Aquino v. United States, 192 F. (2d) 338 (C. C. A. 9th. 1951), cert. den., 343 U. S. 935 (1952). It was not a defect of evidence that the two witnesses to defendant's making of a particular recording for broadcast were unable to testify to its precise content, where the recording was proved to be part of defendant's continuing service to the enemy radio program. Chandler v. United States, *supra*, 942. The First Circuit Court of Appeals there also said that the evidence would not fail though the particular recording contained no propaganda message, where the evidence showed that a planned aspect of the continuing program was to limit propaganda content in order to keep the broadcasts as a whole attractive as entertainment. *Ibid.*

Appendix

I

Omitting grand jury charges and cases in which the enunciation of doctrines of the law of treason figured only incidentally, one may list from the American materials thirty-five instances in which application of the law of treason as defined in the Federal Constitution may be said to have been in question. Classifying these cases, with reference to the vigor of the rules laid down against "treason," as "strong" (*), "moderate" (**), and "restrictive" (***), one emerges with nine instances in which "strong" doctrine is pronounced, one of these in the present war. In the following list, the cases are classified according to the asterisk symbols set out in the preceding sentence.

* Whiskey Rebellion cases: United States v. Vigol, 28 Fed. Cas. 376, No. 16,621 (C. C. D. Pa. 1795); United States v. Mitchell, 26 Fed. Cas. 1,277, No. 15,788 (C. C. D. Pa. 1795). Constructive levying of war, based on forcible resistance to execution of a single statute; the defendants were convicted and later pardoned.

* House tax case: Case of Fries, 9 Fed. Cas. 826, 924, Nos. 5,126, 5,127 (C. C. D. Pa. 1799, 1800). Constructive levying of war by forcible resistance to execution of a single statute; the defendant was convicted and later pardoned, as were other defendants convicted in connected (unreported) prosecutions. In *The Trial of Conrad Marks,*

11 American State Trials (Lawson ed. 1919) 175 (C. C. D. Pa. 1800), the jury was charged on the law of treason as in the other cases, but defendant was acquitted. He later pleaded guilty to a charge of conspiracy. Defendants Gettman and Hainey were found guilty, however, on a charge to the jury similar to that in the *Fries* case. Stahler was acquitted, and *nolle pros.* was entered regarding Desch and Klein, who were held for conspiracy. Carpenter, The Two Trials of John Fries (1800) 210–11.

*** Burr conspiracy: *Ex parte* Bollman, 4 Cranch 75 (U. S. 1807); United States v. Burr, 25 Fed. Cas. 2, 55, Nos. 14,692a, 14,693 (C. C. D. Va. 1807). Conspiracy to levy war held not within constitutional definition as an overt act of levying war; actual assemblage required. Discharge of the prisoners was ordered in the *Bollman* case; the verdict was directed in the *Burr* trial.

** United States v. Lee, 26 Fed. Cas. 907, No. 15,584 (C. C. D. C. 1814). Sale of provisions held a sufficient overt act; mixture of commercial motive does not make intent sufficient. Acquittal.

* United States v. Hodges, 26 Fed. Cas. 332, No. 15,374 (C. C. D. Md. 1815). Obtaining release of prisoners to the enemy is adhering to the enemy; the act shows the intent. Acquittal.

*** United States v. Hoxie, 26 Fed. Cas. 397, No. 15,407 (C. C. D. Vt. 1808). Organized, armed attack of smugglers on troops enforcing embargo is riot and not constructive levying of war. Directed verdict.

*** United States v. Pryor, 27 Fed. Cas. 628, No. 16,096 (C. C. D. Pa. 1814). Proceeding under flag of truce with enemy detachment to help buy provisions is too remote an act to establish adhering to the enemy. Directed verdict.

*** United States v. Hanway, 26 Fed. Cas. 105, No. 15,299 (C. C. E. D. Pa. 1851). Participation in forcible resistance to execution of Fugitive Slave Law held not constructive levying of war in absence of showing of preconceived plan. Directed verdict.

** United States v. Greiner, 26 Fed. Cas. 36, No. 15,262 (E. D. Pa. 1861). Participation as member of state militia company in seizure and holding of a federal fort for the state held a levying of war sufficient to justify binding accused over to await trial when federal court again sits in the rebel area.

** United States v. Greathouse, 26 Fed. Cas. 18, No. 15,254 (C. C.

N. D. Cal. 1863). Fitting out and sailing a privateer held levying of war. Defendants convicted, later pardoned or released on bond upon taking oath of allegiance.

** Cases of confiscation of property or refusal to enforce obligations given in connection with sale of provisions to the Confederacy: Hanauer v. Doane, 12 Wall. 342 (U. S. 1871); Carlisle v. United States, 16 Wall. 147 (U. S. 1873); Sprott v. United States, 20 Wall. 459 (U. S. 1874); United States v. Athens Armory, 24 Fed. Cas. 878, No. 14,473 (N. D. Ga. 1868). Mixed motive, involving commercial profit, does not bar finding of the giving of aid and comfort to the enemy. Other decisions in the Court of Claims are similar.

** United States v. Cathcart and Parmenter, 25 Fed. Cas. 344, No. 14,756 (C. C. S. D. Ohio 1864). Motion to quash and demurrer to indictments for treason by levying war denied and overruled, and argument that the union is only a compact of states rejected.

** Chenoweth's Case [Unreported: see *Ex parte* Vallandigham, 28 Fed. Cas. No. 16,816, at 888 (C. C. S. D. Ohio 1863); Cong. Globe, 37th Cong., 2d Sess. (1862) 2166–67]. Indictment held faulty for alleging aiding and abetting rebels, instead of charging directly the levying of war, as in treason all are principals.

* Druecker v. Salomon, 21 Wis. 621 (1867). In an action for false imprisonment, ruled that detention of defendant lawful because in participating in draft act riot he was guilty of levying war.

*** *In the matter of United States v. Pratt,* (1869) 1 Chi. Legal News 401. Charge of treason by forcing a United States guard and killing several persons in its custody is sufficient justification for detention of petitioners in habeas corpus.

*.** Case of Jefferson Davis, 7 Fed. Cas. 63, No. 3,621a (C. C. D. Va. 1867–1871). Strong arguments were made that treason charges could not properly be brought against those conducting a rebel government which had achieved the status of a recognized belligerent; though the position was not formally conceded, Davis was not eventually brought to trial on the indictment for treason. See 2 Warren, Supreme Court in United States History (Rev. ed. 1937) 485–87; Watson, *Trial of Jefferson Davis* (1915) 24 Yale L. J. 669.

*** Philippine insurrections: United States v. Magtibay, 2 Philipp. 703 (1903), United States v. de los Reyes, 3 Philipp. 349 (1904). Mere possession of rebel commissions held insufficient overt act: defendants' power insufficient to show overt act; strict enforcement of two-witness requirement. Convictions reversed. United States v. Lagnason, 3 Philipp. 472 (1904). An armed effort to overthrow the government held to be levying war.

* United States v. Fricke, 259 Fed. 673 (S. D. N. Y. 1919). Acts "indifferent" on their face held sufficient overt acts where intent is shown.

*** United States v. Robinson, 259 Fed. 685 (S. D. N. Y. 1919). Obiter, acts harmless on their face are insufficient as overt acts; two-witness rule requires two witnesses to acts involving commission of the offense. Directed verdict.

* United States v. Werner, 247 Fed. 708 (E. D. Pa. 1918), *aff'd,* 251 U. S. 466 (1919). Demurrer to indictment overruled; an act indifferent on its face may be sufficient overt act.

*** United States v. Haupt, 136 F.(2d) 661 (C. C. A. 7th, 1943). Strict application of two-witness requirement and of severance of trial where prejudicial evidence regarding some defendants has no proper bearing on others. Inferentially, however, approves acts harmless on their face as sufficient overt acts. Conviction reversed.

* Stephan v. United States, 133 F.(2d) 87 (C. C. A. 6th, 1943). Acts harmless on their face may be sufficient overt acts; firm ruling on intent. Conviction affirmed. Sentence commuted.

*** United States v. Cramer, 325 U. S. 1 (1945). Acts indifferent on their face are insufficient overt acts. Conviction reversed.

*** United States v. Leiner, unreported, (S. D. N. Y. 1943). Acts indifferent on their face are not sufficient overt acts; specific intent must be clearly shown. Directed verdict.

The only reported trials for treason against a state seem to be those of Thomas Wilson Dorr (Rhode Island) and John Brown (Virginia).

** *The Trial of Thomas Wilson Dorr,* 2 American State Trials (Lawson ed. 1914) 5 (R. I. Sup. Ct. 1844). Claim to head a state "government" created by extra-legal elections, enforced by armed effort to seize state arsenal. Defendant was convicted, but subsequently pardoned after serving several years in prison.

** *The Trial of John Brown,* 6 American State Trials (Lawson ed.

1916) 700 (Jefferson Cty. C. C. Va. 1859). Armed insurrection "to free slaves" is treason by levying war. Defendant was convicted and executed.

Certain abortive prosecutions for treason are worth noting.

* Indictments were brought against Joseph Smith and other leaders of the Mormons for treason by levying war against the state of Missouri, in 1838; and again, Smith was arrested on such a charge of treason against the state of Illinois, in 1844. Both charges seem severe, since they followed a long history of mutual recrimination and violence between the Mormons and their neighbors; and it seems likely that on a fair trial a limited purpose of self-defense, rather than intent to set up a rival goverment, could have been made out. See 1 Williams and Shoemaker, History of Missouri (1930) 545; Culmer, New History of Missouri (1938) 212; 1 Roberts, Comprehensive History of the Church of Jesus Christ of Latter-Day Saints (1930) 499, 500, 529, 530; 2 *id.* at 254; Davis, Story of the Church (1943) 244, 283, 305; Ford, History of Illinois (1854) 337; Pease, The Frontier State (1922) 352; Sen. Doc. No. 189, 26th Cong., 2d Sess. (1841). The Missouri charge was not pressed at the time, for political reasons, and the defendants escaped, possibly with the connivance of their jailors; later efforts at extradition failed. Smith was murdered by a mob which took him from his cell shortly after his arrest in Illinois.

** Indictments were brought against Mormon leaders for treason by levying war against the United States, in connection with activities taken to resist Federal troops, in Utah, in 1856–1857; but these charges were immediately nullified by the general pardon granted by President Buchanan. Even the official history of the Church recognizes that, "strictly speaking," there was a levying of war in this case. 4 Roberts, Comprehensive History of the Church of Jesus Christ of Latter-Day Saints (1930) 412–13, 425; see Anderson, Desert Saints (1942) 188.

* Under a strongly partisan charge by the Chief Justice of Pennsylvania, who took the unusual action of addressing a local grand jury, indictments for treason by levying war against the state of Pennsylvania were returned in 1892 against leaders of the Homestead Strike. Commonwealth v. O'Donnell, 12 Pa. Co. 97 (Ct. Oyer & Ter. Allegheny Cty. 1892). The action was subjected to severe criticism, from conservative professional sources, as well as from labor sympathizers; and the prosecutions were quietly dropped after three of the defendants had been acquitted of charges of murder growing out of the clash with the Pinkerton detectives. See notes 44, 47, 48, all in chapter 5 *supra.*

There have also, of course, been many trials by military tribunals on charges amounting to treason. Apart from the issue of free speech involved in the Vallandigham case (*) [see *The Trial of Clement L. Vallandigham,* 1 American State Trials (Lawson ed. 1914) 699], the principal cases seem to have involved conduct clearly within strict definitions of the scope of "treason," and the principal issue has concerned the extent of military jurisdiction. See, *e.g.,* regarding the "Northwest Confederacy conspiracy," Pitman, The Trials for Treason at Indianapolis (1865); Klaus, The Milligan Case (1929) 24; Milton, Abraham Lincoln and the Fifth Column (1942) 170, c. 8. *Cf. Ex Parte* Quirin, 317 U. S. 1 (1942).

Charges of treason were found improperly laid against a state, where the accused was deemed to have acted rather against his allegiance to the United States, in People v. Lynch, 11 Johns. 549 (N. Y. 1814) (**) and in *Ex parte* Quarrier, 2 W. Va. 569 (1866) (**). The conduct involved was in each case within the most strict definition of treason.

II

The following cases (after *United States* v. *Cramer*), in chronological order of the highest authoritative opinion rendered, involved prosecutions for treason.

** Haupt v. United States, 330 U. S. 631 (1947), affirming 152 F.(2d) 771 (C. C. A. 7th. 1946), certiorari granted, 328 U. S. 831 (1946), rehearing denied, 331 U. S. 864 (1947): Harboring known enemy agent, and helping him buy automobile and seek employment to further his mission, held sufficient overt acts of aid. See also 47 F.Supp. 832, 836 (N. D. Ill. 1942), reversed, 136 F.(2d) 661 (C. C. A. 7th. 1943) (first conviction set aside for breach of *McNabb* rule and improper joinder of defendants).

** Chandler v. United States, 171 F.(2d) 921 (C. C. A. 1st 1948), affirming 72 F.Supp. 231 (D. Mass. 1947); certiorari denied, 336 U. S. 918 (1949), rehearing denied, 336 U. S. 947 (1949): Participation in enemy wartime radio propaganda program held sufficient overt act.

** Gillars v. United States, 182 F.(2d) 962 (Ct. App. D. C. 1950): Participation in enemy wartime radio propaganda program held sufficient overt act.

** Best v. United States, 184 F.(2d) 131 (C. C. A. 1st. 1950), affirming 76 F.Supp. 857 (D. Mass. 1948); certiorari denied, 340 U. S. 939 (1951), rehearing denied, 341 U. S. 907 (1951): Participation in enemy wartime radio propaganda program held sufficient overt act. See also 73 F.Supp. 654 (D. Mass. 1947) (sanity hearing); 76 F.Supp. 138 (D. Mass. 1948) (subpoena for witnesses; validity of arrest).

** Burgman v. United States, 188 F.(2d) 637 (Ct. App. D. C. 1951), affirming 87 F.Supp. 568 (Dist. Ct. D. C. 1949), certiorari denied, 342 U. S. 838 (1951): Participation in enemy wartime radio propaganda program held sufficient overt act. See also 89 F.Supp. 288 (Dist. Ct. D. C. 1950) (bail denied pending appeal: in light of Chandler v. United States, no substantial legal question).

** D'Aquino v. United States, 192 F.(2d) 338 (C. C. A. 9th. 1951), rehearing denied, 203 F.(2d) 390 (C. C. A. 9th. 1951), certiorari denied, 343 U. S. 935 (1952), rehearing denied, 343 U. S. 958 (1952), rehearing denied, 345 U. S. 931 (1953): Participation in enemy wartime radio propaganda program held sufficient overt act. See also 180 F.(2d) 271 (C. C. A. 9th. Douglas, Circuit Justice, 1950) (bail allowed pending appeal).

** Kawakita v. United States, 343 U. S. 717 (1952), affirming 96 F.Supp. 824 (S. D. Cal. 1950), as affirmed, 190 F.(2d) 506 (C. C. A. 9th. 1951), certiorari granted, 342 U. S. 932 (1952): Brutalities on U.S. prisoners of war, inflicted by U.S. citizen in wartime Japan, outside his duties as civilian interpreter in war-materials plant, held sufficient overt acts; treasonable intent sufficiently proved by defendant's statements and actions, apart from two-witness evidence. See also 108 F.Supp. 627 (S. D. Cal. 1952) (denial of motion to modify death sentence).

One case was tried by a United States military commission:

**United States v. Shinohara (C. M. O. 9, 1948), p. 280: held, on review by the Office of the Judge Advocate General of the Navy that a military commission had jurisdiction to try for treason a national of Japan, residing in Guam before and during the war, for treason by adhering to and aiding the enemy during the Japanese occupation of Guam; conviction reversed for failure of evidence of the overt acts. See 17 George Washington Law Review 283 (1949).

The following cases involved prosecutions for treason in which the reported decisions did not turn on points of treason doctrine or proof.

United States v. Monti, 100 F.Supp. 209 (E. D. N. Y. 1951), and 168 F.Supp. 671 (E. D. N. Y. 1958): Denials of motions to set aside and vacate judgment of conviction entered on defendant's plea of guilty and confession in open court of treason by aiding enemy by participation in enemy wartime radio propaganda program; venue properly laid, and other points sought to be raised are not properly raised on type of writ defendant filed. See also Ex parte Monti, 79 F.Supp. 651 (E. D. N. Y. 1948): Application to issue writ of habeas corpus denied; held, treason is a crime of such nature that it may be committed in a foreign country, and falls within statute conferring jurisdiction on the federal court.

Provoo v. United States, 215 F.(2d) 531 (C. C. A. 2d 1954), reversing 124 F.Supp. 185 (S. D. N. Y. 1954): Conviction of treason by aiding enemy by conduct while prisoner of war of Japanese, reversed for admission of prejudicial, irrelevant cross examination and error in denying defendant's motion to vacate judgment on basis of newly found evidence offered to show improper venue.

III

Attorney General Rodney recommended that the charge of treason be laid in the *Hoxie* case, as a salutary check on the New England opposition to the Embargo, which had progressed to such a point that Jefferson had proclaimed a state of insurrection and had called out the militia to enforce the law. See Cummings and McFarland, Federal Justice (1937) 68; Moulton, *loc. cit. supra* note 238.

The *Hanway* case arose at a time when conservative Northern opinion was anxious to show to the South evidence of the good faith and practicability of the Fugitive Slave Law as a partial answer to the Abolitionist agitation and the underground railroad. The apparent opportunity to make an early example led the Federal authorities to press the treason charge over the efforts of the state to assert its jurisdiction to prosecute for murder or at least riot. See Smith, Parties and Slavery (1906) 23, 24; 2 Warren, Supreme Court in United States History (Rev. ed. 1937) 229–30; Hensel, *op. cit. supra* Ch. 5, n. 40, at 62. *Cf.* pamphlet by A Member of the Philadelphia Bar, History of the Trial of Castner Hanway (1852) 84–85.

The earlier, and more successful, resort to the broad doctrine of levying of war, in the Whiskey Rebellion cases, likewise reflected a deliberate decision by the administration to employ the dread charge of "treason" as a salutary check to undesirable political tendencies. There is no evidence that the Federalists stirred the insurrection, but they seized on it with obvious relish as a means of tarring their opponents with the stigma of treason. See Baldwin, Whiskey Rebels (1939) 226, 269–70. It is only fair, however, to note that at its peak, the disaffection was close to a state of levying of war even in the strict sense of the term. *Id.* at c. VII.

President Adams' pardon of Fries and his fellows, after their conviction of treason for the forcible rescue from the Federal marshal of prisoners arrested under the hated property excise in 1799, seems to involve in substance an executive construction of the crime of levying war analogous to Mr. Justice Grier's insistence on pre-concert and specific intention to overthrow constituted authority. The questions which Adams posed to his heads of department, in seeking their advice on his disposition of Fries' petition for pardon, indicate clearly the bent of the President's mind: "4. Is it clear beyond all reasonable doubt that the crime of which they stand convicted, amounts to a levying of war against the United States, or, in other words, to treason? . . . 6. *Quo animo* was this insurrection? Was it a design of general resistance to all law, or any particular law? Or was it particular to the place and persons? 7. Was it any thing more than a riot, high-handed, aggravated, daring, and dangerous indeed, for the purpose of a rescue? This is a high crime, but can it strictly amount to treason? 8. Is there not great danger in establishing such a construction of treason, as may be applied to every sudden, ignorant, inconsiderate heat, among a part of the people, wrought up by political disputes, and personal or party animosities? . . . " 9 Works of John Adams (1854) 58.

Though he received unanimous advice that the case was properly held treason and did not in that light establish any undesirable precedent, on May 21, 1800, Adams gave a pardon by proclamation. *Id.* at 178. In a letter of March 31, 1815 to James Lloyd, justifying his conduct, Adams stated that his "judgment was clear, that their crime did not amount to treason," and then repeated the substance of point seven in his memorandum to the heads of departments. He also indicates, however, that his judgment was based largely on his appraisal of the defendants as ignorant of the nature of what they did. 10 *Id.* at 153, 154.

Adams' attitude towards the charge of "treason" against Fries is the more striking because of his strong condemnation of the disturbances, as reflected in his memorandum to the heads of departments, and in his letter to Jefferson, June 30, 1813. *Id.* at 47. 2 Adams, Life of John Adams (1871) 314–18. 1 Works, at 571–74, discusses the pardon, and comments that: "The view of treason opened in this case there is no room here to consider. It must infallibly come up for revision at some time or other in the courts of the United States." *Cf.*Walters, Alexander James Dallas (1943) 79 *ff.*; (Note) 9 Fed. Cas. 934, at 944–47 (1800).

Washington's pardons to those convicted in the Whiskey Rebellion cases apparently imply no similar doubt as to the policy of the legal doctrine under which the convictions were obtained, but represent the ordinary exercise of executive clemency. The leaders had escaped or had signed submissions to the government; the convicted Weigel was probably insane and Mitchell is put down by the historian of the Rebellion as a simpleton. See Baldwin, *op. cit. supra,* at 264.

Grier's charge in the *Hanway* case, as quoted in the text, suggests in part that the intent requisite to make out treason is not shown if it appears that defendants regarded a resort to force as necessary in defense against what they in good faith believe to be an unlawful threat of violence under color of authority. This seems also to be the view suggested by Governor Ford, of Illinois, in his comment upon the dubious character of the charge of treason under which the Mormon leader, Joseph Smith, was arrested in that state in 1844: "The overt act of treason charged against them consisted in the alleged levying of war against the State by declaring martial law in Nauvoo, and in ordering out the legions to resist the *posse comitatus*. Their actual guiltiness of the charge would depend upon circumstances. If their opponents had been seeking to put the law in force in good faith, and nothing more, then an array of military force in open resistance to the *posse comitatus* and the militia of the State, most probably would have amounted to treason. But if those opponents merely intended to use the process of the law, the militia of the State, and the *posse comitatus,* as catspaws to compass the possession of their persons for the purpose of murdering them afterwards, as the sequel demonstrated the fact to be, it might well be doubted whether they were guilty of treason." Ford, History of Illinois (1854) 337.

Here again, obviously, it would be the intent and not the act element of the offense which would be the defendants' bulwark.

IV

In Pennsylvania v. Cribbs, 1 Add. 277 (Westmoreland Cty. Ct., Pa. 1795), an attempt to tar and feather the Federal commissioners sent to adjust the controversy involved in the "Whiskey Rebellion" was treated as riot. *Cf.* Pennsylvania v. Morrison, 1 Add. 274 (Allegheny Cty. Ct., Pa. 1795) (raising a Liberty Pole in disaffected area during visit of Federal commissioners; offense not specified). Even prior to the Fugitive Slave Law efforts to rescue fugitive slaves by force from their masters were charged as riots, though in some instances at least the intent was probably broadly directed against the institution of slavery rather than representing a concern for the particular Negro involved. See, *e.g.,* State v. Connolly, 3 Rich. L. 337 (So. Car. 1831); Clellans v. Commonwealth, 8 Pa. St. 223 (1848); *cf. The Trial of the Rev. Jacob Gruber,* 1 American State Trials (Lawson ed. 1914) 69 (Frederick Cty. Ct., Md. 1819) (inciting slaves to insurrection). It is notable that the Fugitive Slave Law itself created a specific offense to cover such attempts. 9 Stat. 462 (1850).

Vigilantism has been treated as riot, though it represents an unlawful effort to supplant the constituted enforcement authorities. See Crawford v. Ferguson, 5 Okla. Cr. App. 377, 115 Pac. 278 (1911). In *Commonwealth v. Jenkins,* 12 American State Trials (Lawson ed. 1919) 488 (Boston Municipal Ct. 1825), an effort to pull down all brothels was charged to be a riot. Forcible efforts to deprive certain racial, religious, or political groups in the community of the protection of the law have been prosecuted as riots. See, *e.g.,* Charges to Grand Jury in *In re* Riots of 1844, 2 Pa. Law Jour. Rep. 135, 275 (Quarter Sess. and Oyer & Ter., Phila. City and Cty. Ct. 1844); Shouse v. Commonwealth, 5 Pa. St. 83 (1847) ("Know Nothing" clashes with the Irish); *The Trials of Winthrop S. Gilman and John Solomon, and others, for Riot,* 5 American State Trials (Lawson ed. 1916) 528, 589 (Alton Municip. Ct., Ill. 1838) (suppression of Abolitionist agitation—the Lovejoy riot); Bradford v. State, 40 Tex. Cr. 632, 51 S. W. 379 (Tex. Ct. Cr. App. 1899) (against employment of Mexican labor); Bolin v. State, 193 Ind. 302, 139 N. E. 659 (1923) ("the Hunkies must go"). *Cf.* Commonwealth v. Daly, 2 Pa. Law Jour. Rep. 361 (Quarter Ses. Phila. City and Cty. Ct. 1844); Commonwealth v. Hare, *id.* at 467 (1844) (prosecutions for murder growing out of the Know-Nothing riots); People v. Judson, 11 Daly 1 (N. Y. Com. Pleas 1849) (anti-English riot over the actor Macready; twenty-three killed in clash with militia).

And the theory under which the "civil rights" statutes were sought to be applied to the Ku Klux Klan was that of ordinary conspiracy to violate the laws rather than that of constructive treason. See *The Trial of Members of the Ku Klux Klan,* 9 American State Trials (Lawson ed. 1918) 593 *ff.* (C. C. D. S. Car. 1871). Compare the cautiously restricted construction of statutory offenses of conspiracy to prevent by force the execution of the laws, as attempted to be applied against efforts to coerce certain classes of the population, in Baldwin v. Franks, 120 U. S. 678 (1887) (Chinese) [*but cf.* Deady, D. J., *In re* Impaneling and Instructing the Grand Jury, 26 Fed. 749 (D. Ore. 1886)], and Haywood v. United States, 268 Fed. 795 (C. C. A. 7th, 1920) (coercion on government contractors).

Extreme denunciation of organized government in public meetings has been treated as riot or unlawful assembly. People v. Most, 55 Hun 609, 8 N. Y. Supp. 625 (N. Y. Sup. Ct. 1890), *aff'd,* 128 N. Y. 108, 27 N. E. 970 (1891) [*cf.* People v. Most, 171 N. Y. 423, 64 N. E. 175 (1902)]; Commonwealth v. Frishman, 235 Mass. 449, 126 N. E. 838 (1920). Demonstrations to influence the conduct of "relief" policy, eventuating in disturbances which probably were calculated, were prosecuted as riot or unlawful assembly in People v. Dunn, 1 Cal. App.(2d) 556, 36 P.(2d) 1096 (1934); Commonwealth v. Egan, 113 Pa. Super. 375, 173 Atl. 764 (1934); State v. Solomon, 93 Utah 70, 71 P.(2d) 104 (1937); State v. Solomon, 96 Utah 500, 87 P.(2d) 807 (1939), see Ch. 5, n. 51 *supra*; State v. Moe, 174 Wash. 303, 24 P.(2d) 638 (1933). Forcible efforts to prevent execution of process against debtors' property were treated as riot, though they took on the character of attempts to establish general policy rather than merely sympathetic efforts in behalf of particular distressed individuals. See Skilton, *op. cit. supra* Ch. 5, n. 44; Commonwealth v. Frankfeld, 114 Pa. Super. 262, 173 Atl. 834 (1934); State v. Woolman, 84 Utah 23, 33 P.(2d) 640 (1934); State v. Frandsen, 176 Wash. 558, 30 P.(2d) 371 (1934). Demonstrations to influence the conduct of foreign policy, eventuating in breaches of the peace probably foreseen and intended, were prosecuted as riot in Commonwealth v. Spartaco, 104 Pa. Super. 1, 158 Atl. 623 (1932) and Commonwealth v. Kahn, 116 Pa. Super. 28, 176 Atl. 242 (1935).

Commonwealth v. Paul, 145 Pa. Super. 548, 21 A.(2d) 421 (1941), treated as riot what seems probably an attempt by force to prevent technological change. There are of course many cases in which breaches of the peace occurring in the course of labor disputes, usually arising out of picketing, have been prosecuted as riot. The abortive indictments for levying of war in the Homestead Strike (see Ch. 5, n. 46 *supra*) seem to be the only attempt to use the law of treason to suppress labor conflict. That a strong prosecutor might have found a rationalization for this effort which Paxson, C. J., over-looked, is implied in the suggestion in (1892) 31 Am. L. Reg. (n.s.) 691, 700, that it would be treason if strike violence were shown to be intended to enforce a general public policy of collective bargaining. And *Ex parte* Jones, 71 W. Va. 567, 77 S. E. 1029 (1913), over a strong dissent by Robinson, J., employs a rationale derived in part from the broader authorities on "levying war" to sustain the validity of detention of rioters for trial by military tribunals. The decision is not now regarded as sound authority. See Fairman, Law Of Martial Rule (1943) 168-70. A careful definition of the scope of "riot" is necessary to protect a social interest in free speech and a desirable play of competitive claims. See State v. Russell, 45 N. H. 83, 85 (1863);

People v. Edelson, 169 Misc. 386, 7 N. Y. S.(2d) 323 (Kings Cty. Ct. 1938).

For clarity, it is desirable to repeat that the recitation of the foregoing cases is not intended to suggest that in any of them should the prosecution have been for "treason"; quite the contrary. But most of them could have been colorably brought within the 17th and 18th century English precedents as to what constituted levying of war. And since most of them obviously boil up out of tense public situations, the entire absence of any suggestion or attempt to employ the treason charge indicates that the broader reaches of the crime of levying war have been so thoroughly buried under different conceptions of public policy as to make it a clear abuse of power to seek to revive them.

V

On the English material, see Chapter 2; on the history of the Federal Convention of 1787, see pp. 133–134, 144–145 *supra,* and Cramer v. United States, 325 U.S. 1, 28–30 (1945). And see Paterson, C. J., in charge to jury in United States v. Mitchell, 26 Fed. Cas. No. 15,788, at 1,280 (C. C. D. Pa. 1795); Iredell, C. J., Charge to Grand Jury in connection with Case of Fries, 9 Fed. Cas. No. 5,126, at 840 (C. C. D. Pa. 1799); Peters, D. J., in colloquies with counsel on first trial of Fries, *id.* at 891, 916; Iredell, C. J , in charge to jury in first trial of Fries, *id.* at 914, Peters, D. J., in charge to jury in first trial of Fries, *id.* at 909; Chase, C. J., in charge to jury in second trial of Fries, 9 Fed. Cas. No. 5,127, at 931 (C. C. D. Pa. 1800); *Ex parte* Bollman, 4 Cranch 75, 126 (U. S. 1807); United States v. Burr, 25 Fed. Cas. No. 14,692a, at 13–14 (C. C. D. Ky. 1807) (on motion to commit), United States v. Burr, 25 Fed. Cas. No. 14,693, at 168, 169 (C. C. D. Va. 1807) (direction to jury); United States v. Lee, 26 Fed. Cas. 907, No. 15,584 (C. C. D. C. 1814); United States v. Hoxie, 26 Fed. Cas. No. 15,407, at 399, 400 (C. C. D. Vt. 1808); United States v. Pryor, 27 Fed. Cas. No. 16,096, at 628, 630 (C. C. D. Pa. 1814); Story, C. J., Charge to Grand Jury, 30 Fed. Cas. No. 18,275, at 1,046 (C. C. D. R. I. 1842); Sprague, D. J., Charge to Grand Jury, 30 Fed. Cas. No.

18,263, at 1,016 (D. Mass. 1851); Kane, D. J., Charge to Grand Jury, 30 Fed. Cas. No. 18,276, at 1,048 (C. C. E. D. Pa. 1851); Grier, C. J., in charge to jury in United States v. Hanway, 26 Fed. Cas. No. 15,299, at 126 (C. C. E. D. Pa. 1851); United States v. Greiner, 26 Fed. Cas. No. 15,262, at 39 (E. D. Pa. 1861); Field, C. J., in charge to jury in United States v. Greathouse, 26 Fed. Cas. No. 15,254, at 22 (C. C. N. D. Cal. 1863); Mayer, D. J., in charge to jury in United States v. Fricke, 259 Fed. 673, 677 (S. D. N. Y. 1919); Learned Hand, C. J., on motion to direct a verdict in United States v. Robinson, 259 Fed. 685, 690 (S. D. N. Y. 1919); United States v. Werner, 247 Fed. 708, 709–10 (E. D. Pa. 1918); trial court charge in United States v. Stephan, 50 F. Supp. 738, 740, n.1, at 742–43 (E. D. Mich. 1943), *charge approved,* 133 F.(2d) 87, 99 (C. C. A. 6th, 1943); United States v. Cramer, 137 F.(2d) 888, 893 (C. C. A. 2d, 1943); United States v. Magtibay, 2 Philipp. 703, 705 (1903); United States v. de los Reyes, 3 Philipp. 349, 357 (1904); *In Riots of 1844* (charge to grand jury by King, P. J.), 4 Pa. Law Jour. Rep. 29, 35, quoted also at 26 Fed. Cas. 116.

Two cases deviate from the standard distinction of the intent and act elements of the crime. In United States v. Hodges, 26 Fed. Cas. 332, No. 15,374 (C. C. D. Md. 1815), the defendant was indicted for adhering to the enemy by procuring the release of British prisoners by his fervent representations to the guards of British threats to burn his home village in retaliation. Both Duval, C. J., and Houston, D. J., agreed that the judgment on the law as well as on the facts was for the jury. But in his charge, Mr. Justice Duval treated the overt act here charged as itself conclusive evidence of the intent: "First. Hodges is accused of adhering to the enemy, and the overt act laid consists in the delivery of certain prisoners, and I am of opinion that the overt act laid in the indictment and proved by the witness is high treason against the United States.

"Second. When the act itself amounts to treason it involves the intention, and such was the character of this act. No threat of destruction of property will excuse or justify such an act; nothing but a threat of life, and that likely to be put into execution." *Id.* at 334.

Houston, D. J., said that he did not "entirely agree" with the chief justice on these points, but did not specify further his disagreement.

Ibid. The jury acquitted. Duval's charge seems to state an unnecessarily mechanical rule, turning on the showing of an act which "itself amounts to treason;" the facts seem to present the more familiar situation of mixed motives, and the jury might have been charged in conventional terms that a defendant cannot escape the plain consequences of his conduct by pleading a personal motive therefor. The jury's acquittal probably represents a *de facto* rule recognizing an excuse which legal doctrine would find it dangerous to crystallize.

In United States v. Haupt, 136 F.(2d) 661, 665 (C. C. A. 7th, 1943), *rev'g*, 47 F. Supp. 836 (N. D. Ill. 1942), the court rejected defendants' argument that the indictment had improperly joined different offenses, since different overt acts of aid and comfort were alleged, in which not every defendant was charged to have participated. The court said that "the constitutional requirement 'of two Witnesses to the same overt Act' forms no part of the definition of the offense. It relates solely to the proof required before a conviction can be had. The crime itself may be established in the same manner as any other crime, but before there can be a conviction, an act in its promotion must be established by two witnesses. In other words, the two-witness provision of the Constitution is an evidential requirement prerequisite to conviction. Moreover, the constitutional requirement 'of two Witnesses to the same overt Act' appears to be an implied recognition that there may be more than one act committed in the execution of the offense. Otherwise, use of the word 'same' would seem to be superfluous," *Id.* at 665.

The court cites nothing but the words of the constitutional provision for its argument; and on this basis alone, its contention seems extreme, in view of the plain implication of overt acts in the "levying" of war and the "giving aid and comfort." Further, as has been noted, the history of the successive drafts of the treason clause in the Convention reflects an understanding that the crime included a distinct act element. On the merits the court's ruling is open to question; and that the court had some question of it itself is indicated by its caution that if its ruling on the indictment leaves the door open to unfairness, this may be dealt with at the trial stage by allowance of motions for separate trials. In fact, the court reversed in this case because it felt that the trial court had abused its discretion by denying such severance after the evidence for the prosecution was in and showed considerable variations in the charges proven in connection with various defendants. In the context of the history of the case as a whole, the court's ruling thus takes on the character of an awkward rationalization employed to dispose of a point of pleading.

The opinion of Learned Hand, C. J., in United States v. Robinson, 259 Fed. 685, 690 (S. D. N. Y. 1919), does not deny, but rather firmly asserts, according to its own theory, the separate character of the intent and act elements, insisting that the requisite act should be more than such as merely makes out an attempt.

VI

Staundford, Les Plees del Corone (1560) has nothing pertinent to the attempt aspect of "treason," except, like all his successors, he in effect notes that compassing is itself a crime in the nature of an attempt (*"Cest compassement, ou imagination, sauns reducer ceo al effect, est grand treason. . . ."*Lib. I, cap. 2. H). This is not to say that early law would view treason as merely an attempt at some further result, however. Coke begins his treason chapter by noting early authority demonstrating the maxim "voluntas reputabatur pro facto;" *i.e.,* early authority regarded the criminal intent in all serious crimes, at least when something was done towards its effectuation, as dangerous enough to be regarded as the substantive crime itself. Coke, Third Institute (5th ed. 1671) 5. Coke perhaps supports, in his doctrine that a conspiracy to levy war is not the crime of levying war, Judge Hand's theory, expressed in United States v. Robinson, 259 Fed. 685, 689 (S. D. N. Y. 1919), that in early history attempted treason was not treason. Coke, Third Institute (5th ed. 1671) 9.

However, Pollock and Maitland and Holdsworth explain this not as arising from any aversion to treating treason as an attempt, but as arising from the tenacity of the feudal concept of mutuality in the bond of lord and vassal, which entitled the aggrieved vassal to war on a lord who had broken the bond. 2 Pollock and Maitland, History of English Law (1895) 503; 8 Holdsworth, History of English Law (1925) 331.

Quaere, however, whether the crime does not, practically, take on the character of attempt when Coke approvingly states that it is not necessary that there be a great number of persons to levy war. Coke, Third Institute (5th ed. 1671) 9. Coke's stress on the statute's declaration that the defendant be "provablement . . . attaint" (*id.* at 12) might be deemed to support Judge Hand's stress that the object of the overt act requirement is to bar patchwork constructions of evidence; Coke explains this means "upon direct and manifest proof, not upon conjecturall presumptions, or inferences, or straines of wit, but upon good and sufficient proof. . . ." He is not here directly interpreting the meaning of the overt act element; but in the next section, in which he does undertake to do so, he says it "doth also strengthen the former exposition of the word [provablement] that it must be probably, by an open act, which must be manifestly proved." *Id.* at 12. Judge Hand's distinction of adhering and levying from compassing on the ground that in the first two "the treason lay in hostile acts" may be supported by innuendo in Coke's statement that the act requirement "relateth to the severall and distinct treasons before expressed, (and specially to the compassing and imagination of the death of the King, &c. for that it is secret in the heart). . . ." *Id.* at 14.

1 Hale, History of the Pleas of the Crown (Emlyn ed. 1736–1739) 131, 150, in effect introduces into the exposition of the crime of levying war a definition which makes it much of the nature of an attempt, when he says that the mere assembly of men in force, and their marching in military arrays, make out a levying; or the mere assembly in present force alone. *Id.* at 138 (case of the Earl of Essex). And he states that it is not necessary that a blow be struck. *Id.* at 144, 152. His discussion of adherence is very brief, and the examples given are of completed aid and comfort, as by delivery of a castle to the enemy. *Id.* at 167–68.

1 Hawkins, A Treatise of the Pleas of the Crown (7th ed. 1795) 86, 94, in effect makes Judge Hand's point, that the design is itself the complete crime in compassing, citing the case of the regicides. But Hawkins also recognizes that the mere keeping together of armed men against the king's command is a levying of war (*id.* at 90); and that there may be a levying, though there is no actual fighting. *Id.* at 91. He is brief to the point of not being helpful in his definition of

adherence; but he cites with approval the ruling that merely cruising with intent to destroy the king's subjects is adherence when done with the king's enemies. *Id.* at 91.

Foster, A Report of Some Proceedings on the Commission for the Trial of the Rebels in the Year 1746 in the County of Surry; and of other Crown Cases (3d ed. 1792) 195, introduces the first real analysis of underlying policy, when he justifies the doctrine that in compassing the design is itself the completed offense, by pointing to the importance to the security of the community of the king's safety, which supports the wisdom of striking at an early stage at threats to this security. Foster contributes little additional in defining the degree of accomplished resistance to lawful authority that is necessary to constitute levying of war. Regarding adherence, he approves the decisions finding a completed offense, though the aid and comfort was intercepted, "for the party in sending did all he could; the treason was complete *on his part though it had not the effect he intended." Id.* at 217. He simply cites cases and makes no reference to his discussion of the policy behind the broad scope of compassing, though he does take pains to note that the defendants in the cited cases were also charged with compassing. He states that the rulings, considered as defining the crime of adherence, "may very well be supported," but in context this appears to mean only that they are supported by precedents. Lumping both levying and adhering together, he recognizes, without analyzing the underlying policy, that they may be made out without showing that the threat to the state has actually been brought to fruition: "An assembly armed and arrayed in a warlike manner for any treasonable purpose is *bellum levatum,* though not *bellum percussum.* Listing and marching are sufficient overt-acts without coming to a battle or action. So cruising on the King's subjects under a *French* commission, France being then at war with us, was holden to be adhering to the King's enemies, though no other act of hostility was laid or proved." *Id.* at 218.

The upshot of this is scant. Judge Hand really has nothing more than the words of the Statute of Edward III on which to base his argument. Coke and Hale seem to have relied likewise on the contrast between the terms in which the three main branches of treason are there described, to explain why the conspiracy to levy war was not sufficient to make out a levying of war. But the scope of levying war seems, from Coke on, to make that offense analogous to an attempt in the solicitude shown for taking preventive action against a threat to state security. Analysis of the crime of adherence is almost wholly lacking, and, when it appears, amounts to no more than a citation of decisions which look in the same direction as developments under the head of levying war.

Index

*The Law of Treason in the
United States* was composed in
Linotron 505 Baskerville by Black Dot, Inc.,
Crystal Lake, Illinois. The Bulmer display type was
supplied by The Book Press, Brattleboro, Vermont.
Printed by Litho Crafters, Inc.
Ann Arbor, Michigan